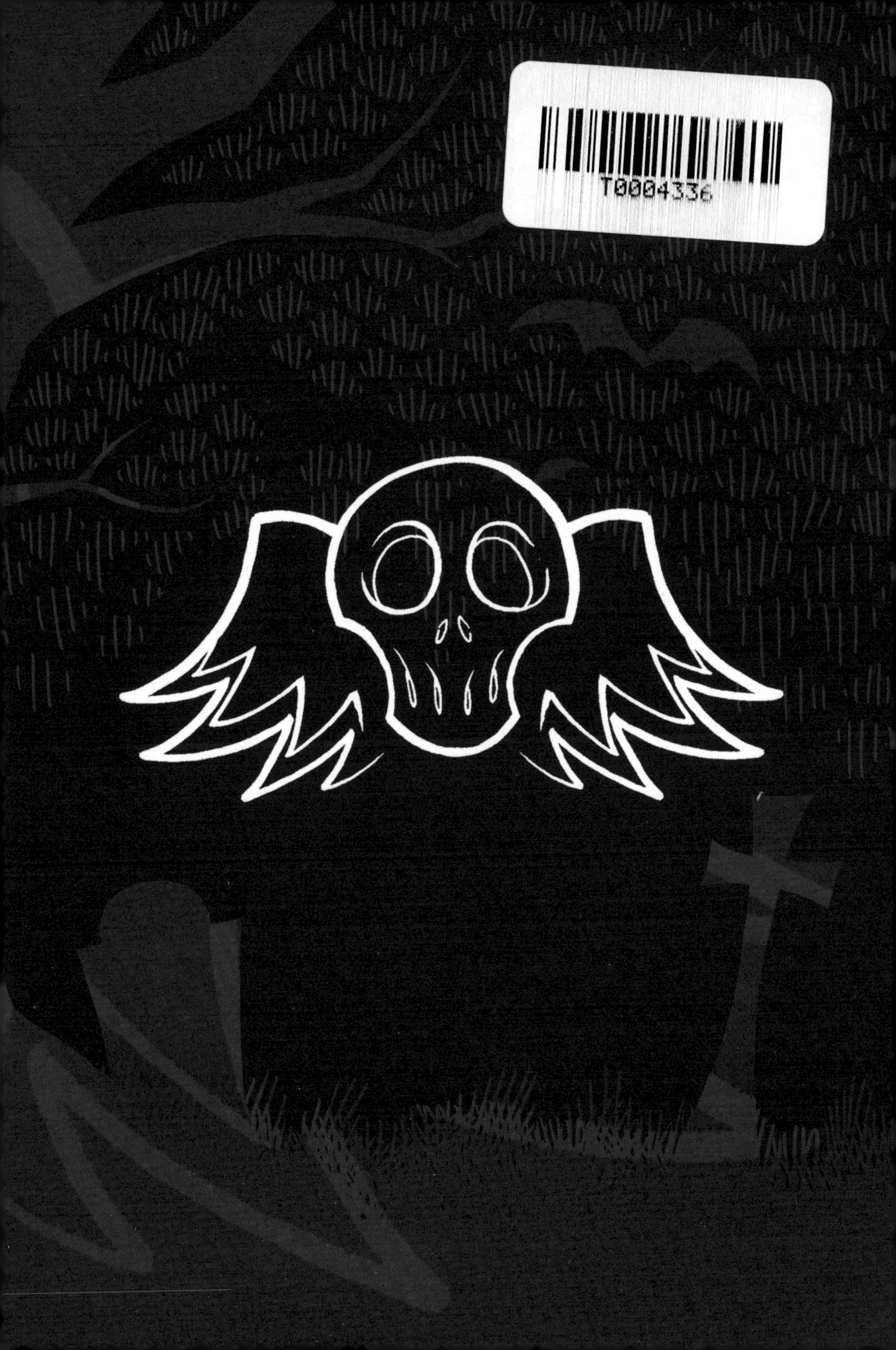

UNDEADED

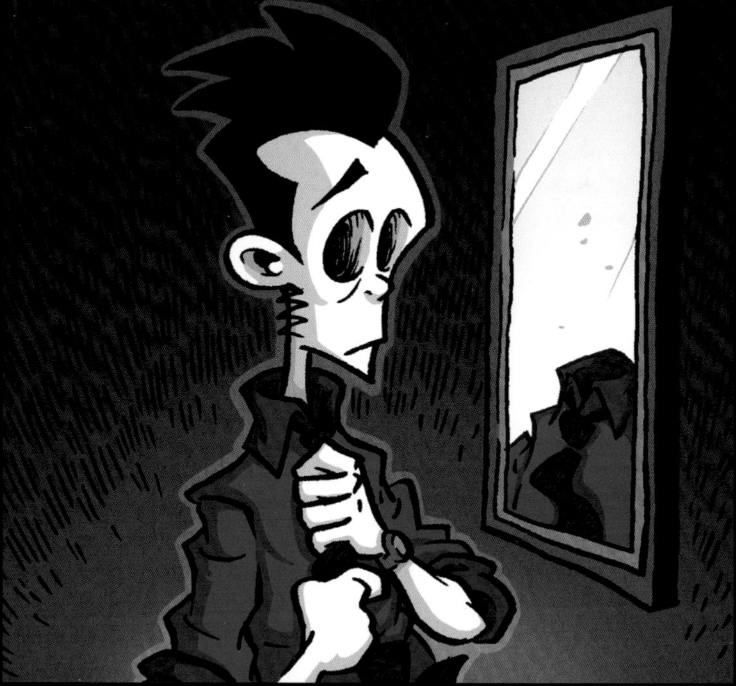

BY

BOREDMAN

Rocketship™ Rocketship Entertainment, LLC
rocketshipent.com

Tom Akel, CEO & Publisher • **Rob Feldman,** CTO • **Jeanmarie McNeely,** CFO
Brandon Freeberg, Dir. of Campaign Mgmt. • **Phil Smith,** Art Director • **Aram Alekyan,** Designer
Jimmy Deoquino, Designer • **Jed Keith,** Social Media • **Jerrod Clark,** Publicity

UndeadEd volume 1 | Softcover Edition ISBN: 978-1-952126-65-9 | Hardcover Edition ISBN: 978-1-952126-67-3

Created in December 2014 as an entry
for the Webtoon Challenge League Contest,
UndeadEd is the story of a dead man
trying to go on with his life.

Which, in addition to being paradoxical,
certainly isn't easy.

The series was later picked up
by Webtoon and became available
as a Slidetoon, updating three times
a week from the 8th of May 2015
to the 7th of February 2016

Special thanks to my friend Damien
for letting me know about the contest,
to my editor David for giving me a chance,
and to Elie, Anna and Vane for feeding me
ideas and support throughout the way.

UndeadEd is dedicated to my grandfather,
who passed away during its early beginnings.

2

TABLE OF CONTENTS

Chapter

-Denial-

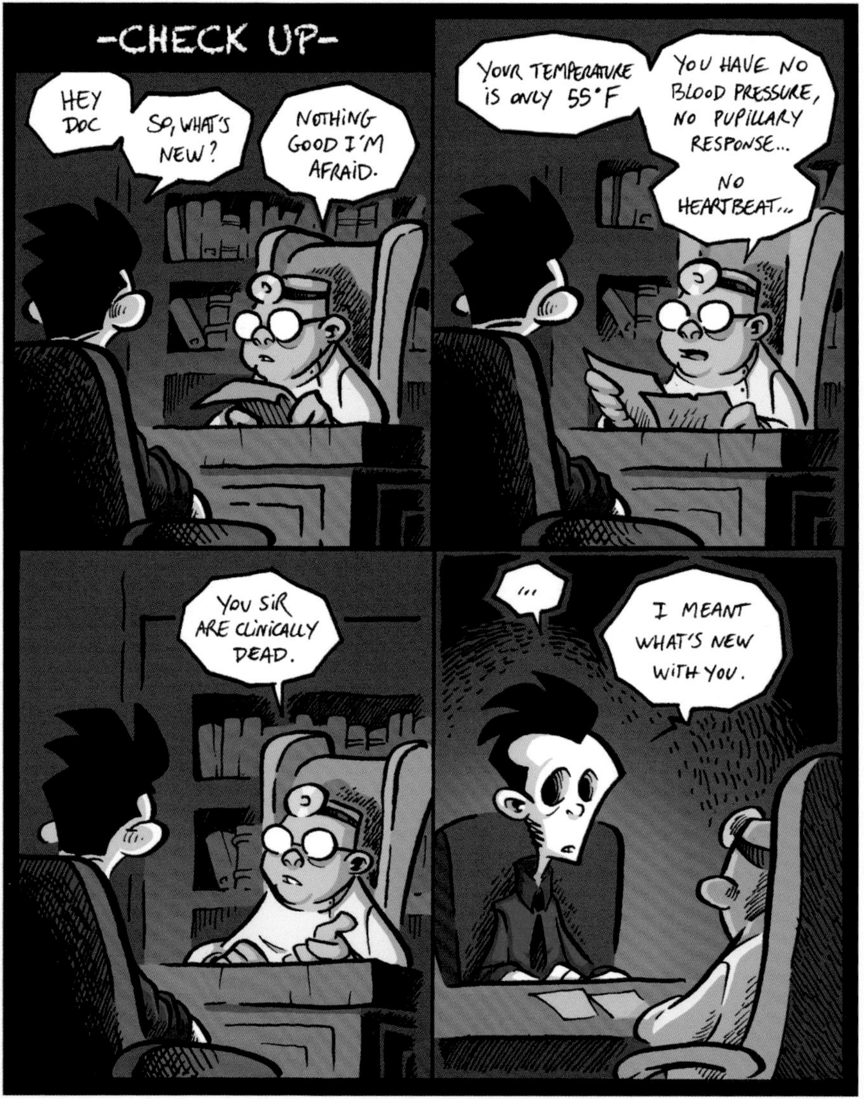
-CHECK UP-
HEY DOC
SO, WHAT'S NEW?
NOTHING GOOD I'M AFRAID.
YOUR TEMPERATURE IS ONLY 55°F
YOU HAVE NO BLOOD PRESSURE, NO PUPILLARY RESPONSE...
NO HEARTBEAT...
YOU SIR ARE CLINICALLY DEAD.
...
I MEANT WHAT'S NEW WITH YOU.

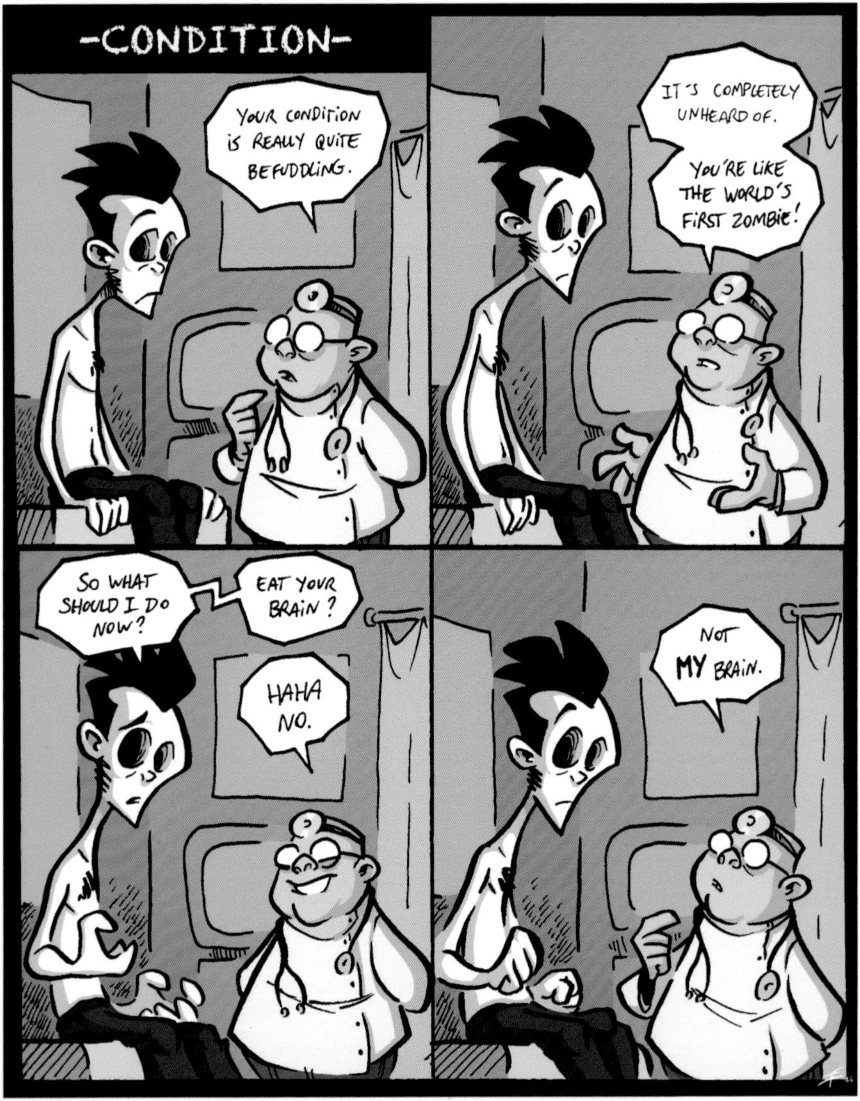
-CONDITION-
YOUR CONDITION IS REALLY QUITE BEFUDDLING.
IT'S COMPLETELY UNHEARD OF.
YOU'RE LIKE THE WORLD'S FIRST ZOMBIE!
SO WHAT SHOULD I DO NOW?
EAT YOUR BRAIN?
HAHA NO.
NOT MY BRAIN.

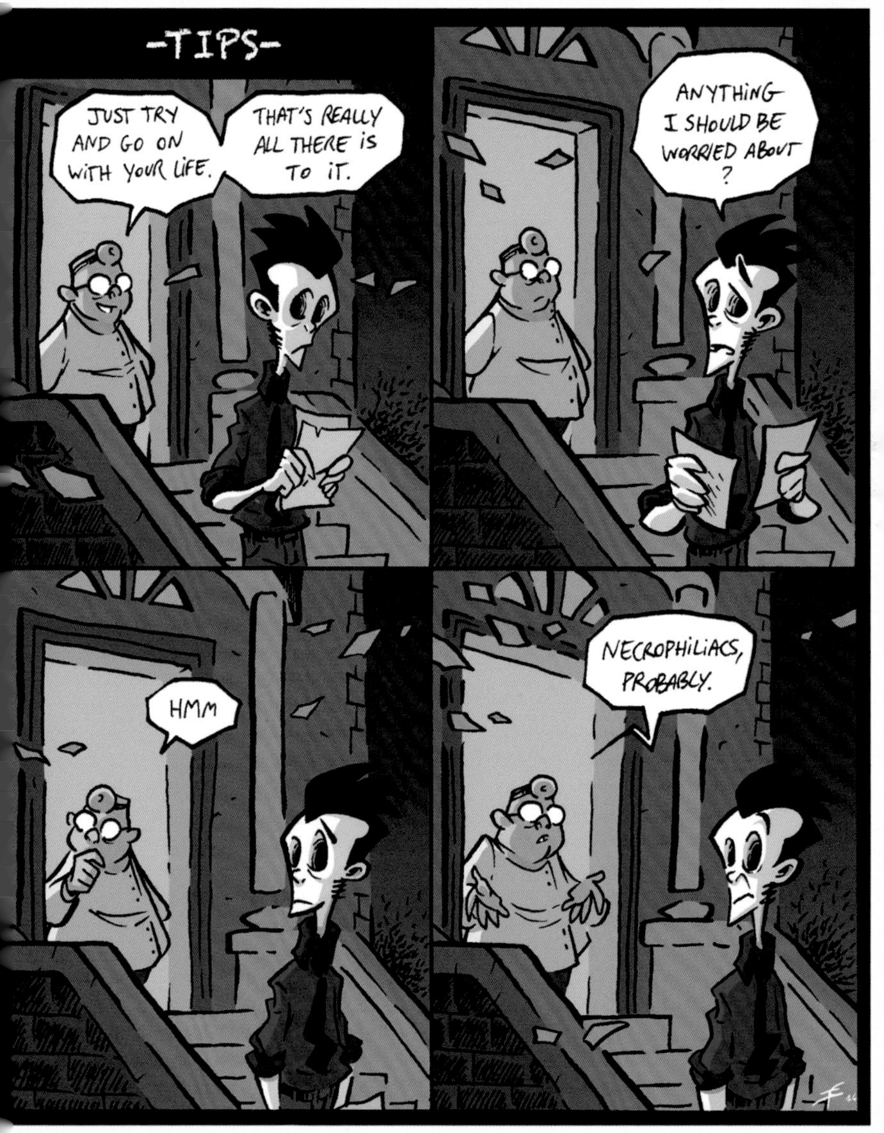
-TIPS-
JUST TRY AND GO ON WITH YOUR LIFE.
THAT'S REALLY ALL THERE IS TO IT.
ANYTHING I SHOULD BE WORRIED ABOUT?
HMM
NECROPHILIACS, PROBABLY.

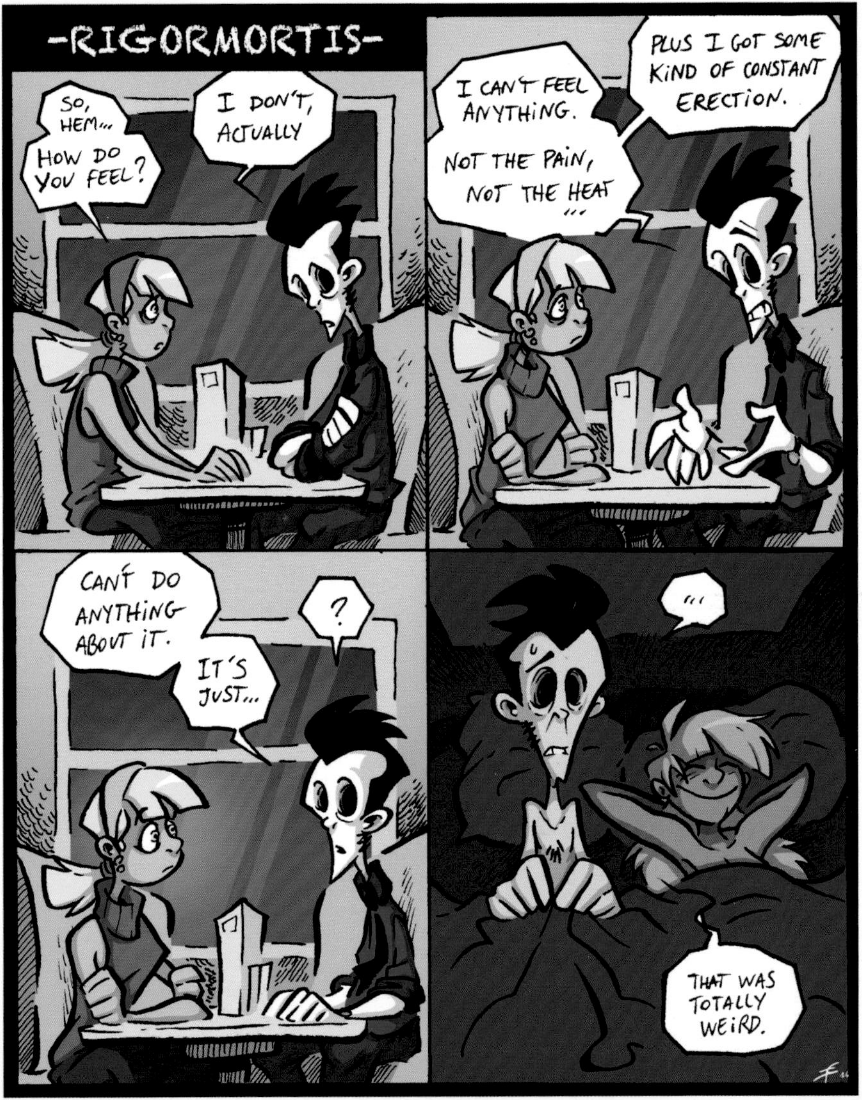
-RIGORMORTIS-
SO, HEM... HOW DO YOU FEEL?
I DON'T, ACTUALLY
I CAN'T FEEL ANYTHING.
NOT THE PAIN, NOT THE HEAT ...
PLUS I GOT SOME KIND OF CONSTANT ERECTION.
CAN'T DO ANYTHING ABOUT IT.
IT'S JUST...
?
...
THAT WAS TOTALLY WEIRD.

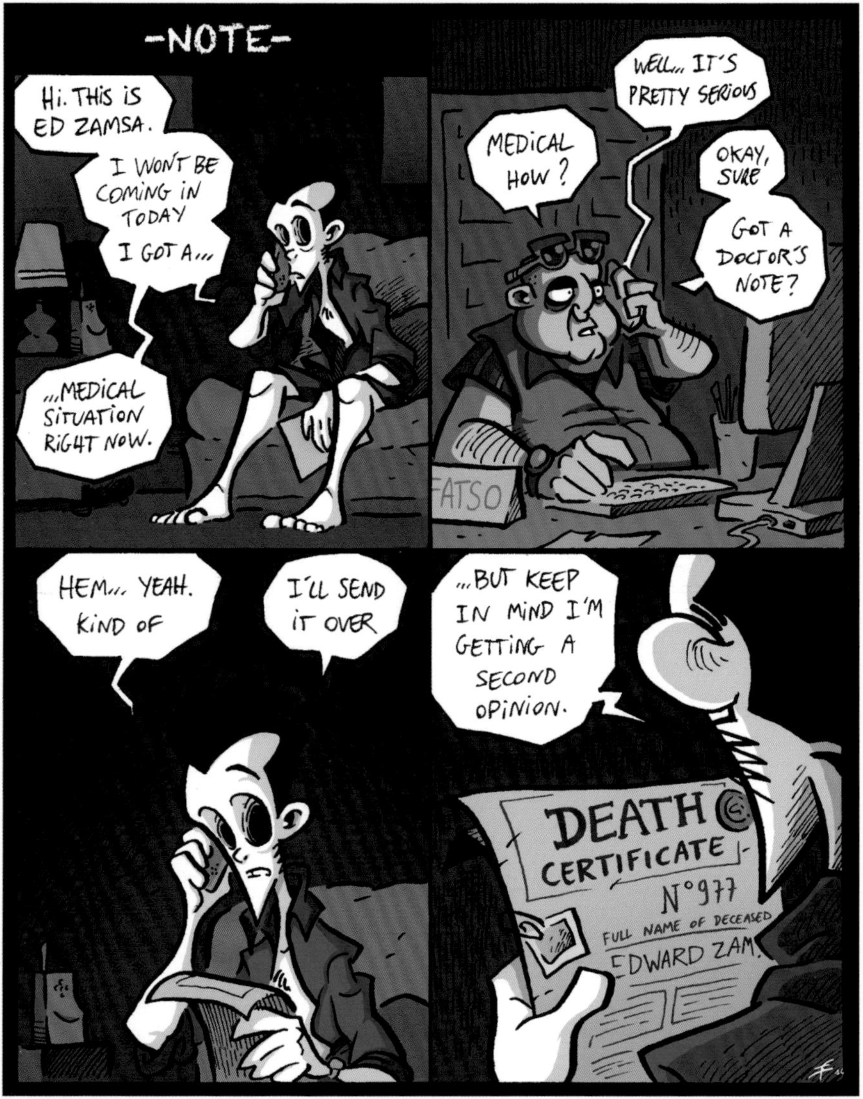
-NOTE-
Hi. THIS IS ED ZAMSA.
I WON'T BE COMING IN TODAY
I GOT A...
...MEDICAL SITUATION RIGHT NOW.
MEDICAL HOW?
WELL... IT'S PRETTY SERIOUS
OKAY, SURE
GOT A DOCTOR'S NOTE?
FATSO
HEM... YEAH. KIND OF
I'LL SEND IT OVER
...BUT KEEP IN MIND I'M GETTING A SECOND OPINION.
DEATH CERTIFICATE
N°977
FULL NAME OF DECEASED
EDWARD ZAM

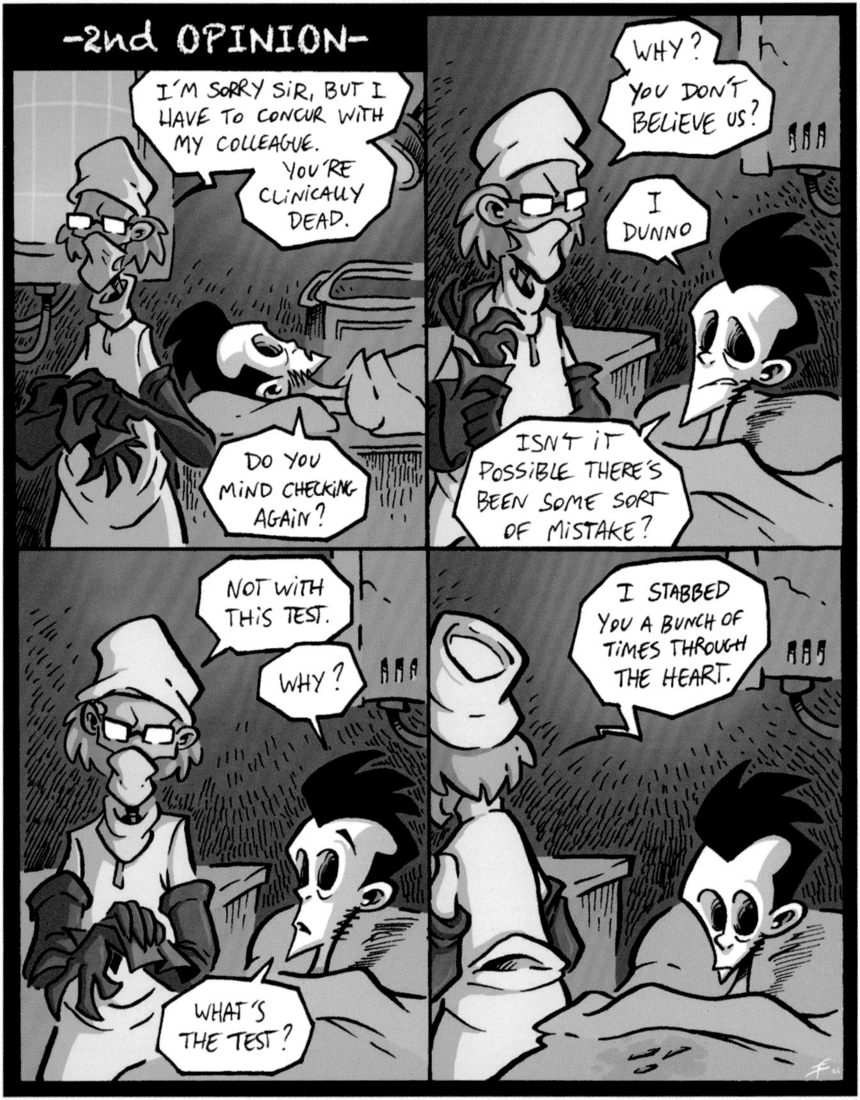
-2nd OPINION-
I'M SORRY SIR, BUT I HAVE TO CONCUR WITH MY COLLEAGUE.
YOU'RE CLINICALLY DEAD.
DO YOU MIND CHECKING AGAIN?
WHY? YOU DON'T BELIEVE US?
I DUNNO
ISN'T IT POSSIBLE THERE'S BEEN SOME SORT OF MISTAKE?
NOT WITH THIS TEST.
WHY?
WHAT'S THE TEST?
I STABBED YOU A BUNCH OF TIMES THROUGH THE HEART.

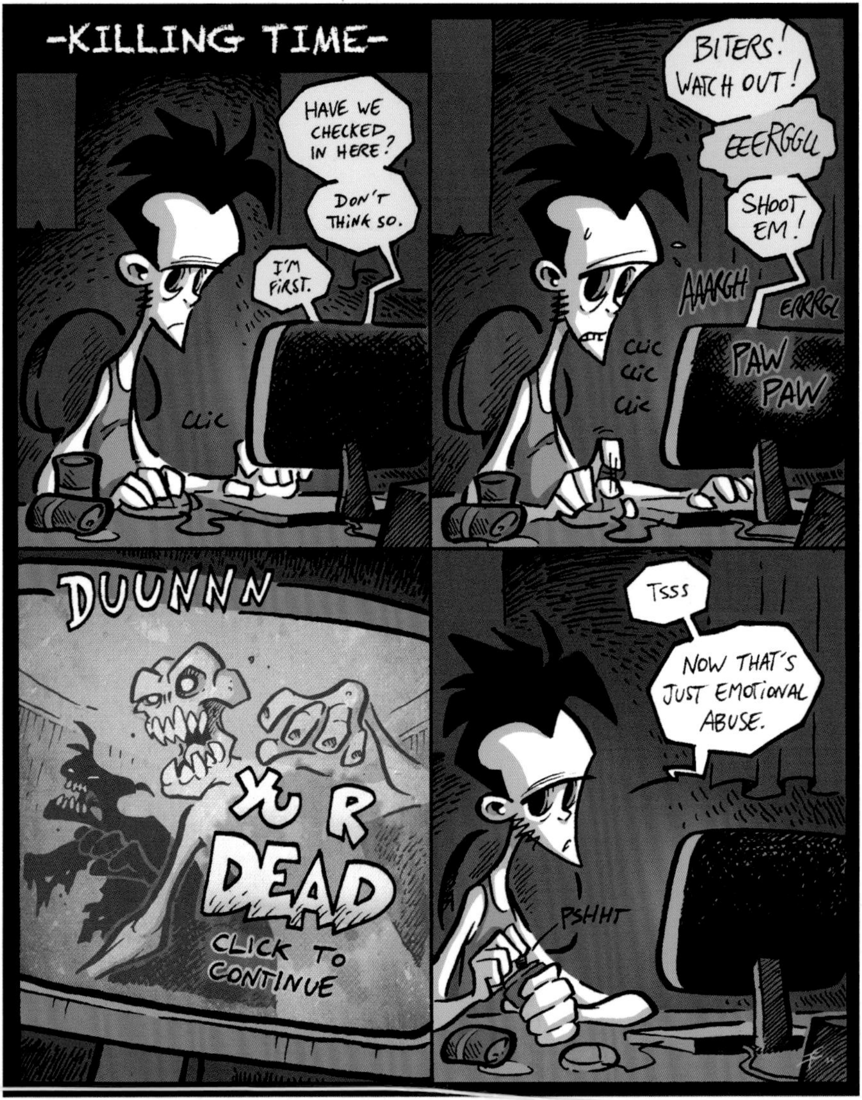
-KILLING TIME-
HAVE WE CHECKED IN HERE?
DON'T THINK SO.
I'M FIRST.
CLIC
BITERS! WATCH OUT!
EEERGGL
SHOOT, EM!
AAARGH
ERRRGL
CLIC CLIC CLIC
PAW PAW
DUUNNN
YU R DEAD
CLICK TO CONTINUE
TSSS
NOW THAT'S JUST EMOTIONAL ABUSE.
PSHHT

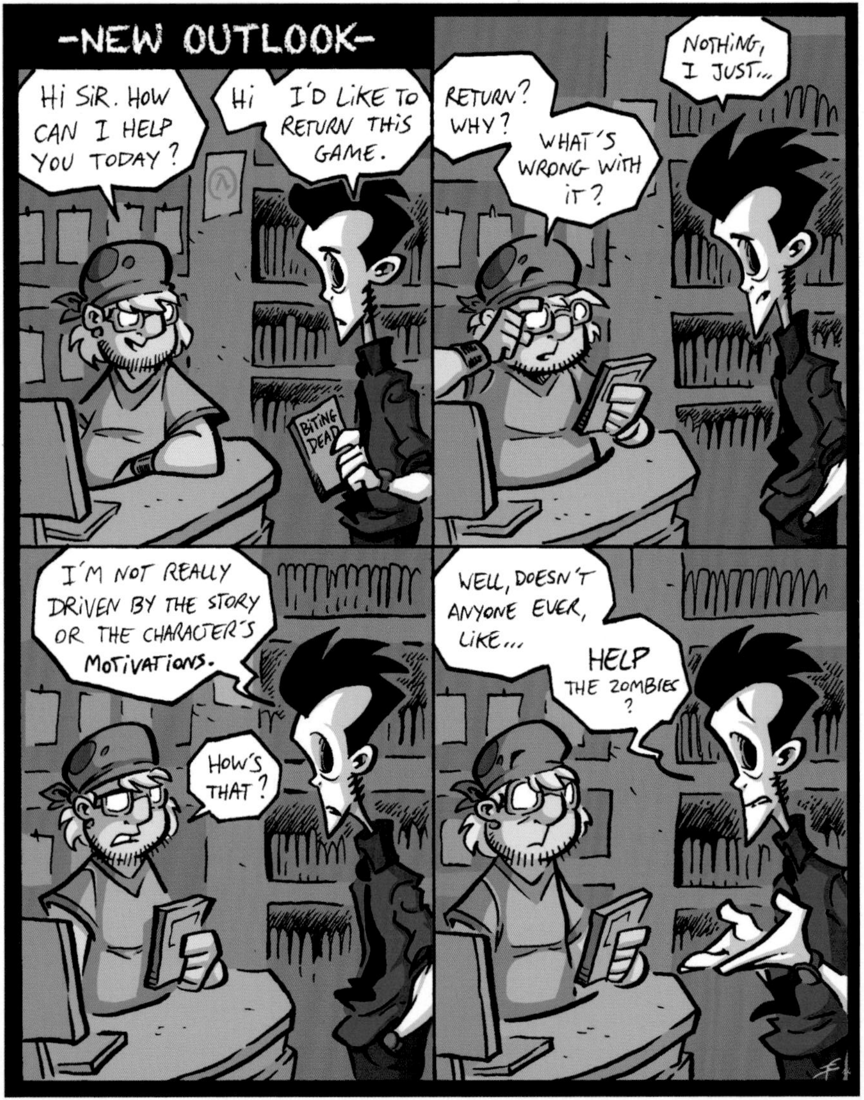
-NEW OUTLOOK-
Hi SIR. HOW CAN I HELP YOU TODAY?
Hi
I'D LIKE TO RETURN THIS GAME.
BITING DEAD
RETURN? WHY?
WHAT'S WRONG WITH IT?
NOTHING, I JUST...
I'M NOT REALLY DRIVEN BY THE STORY OR THE CHARACTER'S MOTIVATIONS.
HOW'S THAT?
WELL, DOESN'T ANYONE EVER, LIKE...
HELP THE ZOMBIES?

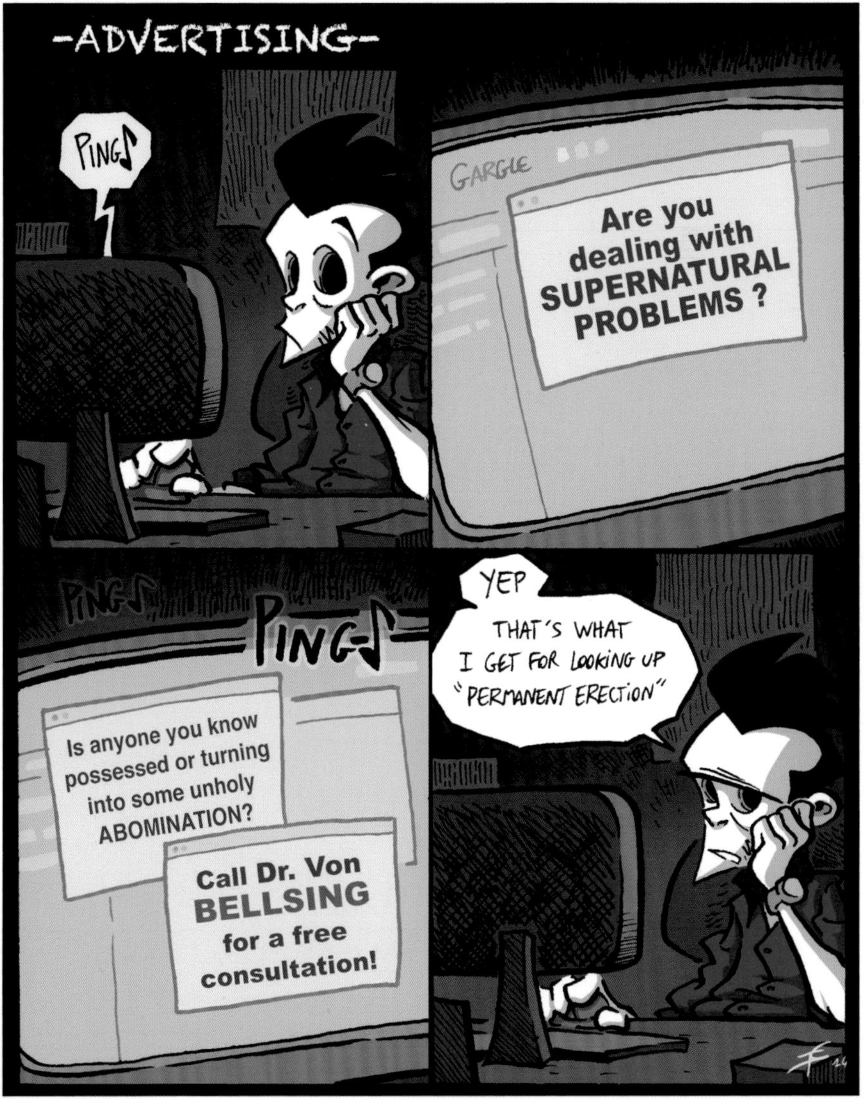
-ADVERTISING-
PING♪
GARGLE
Are you dealing with SUPERNATURAL PROBLEMS ?
PING♪
PING♪
Is anyone you know possessed or turning into some unholy ABOMINATION?
Call Dr. Von BELLSING for a free consultation!
YEP
THAT'S WHAT I GET FOR LOOKING UP "PERMANENT ERECTION"

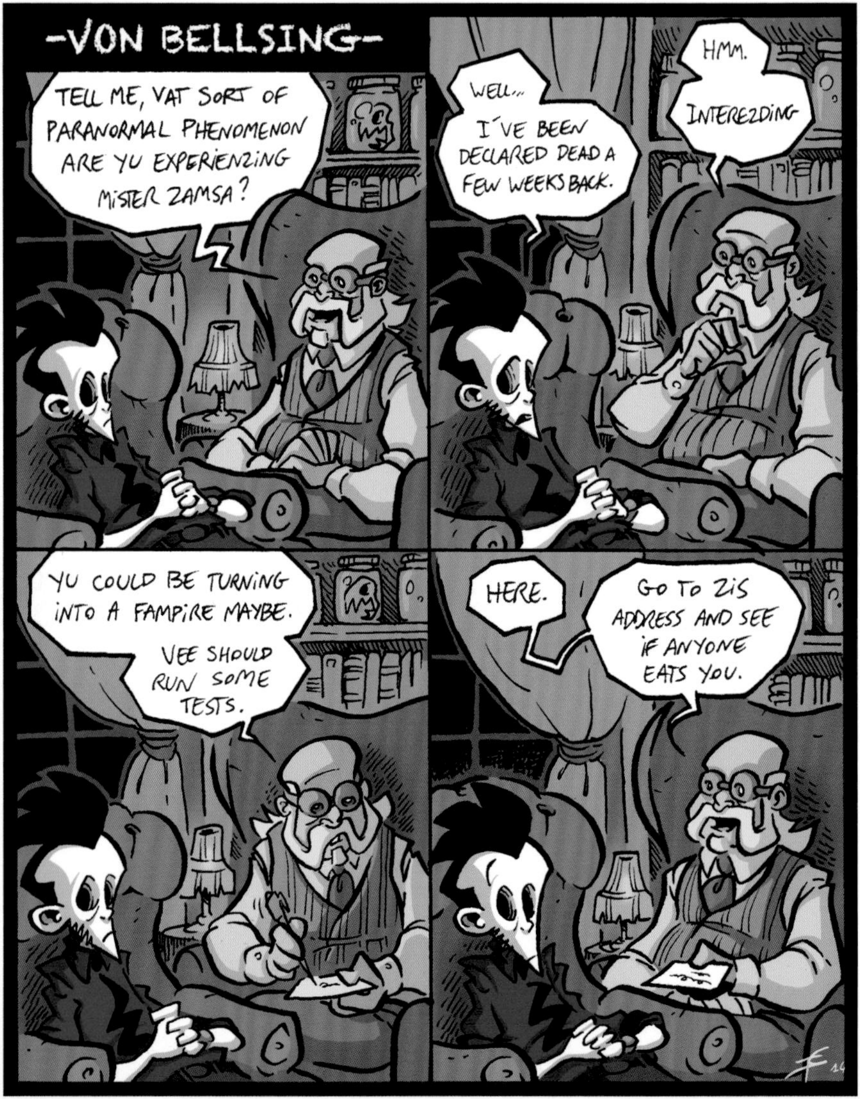
-VON BELLSING-
TELL ME, VAT SORT OF PARANORMAL PHENOMENON ARE YU EXPERIENZING MISTER ZAMSA?
WELL... I'VE BEEN DECLARED DEAD A FEW WEEKS BACK.
HMM. INTEREZDING
YU COULD BE TURNING INTO A FAMPIRE MAYBE.
VEE SHOULD RUN SOME TESTS.
HERE.
GO TO ZIS ADDRESS AND SEE IF ANYONE EATS YOU.

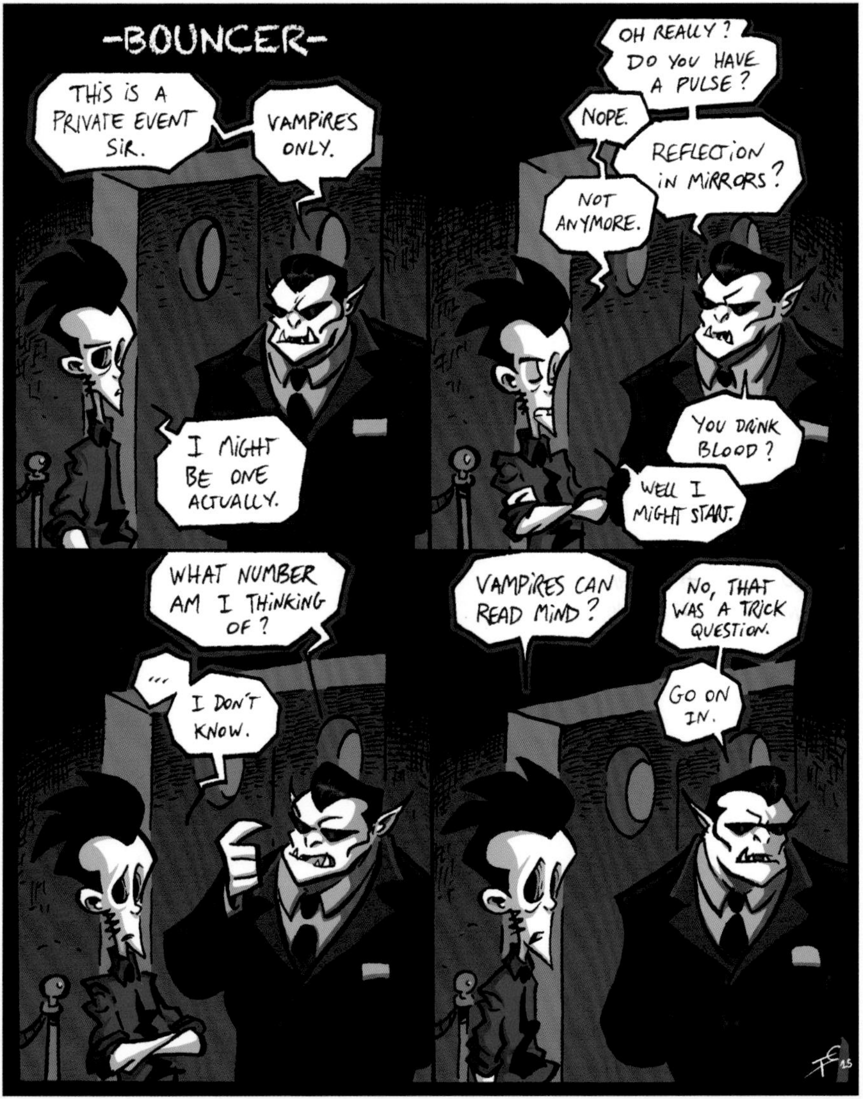
-BOUNCER-
THIS IS A PRIVATE EVENT SIR.
VAMPIRES ONLY.
I MIGHT BE ONE ACTUALLY.
OH REALLY? DO YOU HAVE A PULSE?
NOPE.
REFLECTION IN MIRRORS?
NOT ANYMORE.
YOU DRINK BLOOD?
WELL I MIGHT START.
WHAT NUMBER AM I THINKING OF?
...
I DON'T KNOW.
VAMPIRES CAN READ MIND?
NO, THAT WAS A TRICK QUESTION.
GO ON IN.

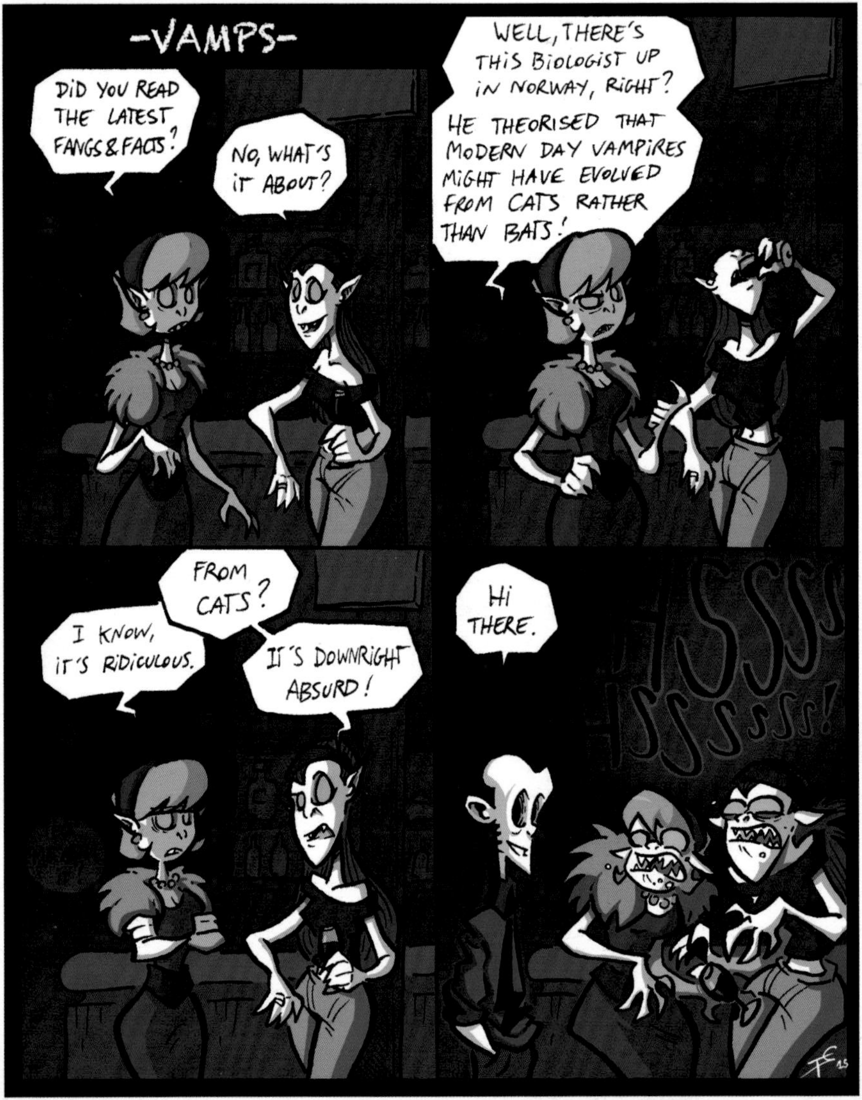
-VAMPS-
DID YOU READ THE LATEST FANGS & FACTS?
NO, WHAT'S IT ABOUT?
WELL, THERE'S THIS BIOLOGIST UP IN NORWAY, RIGHT?
HE THEORISED THAT MODERN DAY VAMPIRES MIGHT HAVE EVOLVED FROM CATS RATHER THAN BATS!
FROM CATS?
I KNOW, IT'S RIDICULOUS.
IT'S DOWNRIGHT ABSURD!
HI THERE.
HSSSSS SSSSSS!

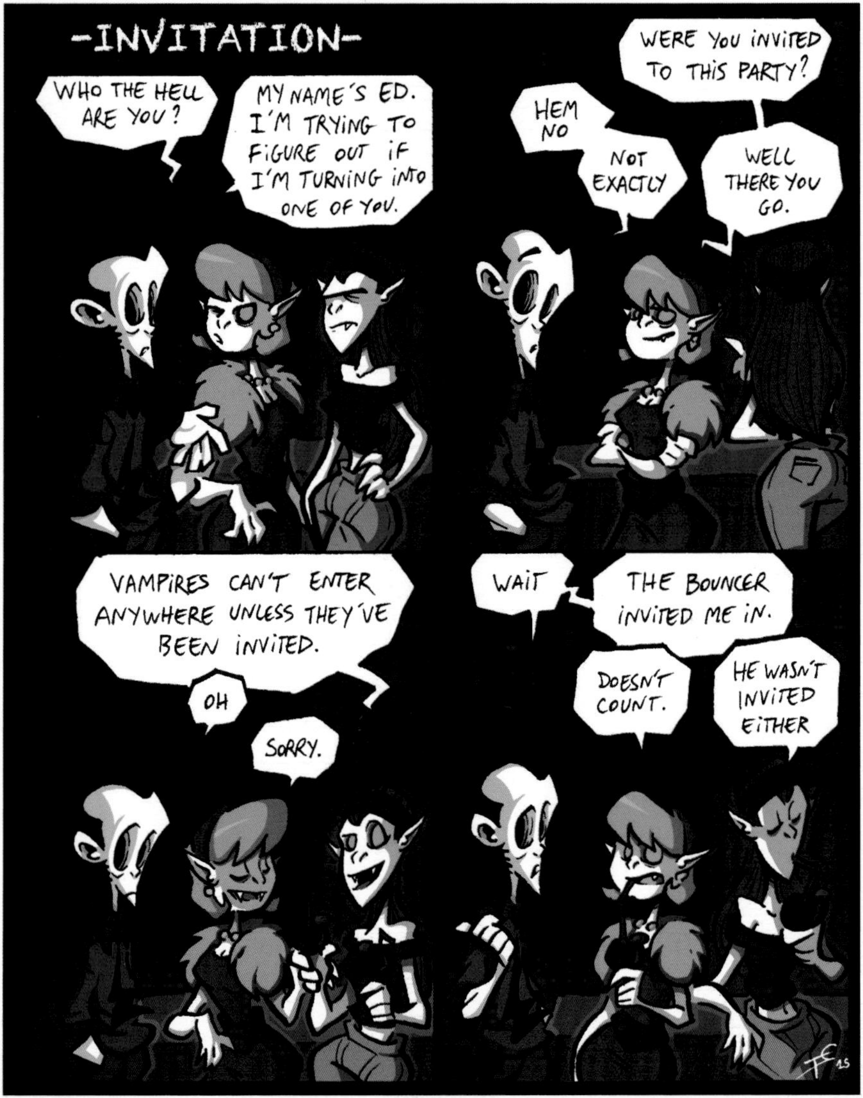
-INVITATION-
WHO THE HELL ARE YOU?
MY NAME'S ED. I'M TRYING TO FIGURE OUT IF I'M TURNING INTO ONE OF YOU.
WERE YOU INVITED TO THIS PARTY?
HEM NO
NOT EXACTLY
WELL THERE YOU GO.
VAMPIRES CAN'T ENTER ANYWHERE UNLESS THEY'VE BEEN INVITED.
OH
SORRY.
WAIT
THE BOUNCER INVITED ME IN.
DOESN'T COUNT.
HE WASN'T INVITED EITHER

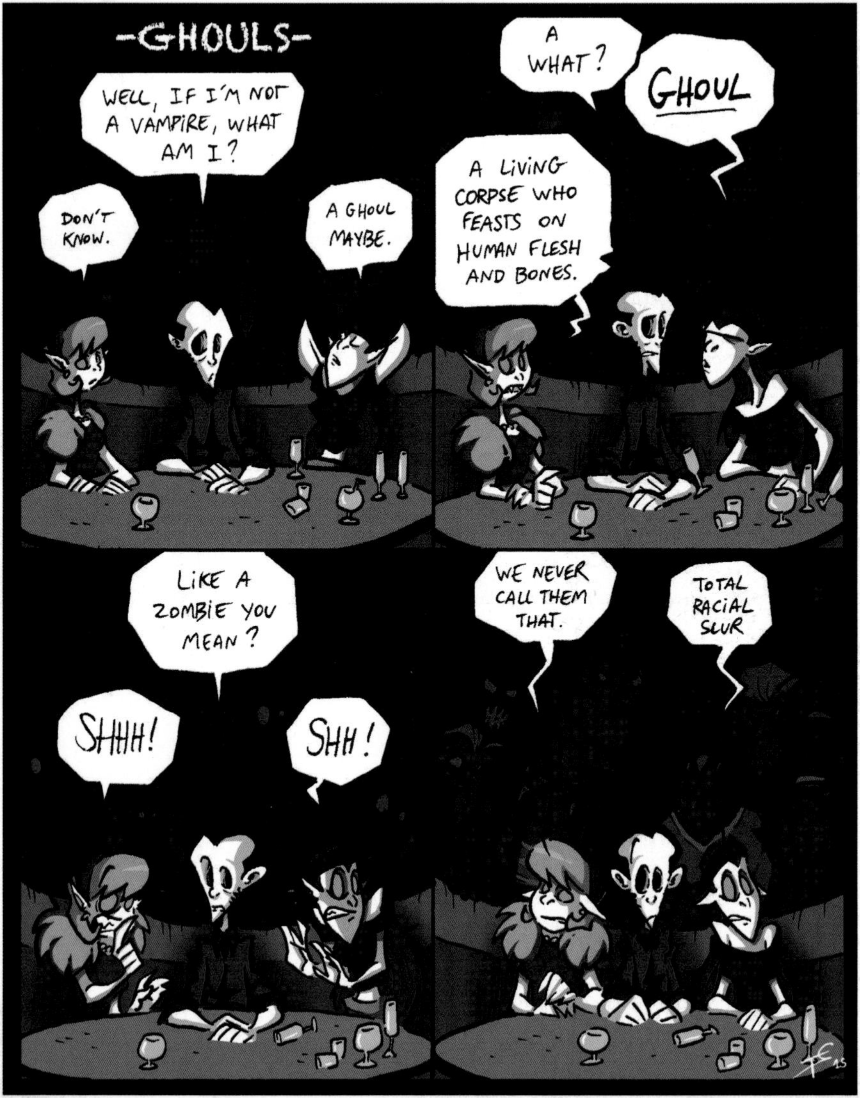
-GHOULS-
WELL, IF I'M NOT A VAMPIRE, WHAT AM I?
DON'T KNOW.
A GHOUL MAYBE.
A WHAT?
GHOUL
A LIVING CORPSE WHO FEASTS ON HUMAN FLESH AND BONES.
LIKE A ZOMBIE YOU MEAN?
SHHH!
SHH!
WE NEVER CALL THEM THAT.
TOTAL RACIAL SLUR

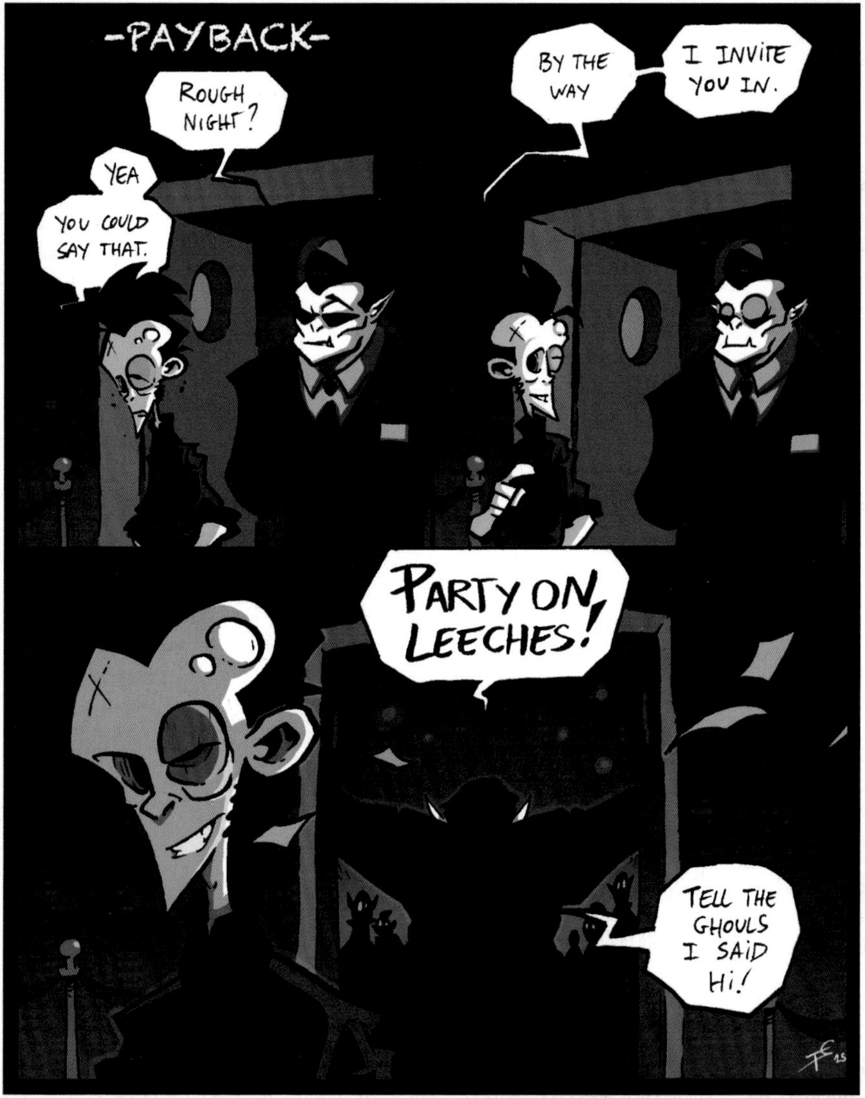
-PAYBACK-
ROUGH NIGHT?
YEA
YOU COULD SAY THAT.
BY THE WAY
I INVITE YOU IN.
PARTY ON, LEECHES!
TELL THE GHOULS I SAID HI!

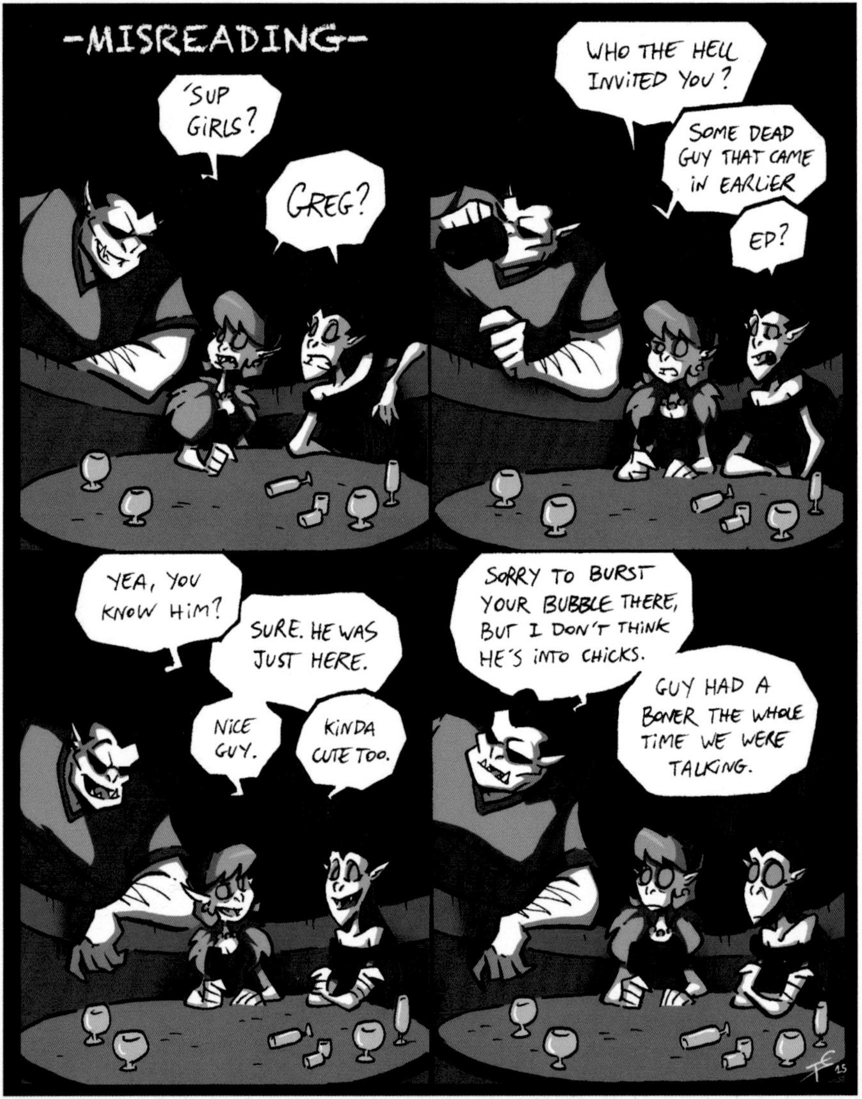
-MISREADING-
'SUP GIRLS?
GREG?
WHO THE HELL INVITED YOU?
SOME DEAD GUY THAT CAME IN EARLIER
ED?
YEA, YOU KNOW HIM?
SURE. HE WAS JUST HERE.
NICE GUY.
KINDA CUTE TOO.
SORRY TO BURST YOUR BUBBLE THERE, BUT I DON'T THINK HE'S INTO CHICKS.
GUY HAD A BONER THE WHOLE TIME WE WERE TALKING.

As if
life wasn't
hard enough
without being
dead.

Chapter

-Anger-

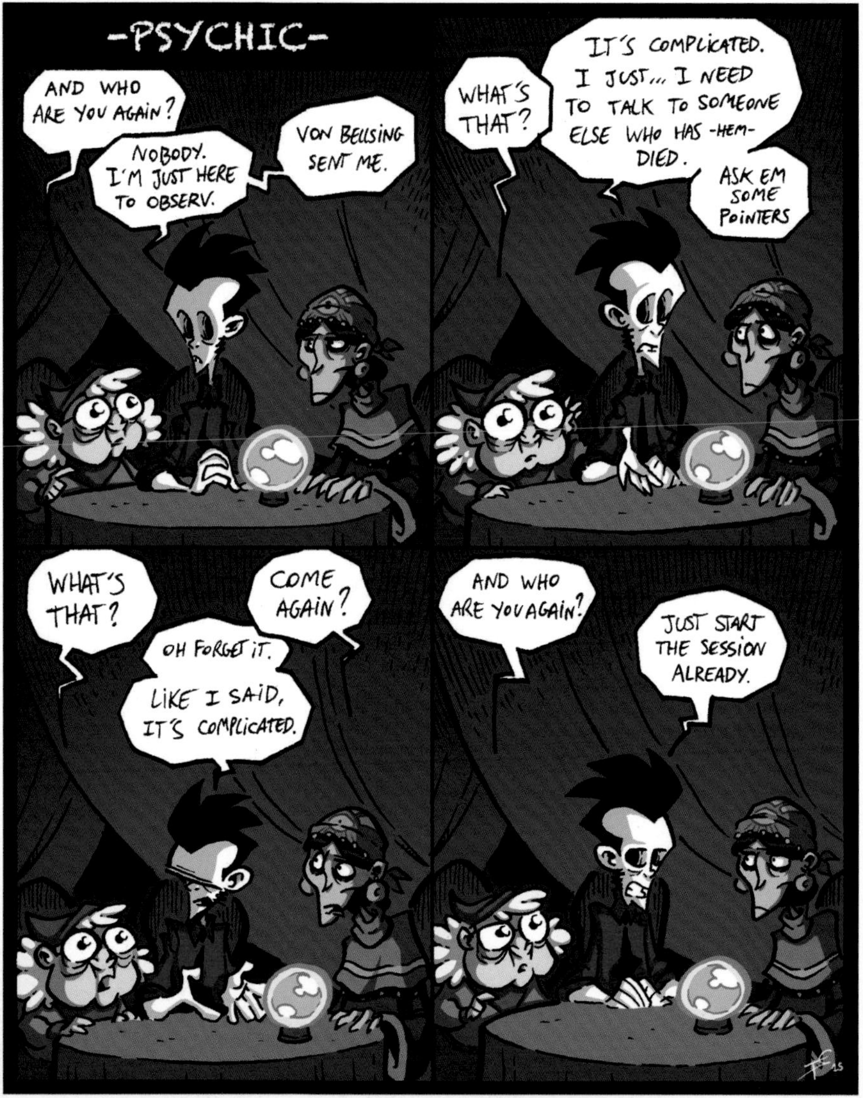
-PSYCHIC-
AND WHO ARE YOU AGAIN?
NOBODY. I'M JUST HERE TO OBSERV.
VON BELLSING SENT ME.
WHAT'S THAT?
IT'S COMPLICATED. I JUST... I NEED TO TALK TO SOMEONE ELSE WHO HAS -HEM- DIED.
ASK EM SOME POINTERS
WHAT'S THAT?
COME AGAIN?
OH FORGET IT.
LIKE I SAID, IT'S COMPLICATED.
AND WHO ARE YOU AGAIN?
JUST START THE SESSION ALREADY.

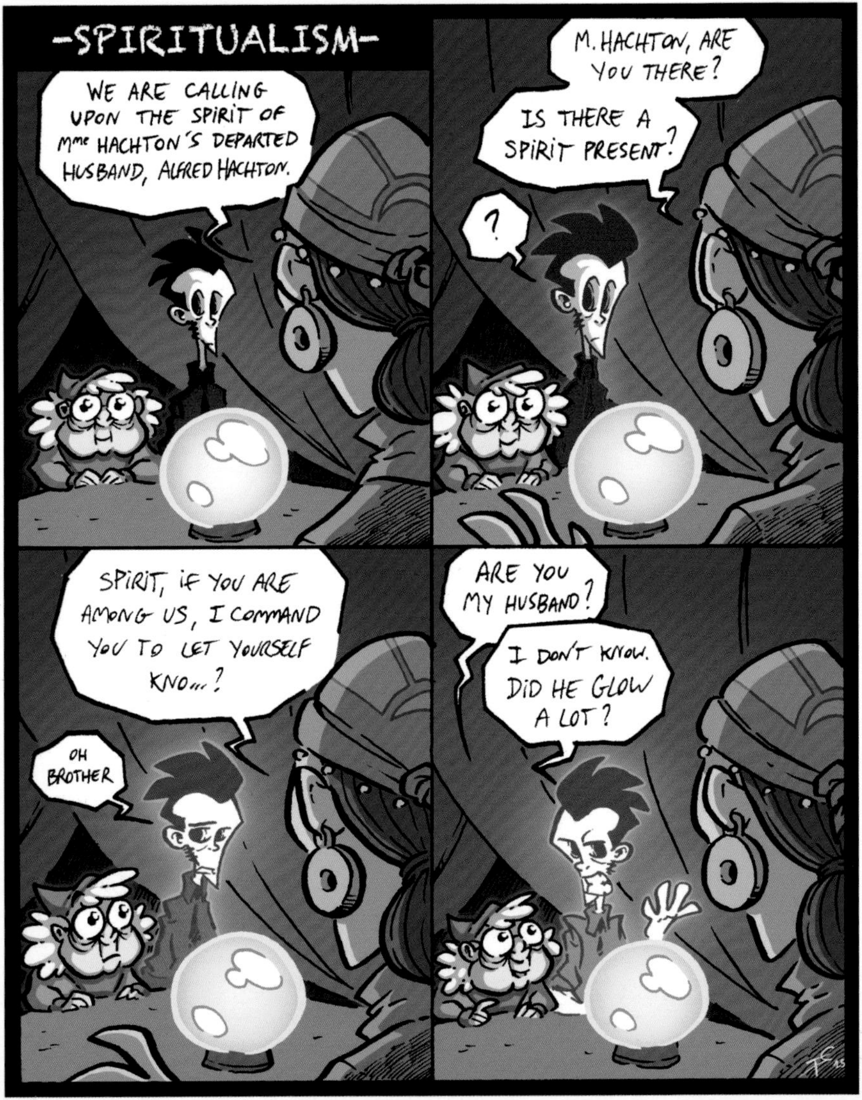
-SPIRITUALISM-
WE ARE CALLING UPON THE SPIRIT OF Mme HACHTON'S DEPARTED HUSBAND, ALFRED HACHTON.
M. HACHTON, ARE YOU THERE?
IS THERE A SPIRIT PRESENT?
?
SPIRIT, IF YOU ARE AMONG US, I COMMAND YOU TO LET YOURSELF KNO...?
OH BROTHER
ARE YOU MY HUSBAND?
I DON'T KNOW. DID HE GLOW A LOT?

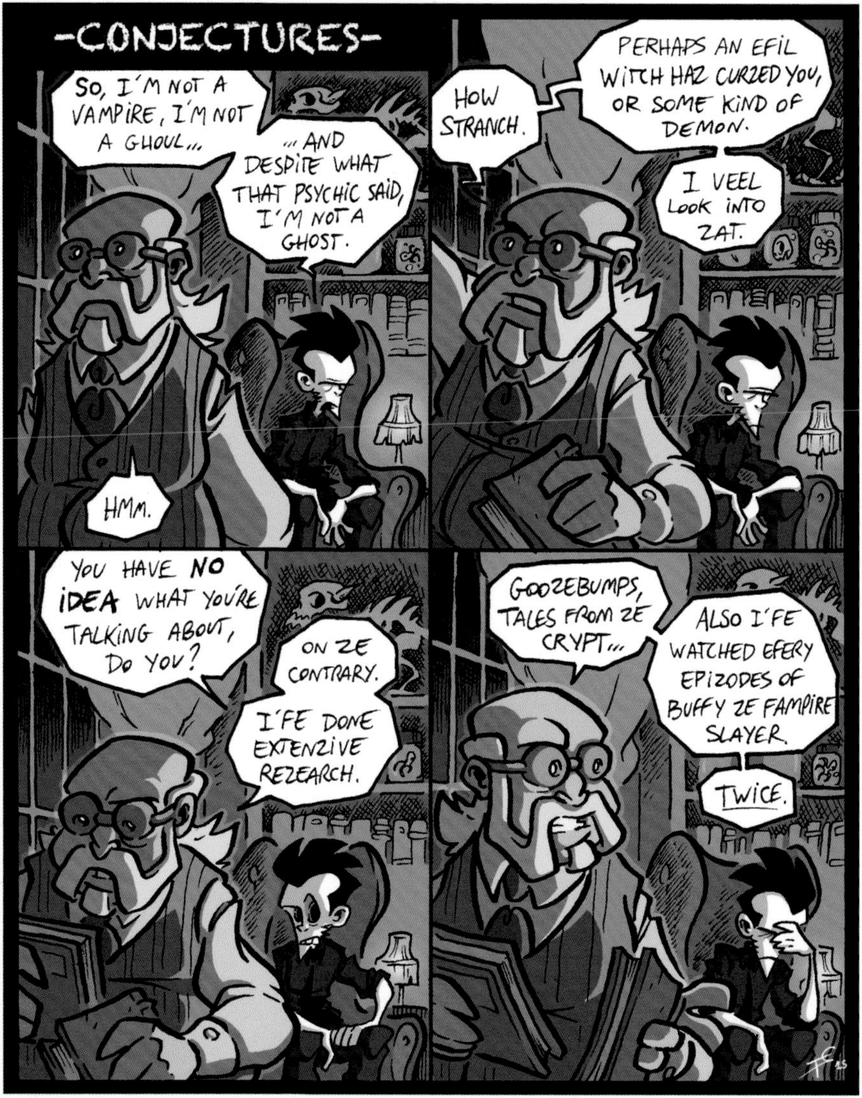
-CONJECTURES-
SO, I'M NOT A VAMPIRE, I'M NOT A GHOUL...
...AND DESPITE WHAT THAT PSYCHIC SAID, I'M NOT A GHOST.
HMM.
HOW STRANCH.
PERHAPS AN EFIL WITCH HAZ CURZED YOU, OR SOME KIND OF DEMON.
I VEEL LOOK INTO ZAT.
YOU HAVE NO IDEA WHAT YOU'RE TALKING ABOUT, DO YOU?
ON ZE CONTRARY.
I'FE DONE EXTENZIVE REZEARCH.
GOOZEBUMPS, TALES FROM ZE CRYPT...
ALSO I'FE WATCHED EFERY EPIZODES OF BUFFY ZE FAMPIRE SLAYER.
TWICE.

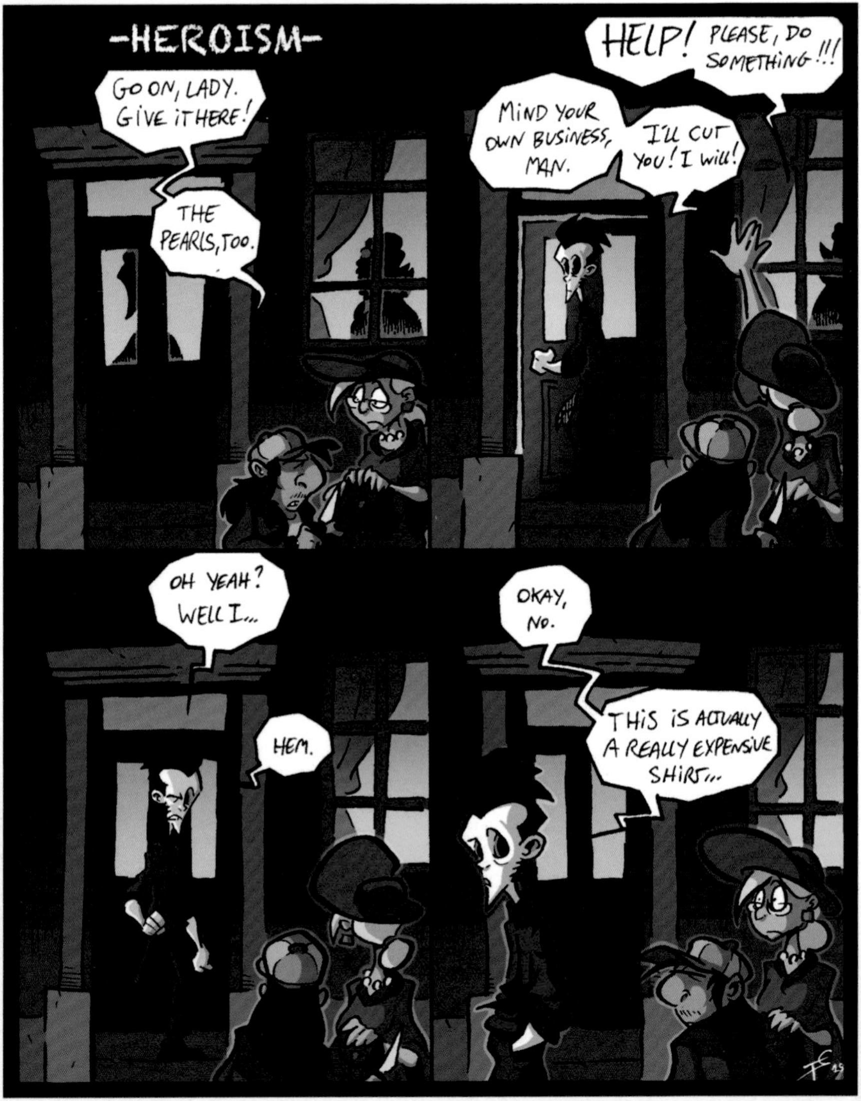
-HEROISM-
GO ON, LADY. GIVE IT HERE!
THE PEARLS, TOO.
HELP! PLEASE, DO SOMETHING!!!
MIND YOUR OWN BUSINESS, MAN.
I'LL CUT YOU! I WILL!
OH YEAH? WELL I...
HEM.
OKAY, NO.
THIS IS ACTUALLY A REALLY EXPENSIVE SHIRT...

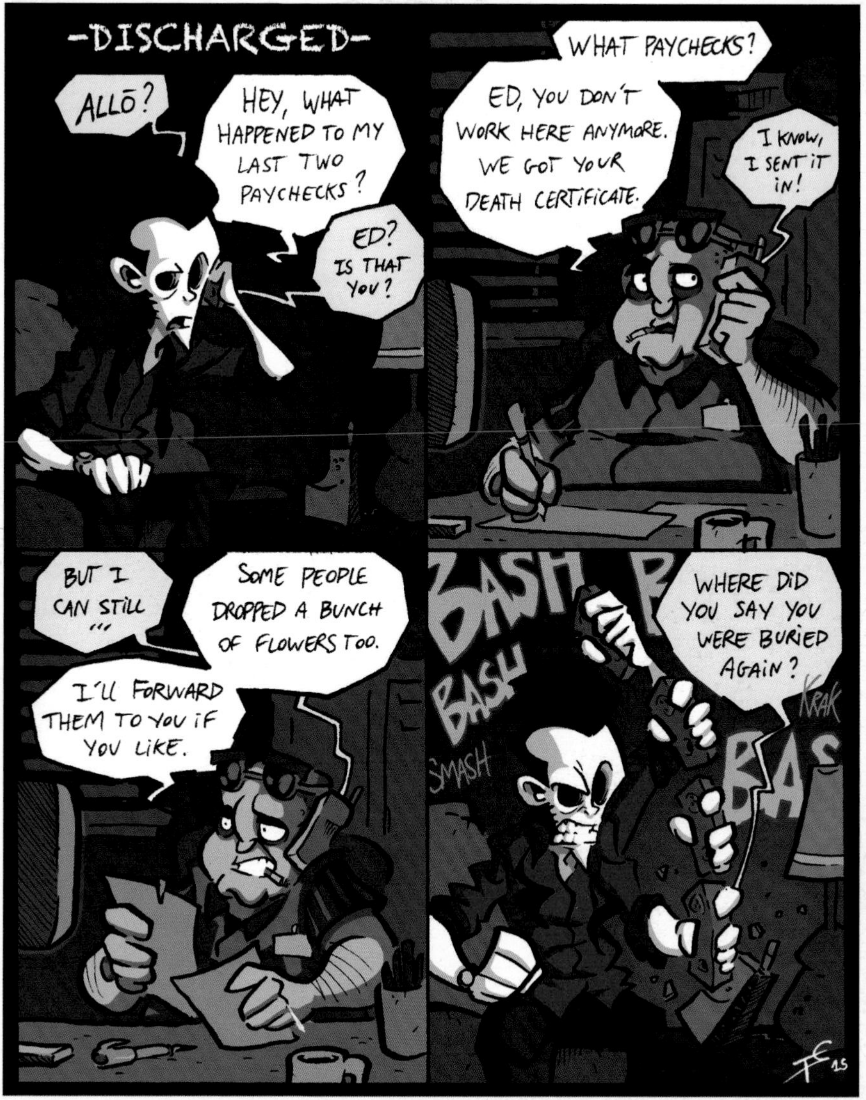
-DISCHARGED-
ALLŌ?
HEY, WHAT HAPPENED TO MY LAST TWO PAYCHECKS?
ED? IS THAT YOU?
WHAT PAYCHECKS?
ED, YOU DON'T WORK HERE ANYMORE. WE GOT YOUR DEATH CERTIFICATE.
I KNOW, I SENT IT IN!
BUT I CAN STILL ...
SOME PEOPLE DROPPED A BUNCH OF FLOWERS TOO.
I'LL FORWARD THEM TO YOU IF YOU LIKE.
BASH
BASH
SMASH
KRAK
WHERE DID YOU SAY YOU WERE BURIED AGAIN?
FC 15

-BLACKMAIL-

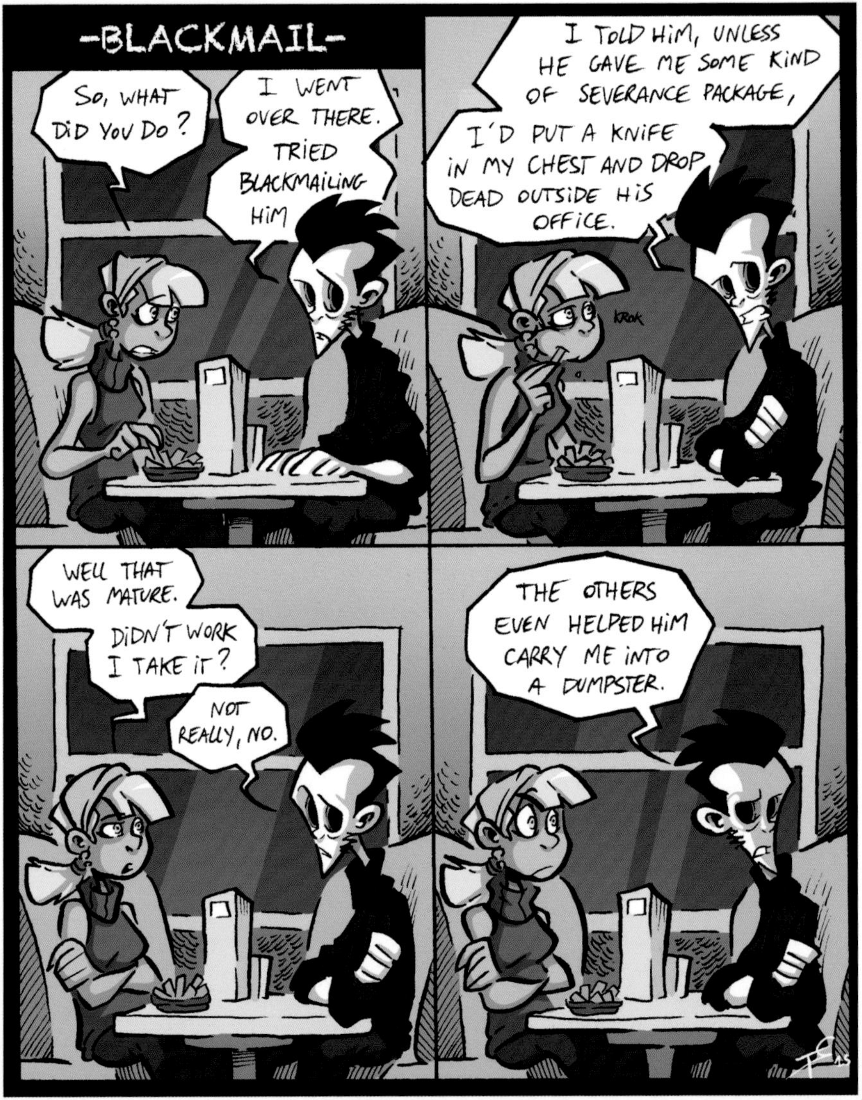

SO, WHAT DID YOU DO?
I WENT OVER THERE.
TRIED BLACKMAILING HIM
I TOLD HIM, UNLESS HE GAVE ME SOME KIND OF SEVERANCE PACKAGE,
I'D PUT A KNIFE IN MY CHEST AND DROP DEAD OUTSIDE HIS OFFICE.
KROK
WELL THAT WAS MATURE.
DIDN'T WORK I TAKE IT?
NOT REALLY, NO.
THE OTHERS EVEN HELPED HIM CARRY ME INTO A DUMPSTER.

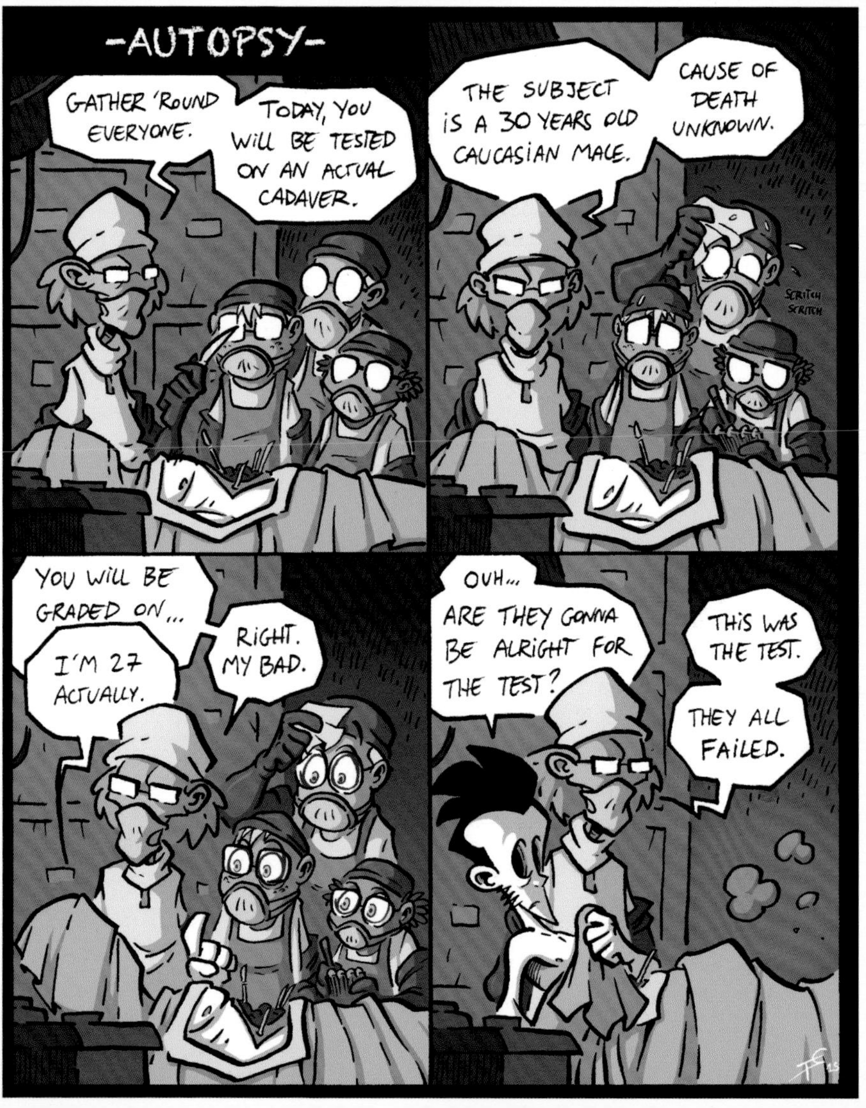
-AUTOPSY-
GATHER 'ROUND EVERYONE.
TODAY, YOU WILL BE TESTED ON AN ACTUAL CADAVER.
THE SUBJECT IS A 30 YEARS OLD CAUCASIAN MALE.
CAUSE OF DEATH UNKNOWN.
SCRITCH SCRITCH
YOU WILL BE GRADED ON...
I'M 27 ACTUALLY.
RIGHT. MY BAD.
OUH... ARE THEY GONNA BE ALRIGHT FOR THE TEST?
THIS WAS THE TEST.
THEY ALL FAILED.

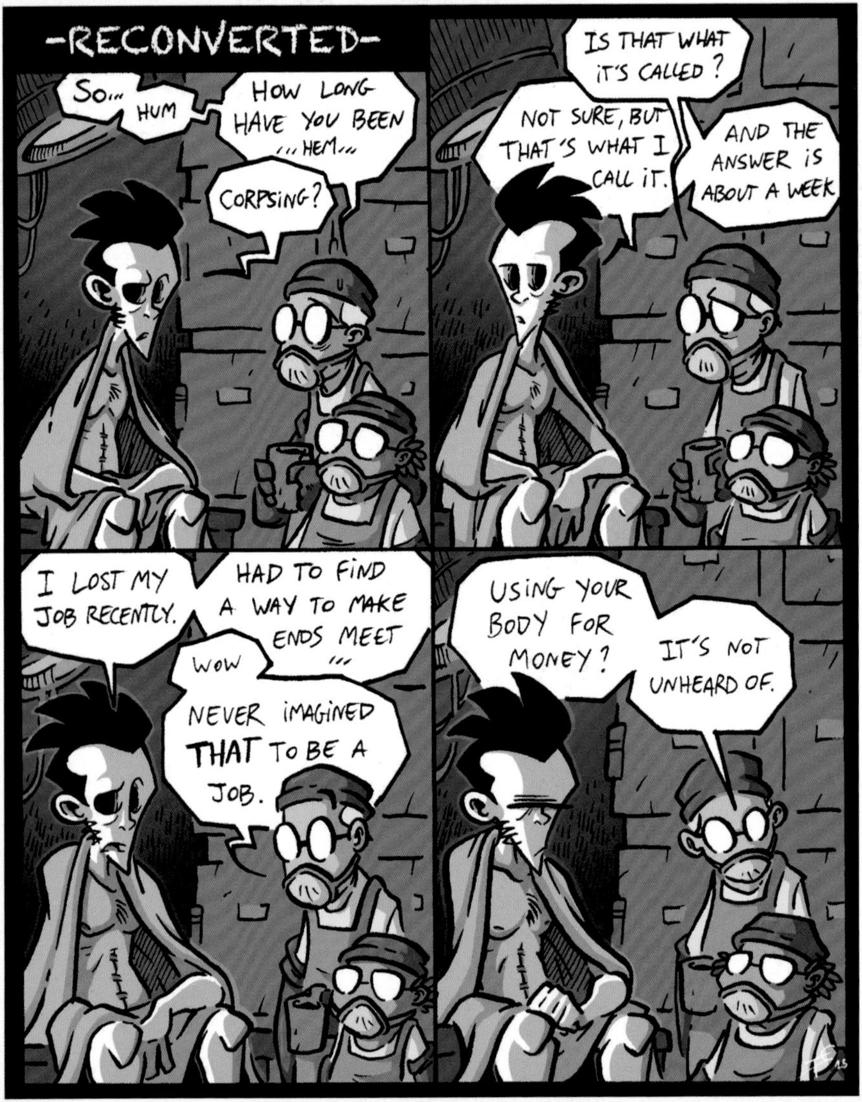
-RECONVERTED-
SO... HUM
HOW LONG HAVE YOU BEEN ...HEM...
CORPSING?
IS THAT WHAT IT'S CALLED?
NOT SURE, BUT THAT'S WHAT I CALL IT.
AND THE ANSWER IS ABOUT A WEEK
I LOST MY JOB RECENTLY.
HAD TO FIND A WAY TO MAKE ENDS MEET ...
WOW
NEVER IMAGINED THAT TO BE A JOB.
USING YOUR BODY FOR MONEY?
IT'S NOT UNHEARD OF.

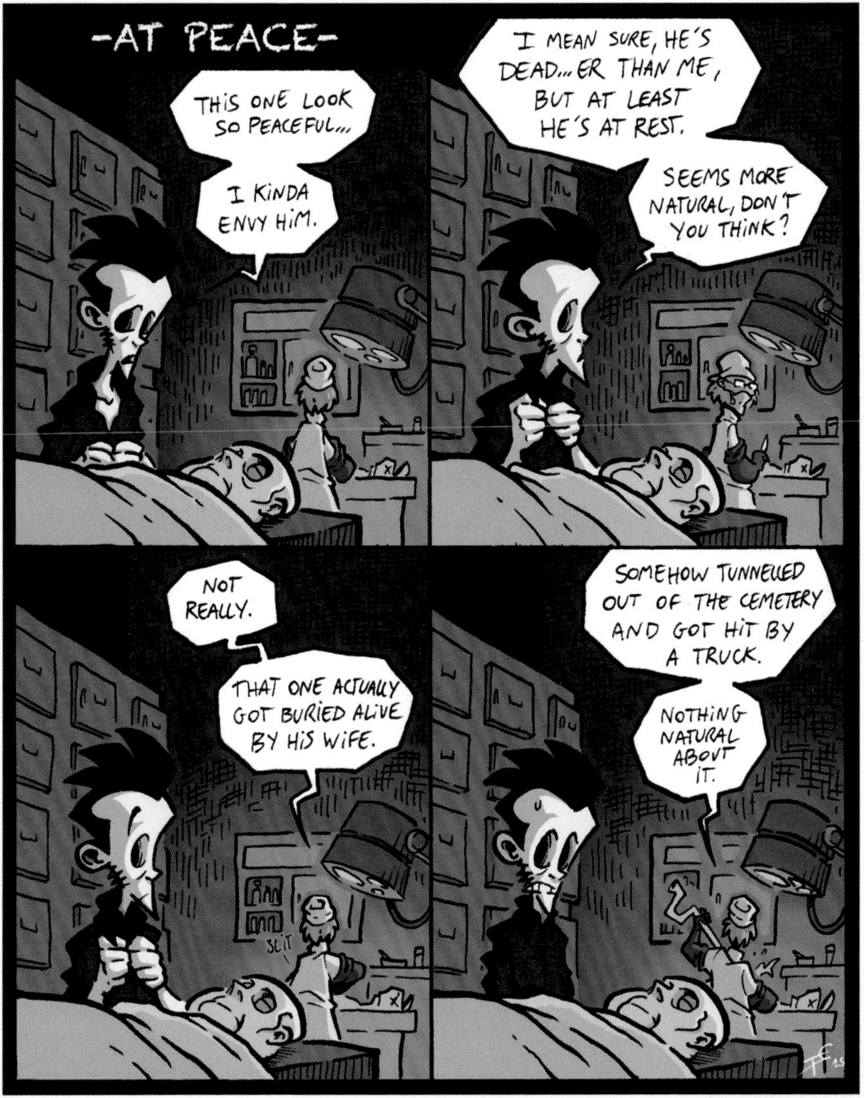
-AT PEACE-
THIS ONE LOOK SO PEACEFUL...
I KINDA ENVY HIM.
I MEAN SURE, HE'S DEAD...ER THAN ME, BUT AT LEAST HE'S AT REST.
SEEMS MORE NATURAL, DON'T YOU THINK?
NOT REALLY.
THAT ONE ACTUALLY GOT BURIED ALIVE BY HIS WIFE.
SLIT
SOMEHOW TUNNELLED OUT OF THE CEMETERY AND GOT HIT BY A TRUCK.
NOTHING NATURAL ABOUT IT.

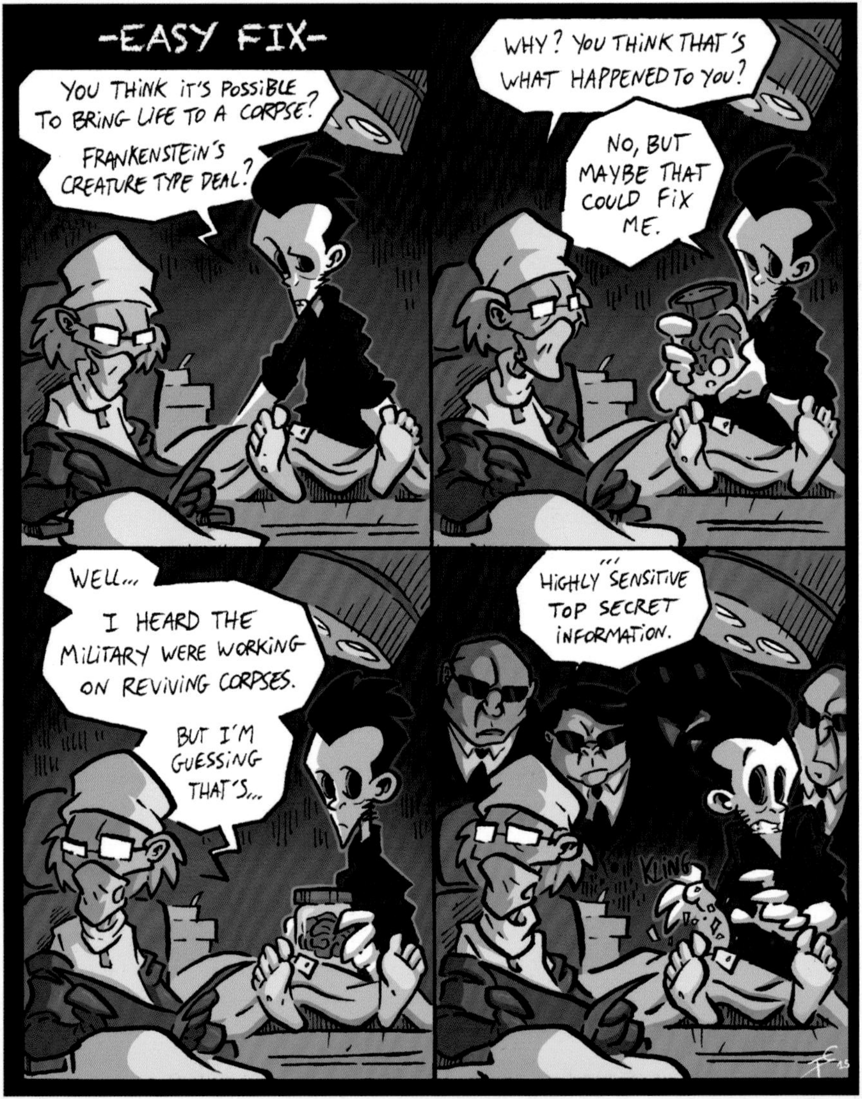
-EASY FIX-
YOU THINK IT'S POSSIBLE TO BRING LIFE TO A CORPSE?
FRANKENSTEIN'S CREATURE TYPE DEAL?
WHY? YOU THINK THAT'S WHAT HAPPENED TO YOU?
NO, BUT MAYBE THAT COULD FIX ME.
WELL...
I HEARD THE MILITARY WERE WORKING ON REVIVING CORPSES.
BUT I'M GUESSING THAT'S...
...HIGHLY SENSITIVE TOP SECRET INFORMATION.
KLING

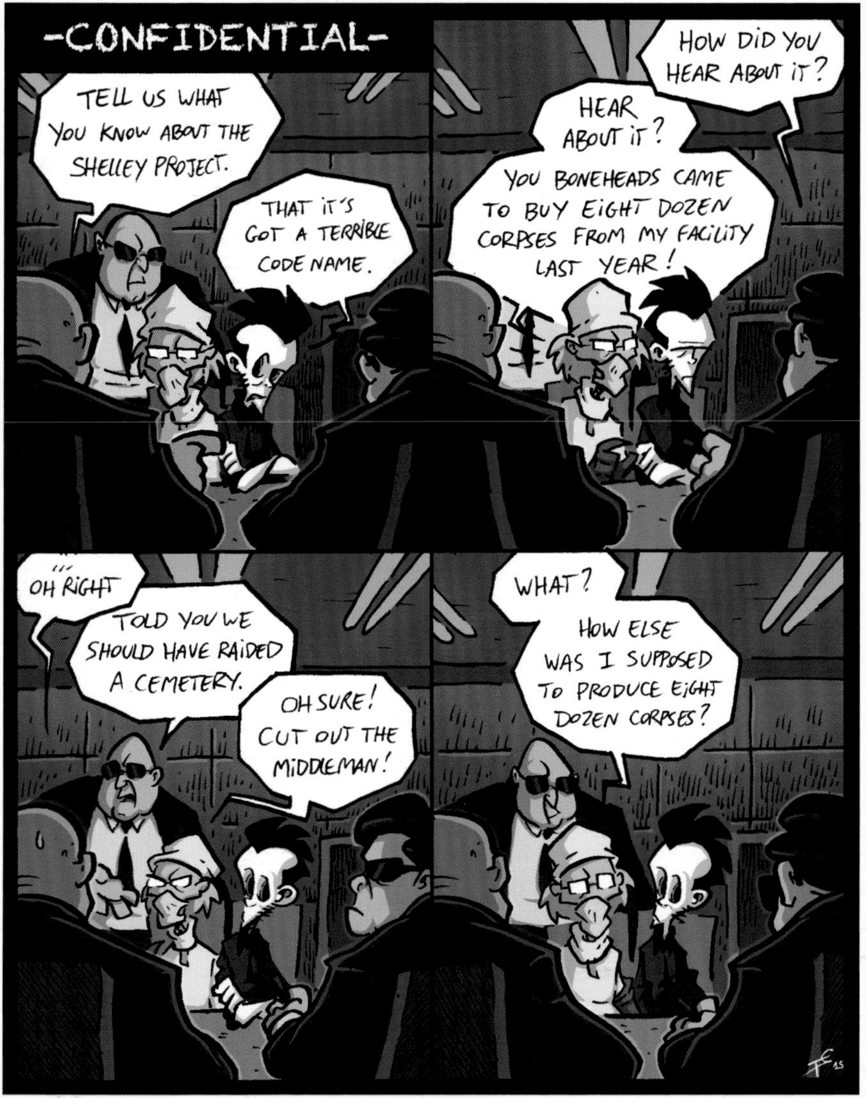
-CONFIDENTIAL-
TELL US WHAT YOU KNOW ABOUT THE SHELLEY PROJECT.
THAT IT'S GOT A TERRIBLE CODE NAME.
HOW DID YOU HEAR ABOUT IT?
HEAR ABOUT IT?
YOU BONEHEADS CAME TO BUY EIGHT DOZEN CORPSES FROM MY FACILITY LAST YEAR!
... OH RIGHT
TOLD YOU WE SHOULD HAVE RAIDED A CEMETERY.
OH SURE! CUT OUT THE MIDDLEMAN!
WHAT?
HOW ELSE WAS I SUPPOSED TO PRODUCE EIGHT DOZEN CORPSES?

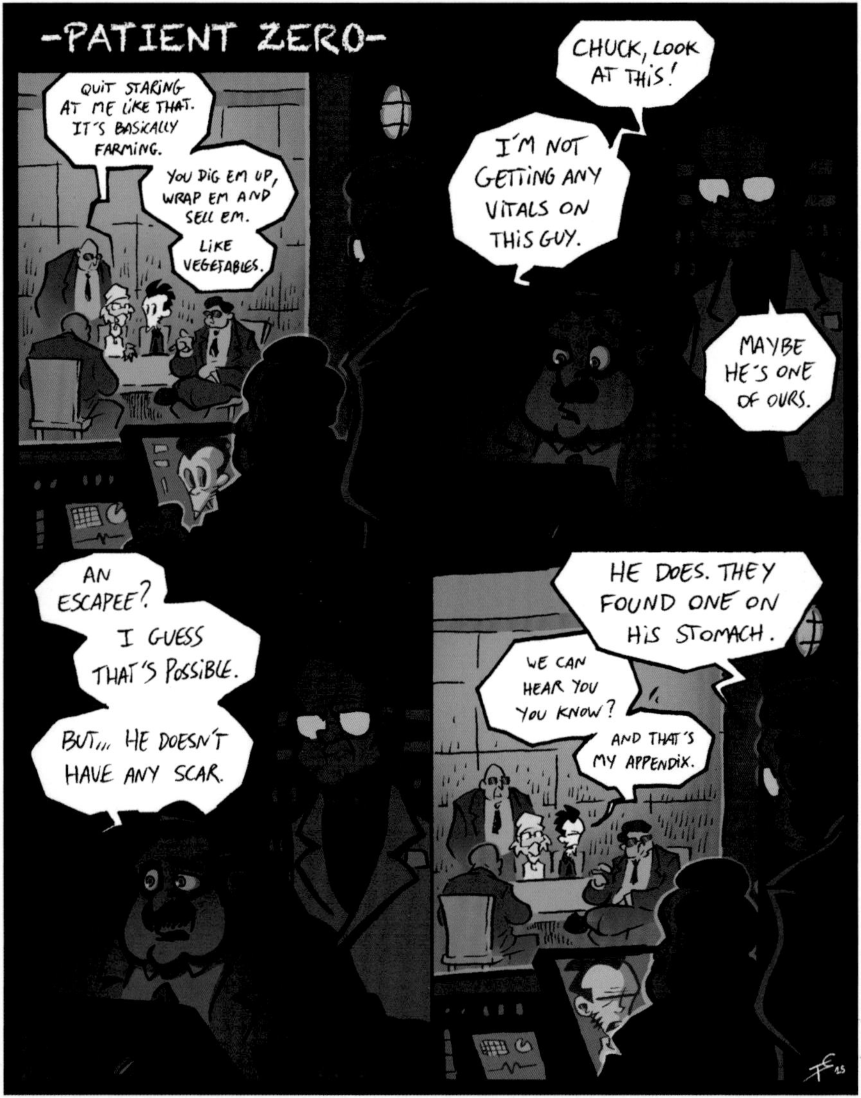
-PATIENT ZERO-
QUIT STARING AT ME LIKE THAT. IT'S BASICALLY FARMING.
YOU DIG EM UP, WRAP EM AND SELL EM.
LIKE VEGETABLES.
CHUCK, LOOK AT THIS!
I'M NOT GETTING ANY VITALS ON THIS GUY.
MAYBE HE'S ONE OF OURS.
AN ESCAPEE?
I GUESS THAT'S POSSIBLE.
BUT... HE DOESN'T HAVE ANY SCAR.
HE DOES. THEY FOUND ONE ON HIS STOMACH.
WE CAN HEAR YOU YOU KNOW?
AND THAT'S MY APPENDIX.

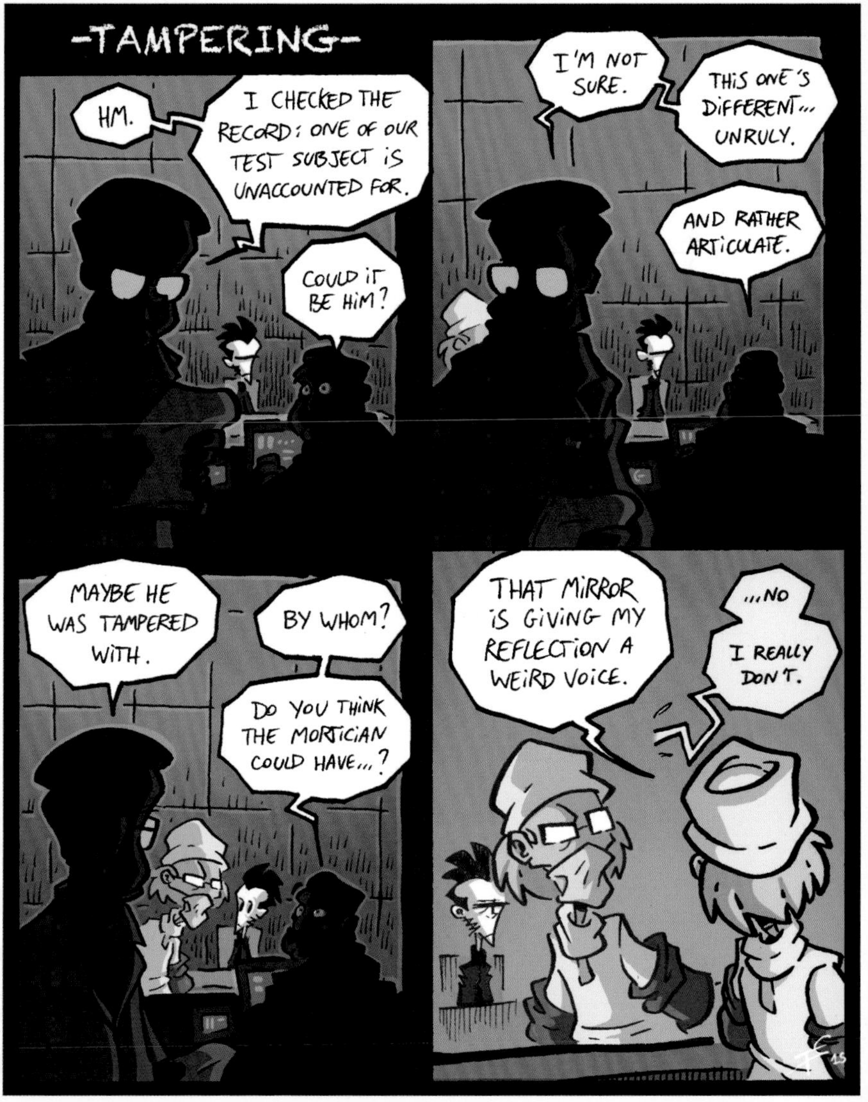
-TAMPERING-
HM.
I CHECKED THE RECORD: ONE OF OUR TEST SUBJECT IS UNACCOUNTED FOR.
COULD IT BE HIM?
I'M NOT SURE.
THIS ONE'S DIFFERENT... UNRULY.
AND RATHER ARTICULATE.
MAYBE HE WAS TAMPERED WITH.
BY WHOM?
DO YOU THINK THE MORTICIAN COULD HAVE...?
THAT MIRROR IS GIVING MY REFLECTION A WEIRD VOICE.
...NO
I REALLY DON'T.

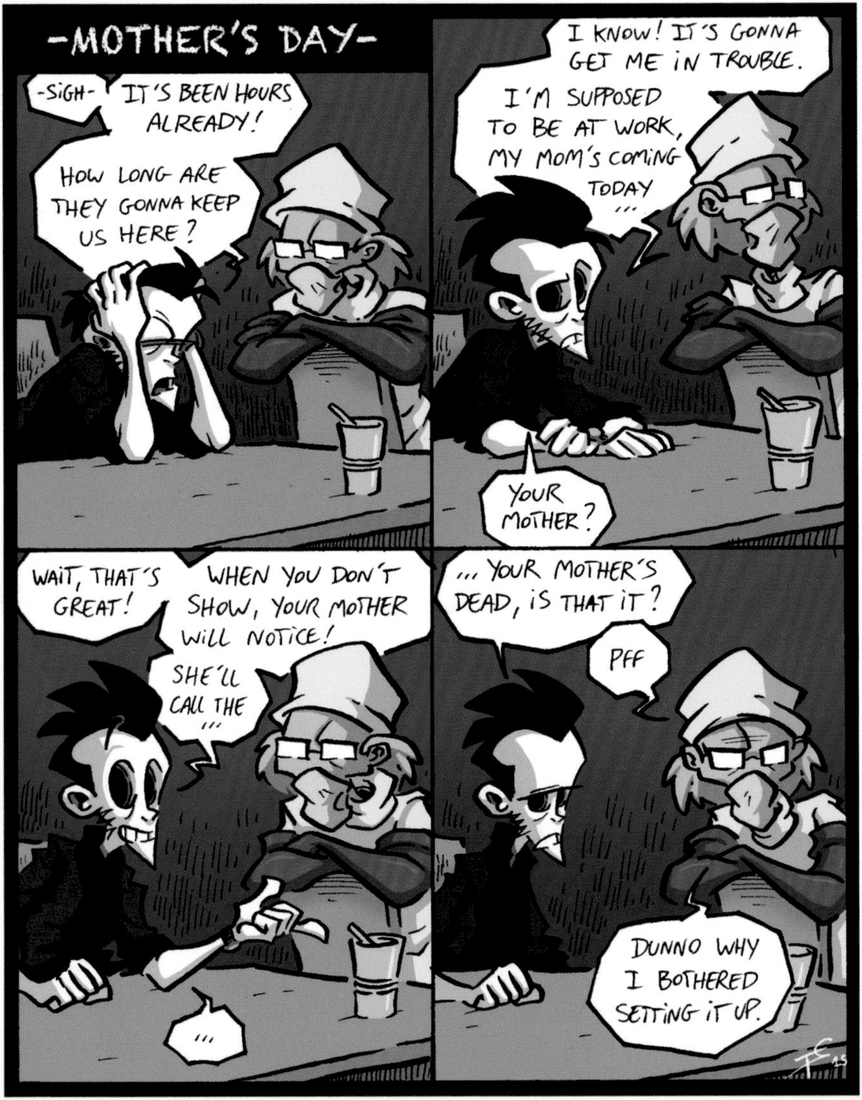
-MOTHER'S DAY-
-SIGH-
IT'S BEEN HOURS ALREADY!
HOW LONG ARE THEY GONNA KEEP US HERE?
I KNOW! IT'S GONNA GET ME IN TROUBLE.
I'M SUPPOSED TO BE AT WORK, MY MOM'S COMING TODAY ...
YOUR MOTHER?
WAIT, THAT'S GREAT!
WHEN YOU DON'T SHOW, YOUR MOTHER WILL NOTICE!
SHE'LL CALL THE ...
...
... YOUR MOTHER'S DEAD, IS THAT IT?
PFF
DUNNO WHY I BOTHERED SETTING IT UP.

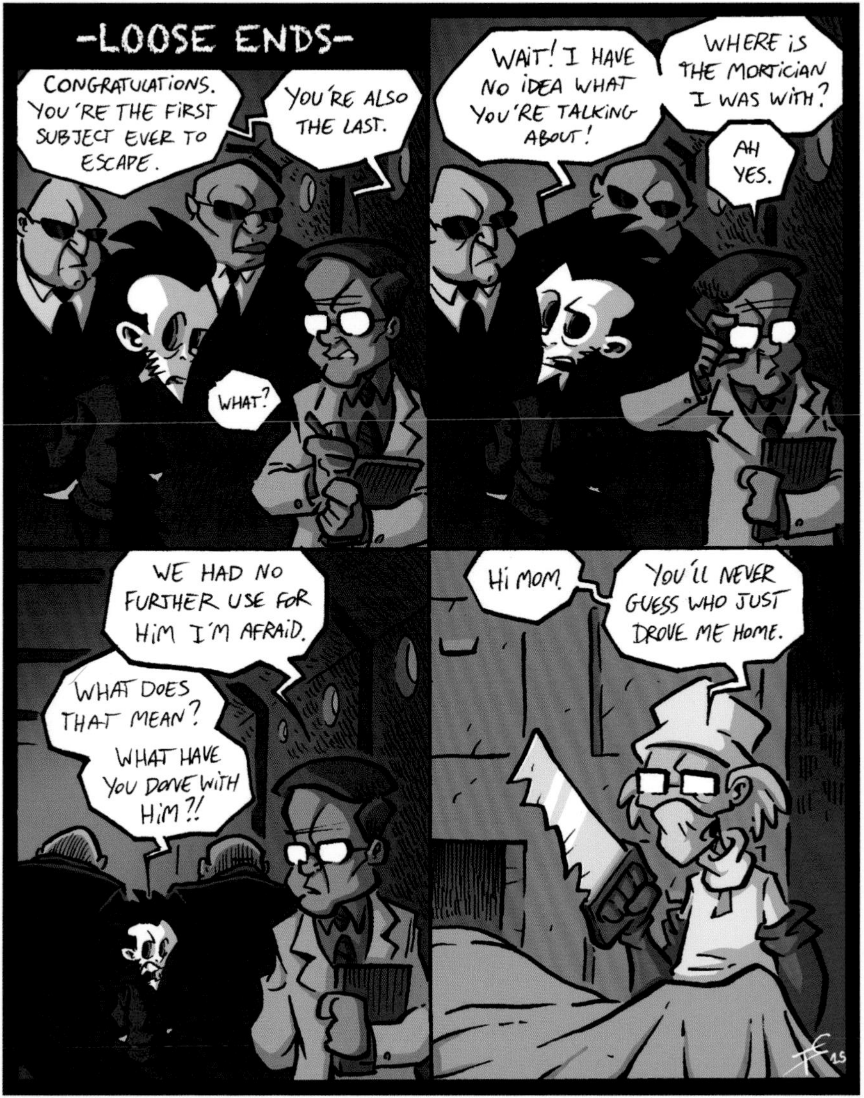
-LOOSE ENDS-
CONGRATULATIONS. YOU'RE THE FIRST SUBJECT EVER TO ESCAPE.
YOU'RE ALSO THE LAST.
WHAT?
WAIT! I HAVE NO IDEA WHAT YOU'RE TALKING ABOUT!
WHERE IS THE MORTICIAN I WAS WITH?
AH YES.
WE HAD NO FURTHER USE FOR HIM I'M AFRAID.
WHAT DOES THAT MEAN?
WHAT HAVE YOU DONE WITH HIM?!
Hi MOM.
YOU'LL NEVER GUESS WHO JUST DROVE ME HOME.

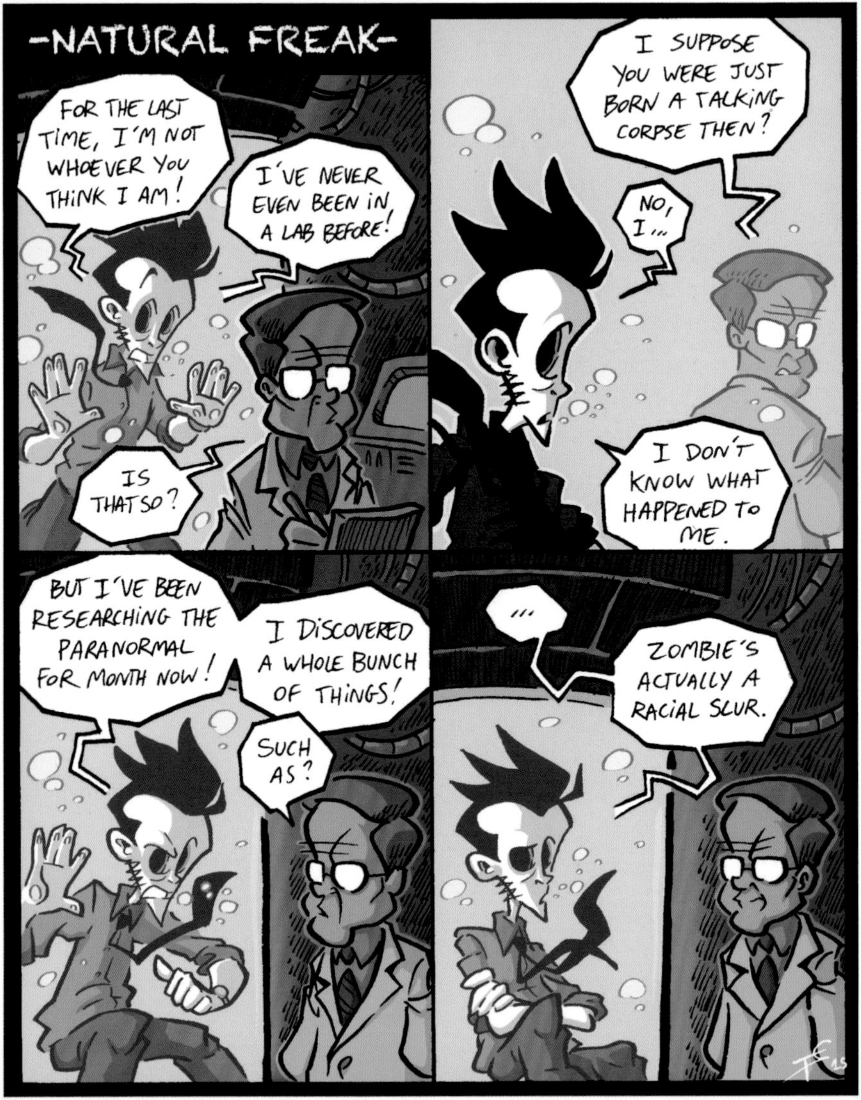
-NATURAL FREAK-
FOR THE LAST TIME, I'M NOT WHOEVER YOU THINK I AM!
I'VE NEVER EVEN BEEN IN A LAB BEFORE!
IS THAT SO?
I SUPPOSE YOU WERE JUST BORN A TALKING CORPSE THEN?
NO, I...
I DON'T KNOW WHAT HAPPENED TO ME.
BUT I'VE BEEN RESEARCHING THE PARANORMAL FOR MONTH NOW!
I DISCOVERED A WHOLE BUNCH OF THINGS!
SUCH AS?
...
ZOMBIE'S ACTUALLY A RACIAL SLUR.

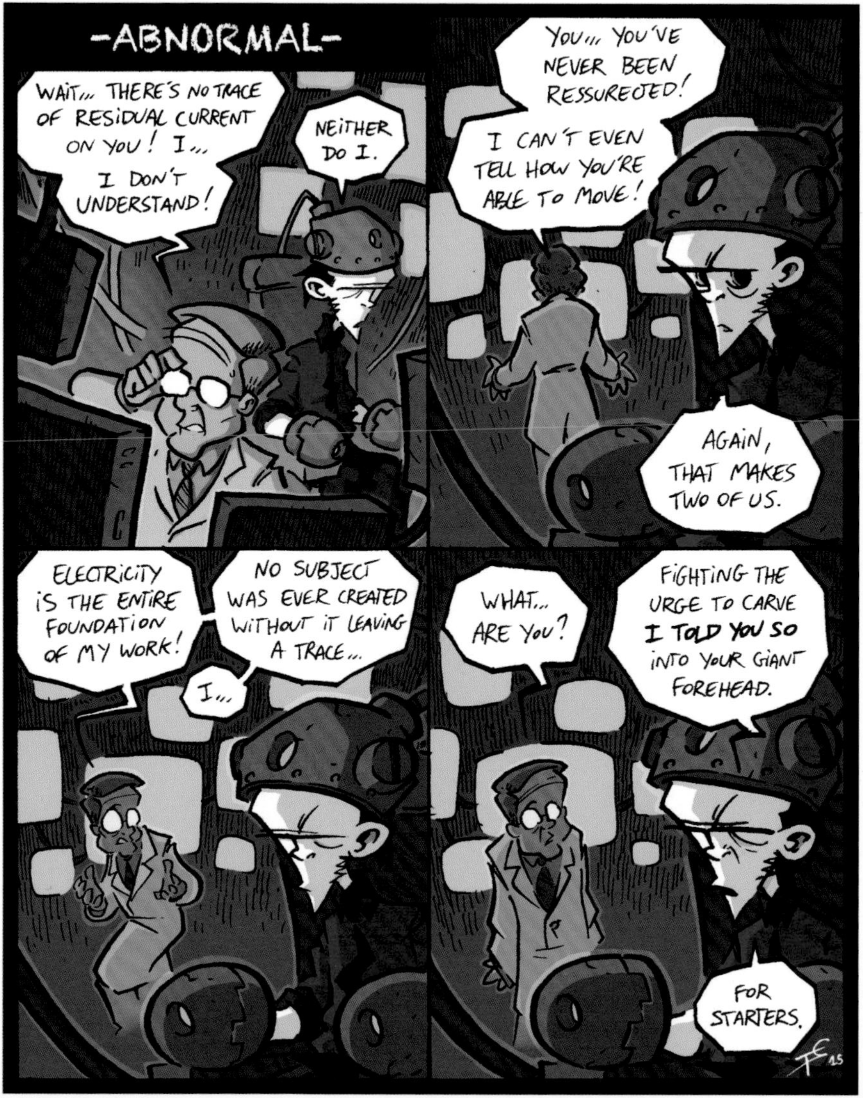
-ABNORMAL-
WAIT... THERE'S NO TRACE OF RESIDUAL CURRENT ON YOU! I...
I DON'T UNDERSTAND!
NEITHER DO I.
YOU... YOU'VE NEVER BEEN RESSURECTED!
I CAN'T EVEN TELL HOW YOU'RE ABLE TO MOVE!
AGAIN, THAT MAKES TWO OF US.
ELECTRICITY IS THE ENTIRE FOUNDATION OF MY WORK!
NO SUBJECT WAS EVER CREATED WITHOUT IT LEAVING A TRACE...
I...
WHAT... ARE YOU?
FIGHTING THE URGE TO CARVE **I TOLD YOU SO** INTO YOUR GIANT FOREHEAD.
FOR STARTERS.

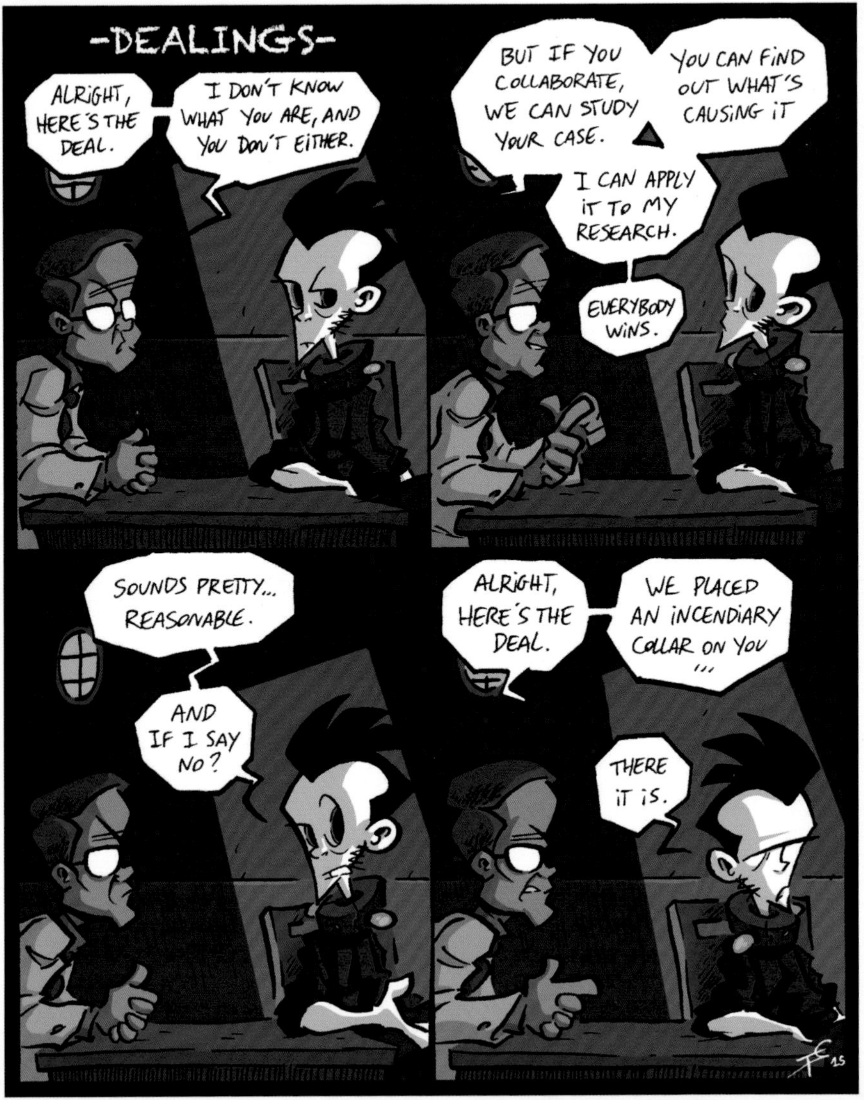
-DEALINGS-
ALRIGHT, HERE'S THE DEAL.
I DON'T KNOW WHAT YOU ARE, AND YOU DON'T EITHER.
BUT IF YOU COLLABORATE, WE CAN STUDY YOUR CASE.
YOU CAN FIND OUT WHAT'S CAUSING IT
I CAN APPLY IT TO MY RESEARCH.
EVERYBODY WINS.
SOUNDS PRETTY... REASONABLE.
AND IF I SAY NO?
ALRIGHT, HERE'S THE DEAL.
WE PLACED AN INCENDIARY COLLAR ON YOU ...
THERE IT IS.

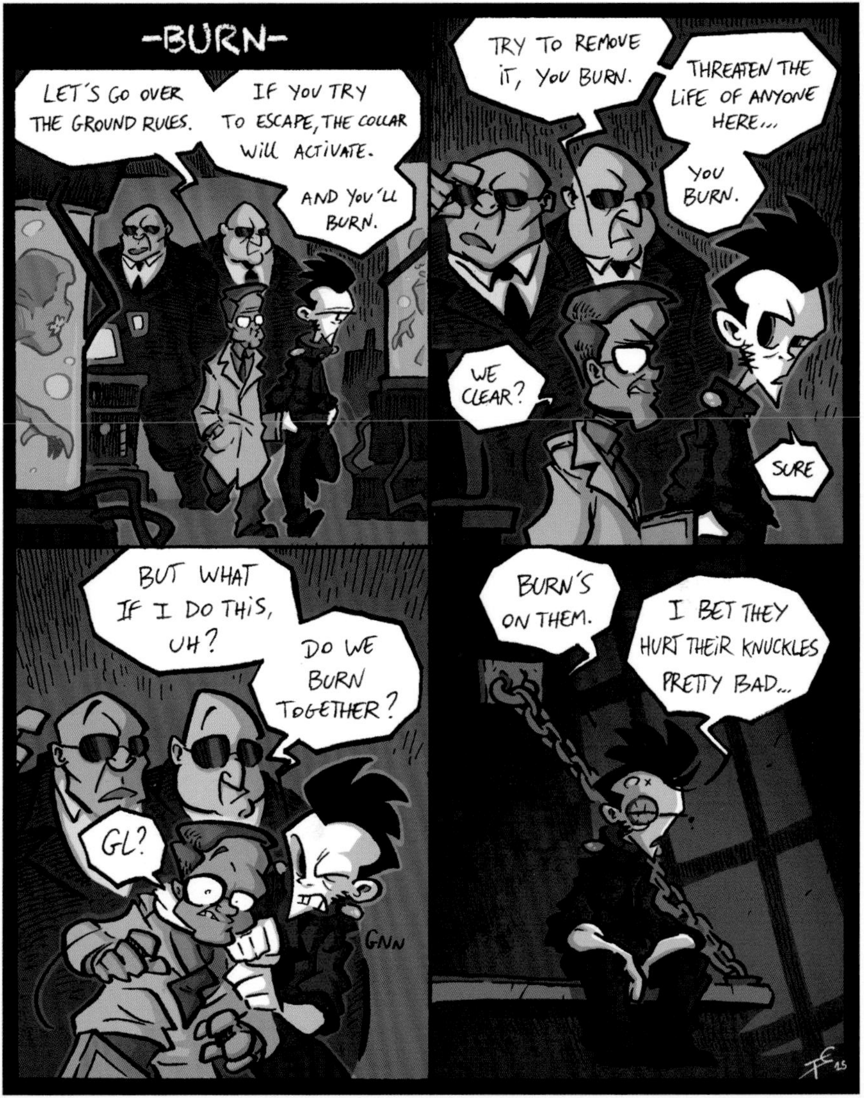
-BURN-
LET'S GO OVER THE GROUND RULES.
IF YOU TRY TO ESCAPE, THE COLLAR WILL ACTIVATE.
AND YOU'LL BURN.
TRY TO REMOVE IT, YOU BURN.
THREATEN THE LIFE OF ANYONE HERE...
YOU BURN.
WE CLEAR?
SURE
BUT WHAT IF I DO THIS, UH?
DO WE BURN TOGETHER?
GL?
GNN
BURN'S ON THEM.
I BET THEY HURT THEIR KNUCKLES PRETTY BAD...

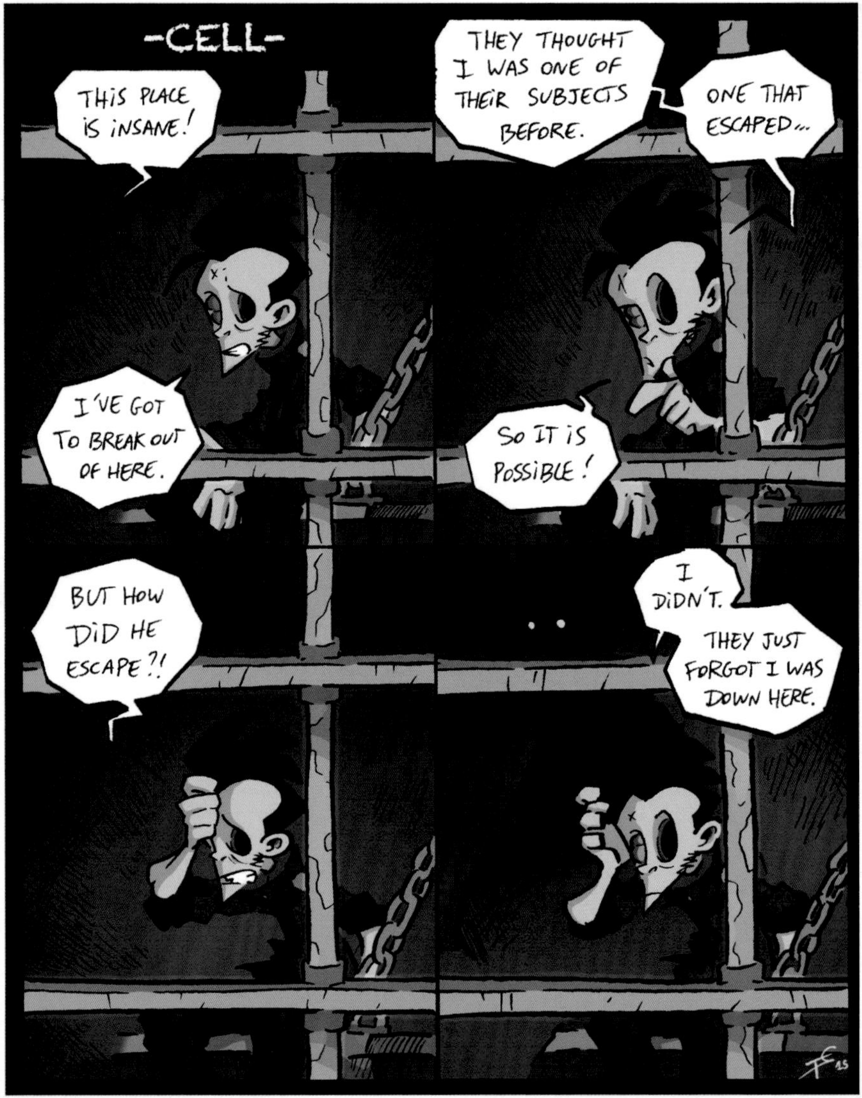
-CELL-
THIS PLACE IS INSANE!
I'VE GOT TO BREAK OUT OF HERE.
THEY THOUGHT I WAS ONE OF THEIR SUBJECTS BEFORE.
ONE THAT ESCAPED...
SO IT IS POSSIBLE!
BUT HOW DID HE ESCAPE?!
I DIDN'T.
THEY JUST FORGOT I WAS DOWN HERE.

They say
life is pain.

But death
is no picnic
either.

Chapter III
-Bargaining-

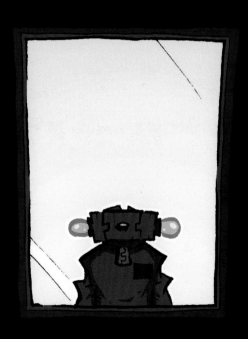

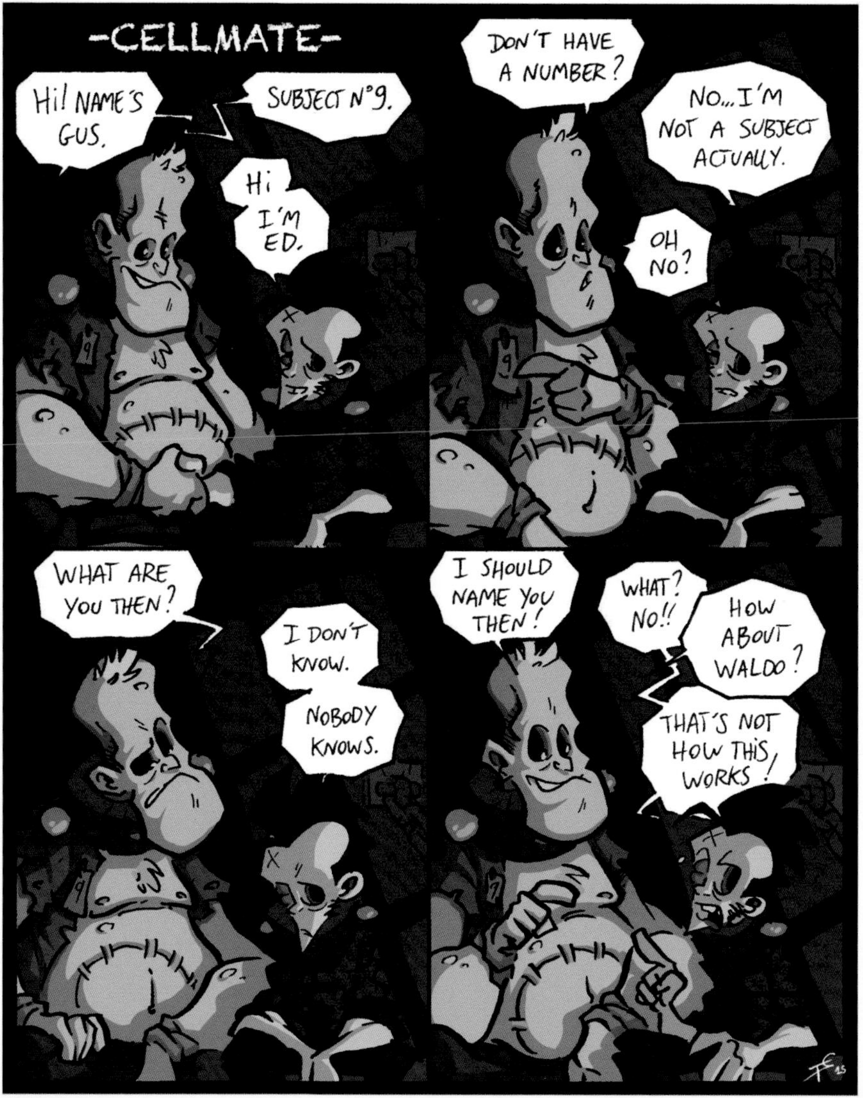
-CELLMATE-
Hi! NAME'S GUS.
SUBJECT N°9.
Hi I'M ED.
DON'T HAVE A NUMBER?
NO... I'M NOT A SUBJECT ACTUALLY.
OH NO?
WHAT ARE YOU THEN?
I DON'T KNOW.
NOBODY KNOWS.
I SHOULD NAME YOU THEN!
WHAT? NO!!
HOW ABOUT WALDO?
THAT'S NOT HOW THIS WORKS!

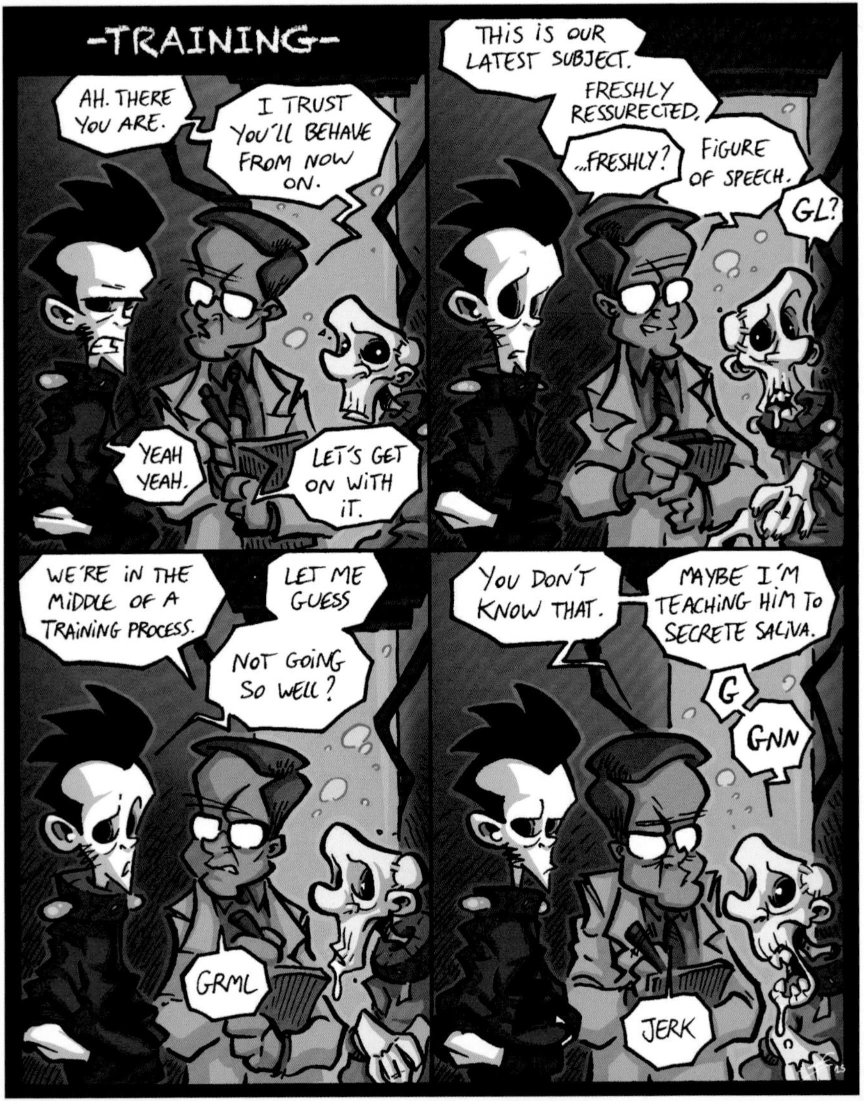
-TRAINING-
AH. THERE YOU ARE.
I TRUST YOU'LL BEHAVE FROM NOW ON.
YEAH YEAH.
LET'S GET ON WITH IT.
THIS IS OUR LATEST SUBJECT.
FRESHLY RESSURECTED.
...FRESHLY?
FIGURE OF SPEECH.
GL?
WE'RE IN THE MIDDLE OF A TRAINING PROCESS.
LET ME GUESS
NOT GOING SO WELL?
GRML
YOU DON'T KNOW THAT.
MAYBE I'M TEACHING HIM TO SECRETE SALIVA.
G
GNN
JERK

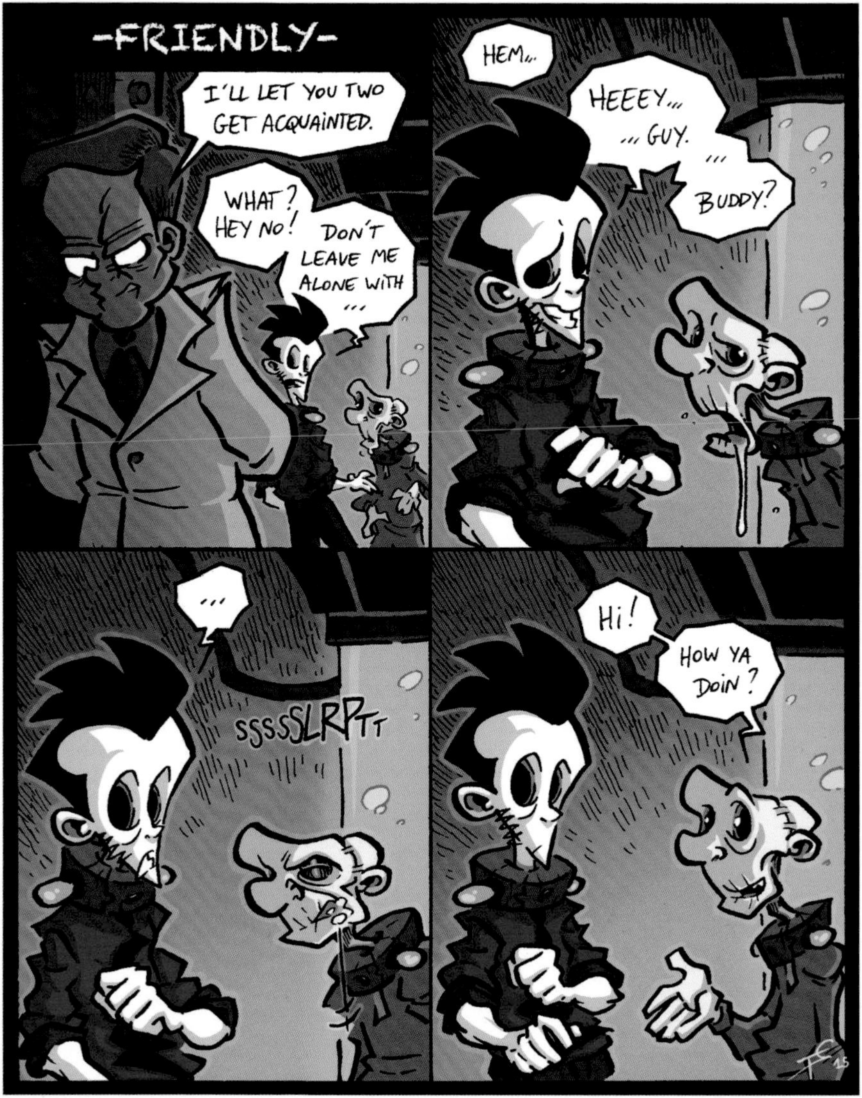
-FRIENDLY-
I'LL LET YOU TWO GET ACQUAINTED.
WHAT? HEY NO!
DON'T LEAVE ME ALONE WITH ...
HEM...
HEEEY... ...GUY.
... BUDDY?
...
SSSSSLRPTT
Hi!
HOW YA DOIN?

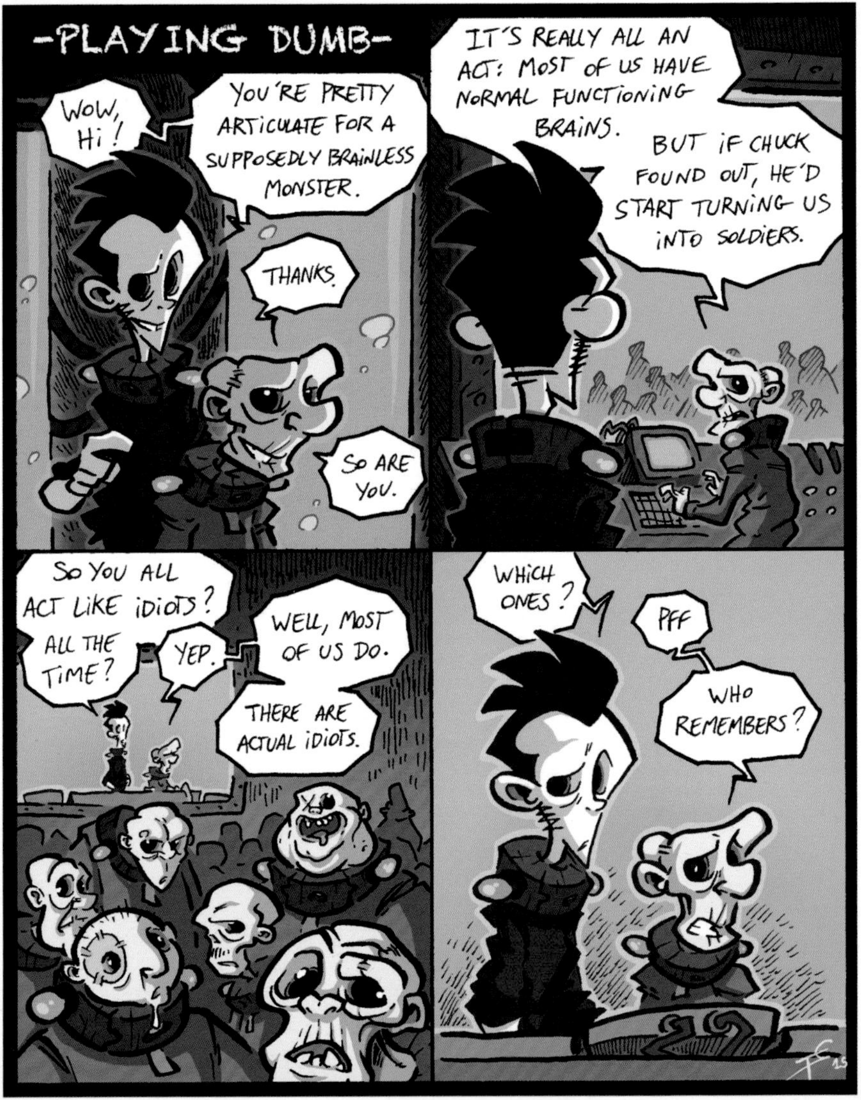
-PLAYING DUMB-
WOW, HI!
YOU'RE PRETTY ARTICULATE FOR A SUPPOSEDLY BRAINLESS MONSTER.
THANKS.
SO ARE YOU.
IT'S REALLY ALL AN ACT: MOST OF US HAVE NORMAL FUNCTIONING BRAINS.
BUT IF CHUCK FOUND OUT, HE'D START TURNING US INTO SOLDIERS.
SO YOU ALL ACT LIKE IDIOTS?
ALL THE TIME?
YEP.
WELL, MOST OF US DO.
THERE ARE ACTUAL IDIOTS.
WHICH ONES?
PFF
WHO REMEMBERS?

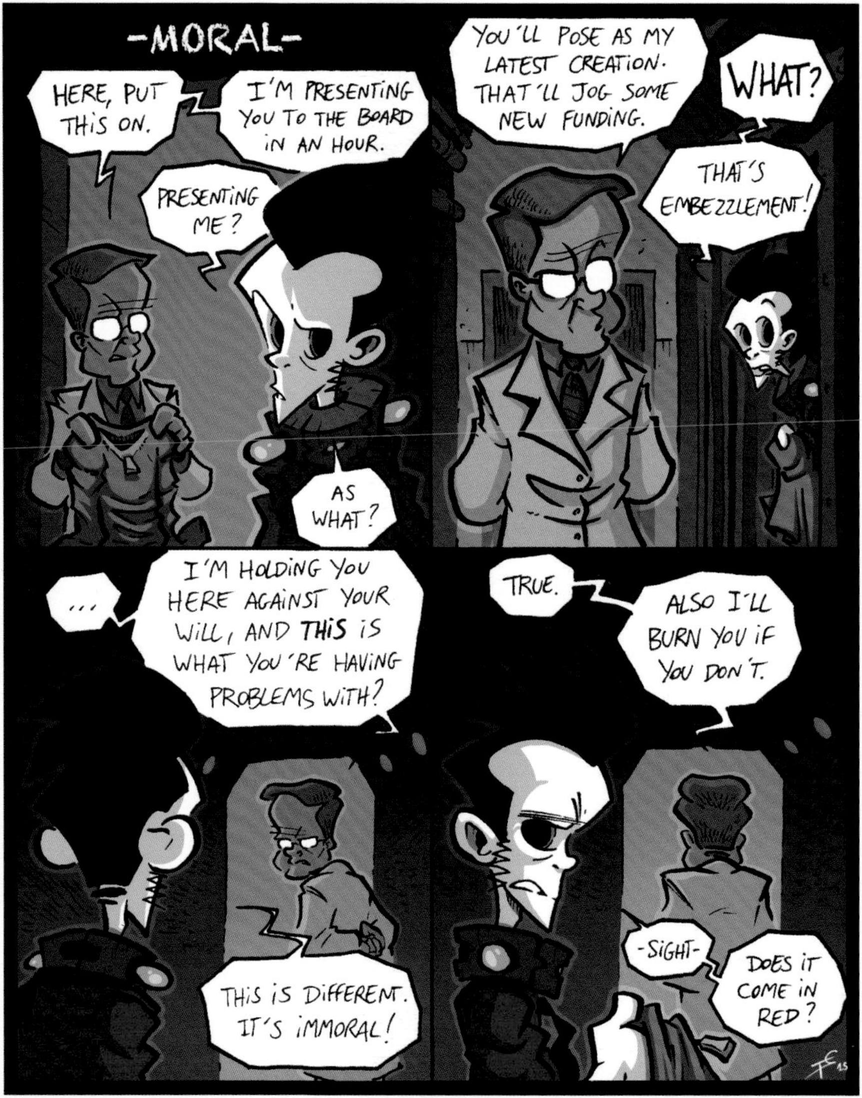

-MORAL-
HERE, PUT THIS ON.
I'M PRESENTING YOU TO THE BOARD IN AN HOUR.
PRESENTING ME?
AS WHAT?
YOU'LL POSE AS MY LATEST CREATION. THAT'LL JOG SOME NEW FUNDING.
WHAT?
THAT'S EMBEZZLEMENT!
...
I'M HOLDING YOU HERE AGAINST YOUR WILL, AND THIS IS WHAT YOU'RE HAVING PROBLEMS WITH?
THIS IS DIFFERENT. IT'S IMMORAL!
TRUE.
ALSO I'LL BURN YOU IF YOU DON'T.
-SIGH-
DOES IT COME IN RED?

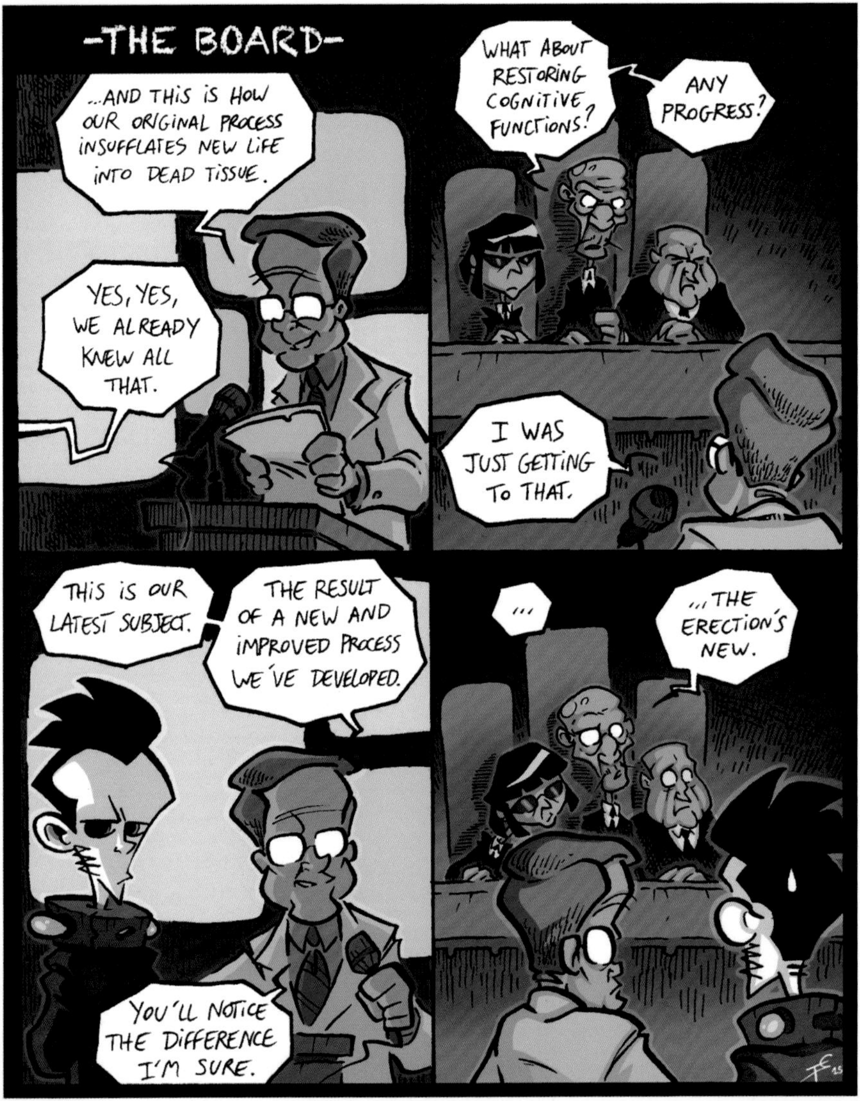
-THE BOARD-
...AND THIS IS HOW OUR ORIGINAL PROCESS INSUFFLATES NEW LIFE INTO DEAD TISSUE.
YES, YES, WE ALREADY KNEW ALL THAT.
WHAT ABOUT RESTORING COGNITIVE FUNCTIONS?
ANY PROGRESS?
I WAS JUST GETTING TO THAT.
THIS IS OUR LATEST SUBJECT.
THE RESULT OF A NEW AND IMPROVED PROCESS WE'VE DEVELOPED.
YOU'LL NOTICE THE DIFFERENCE I'M SURE.
...
...THE ERECTION'S NEW.

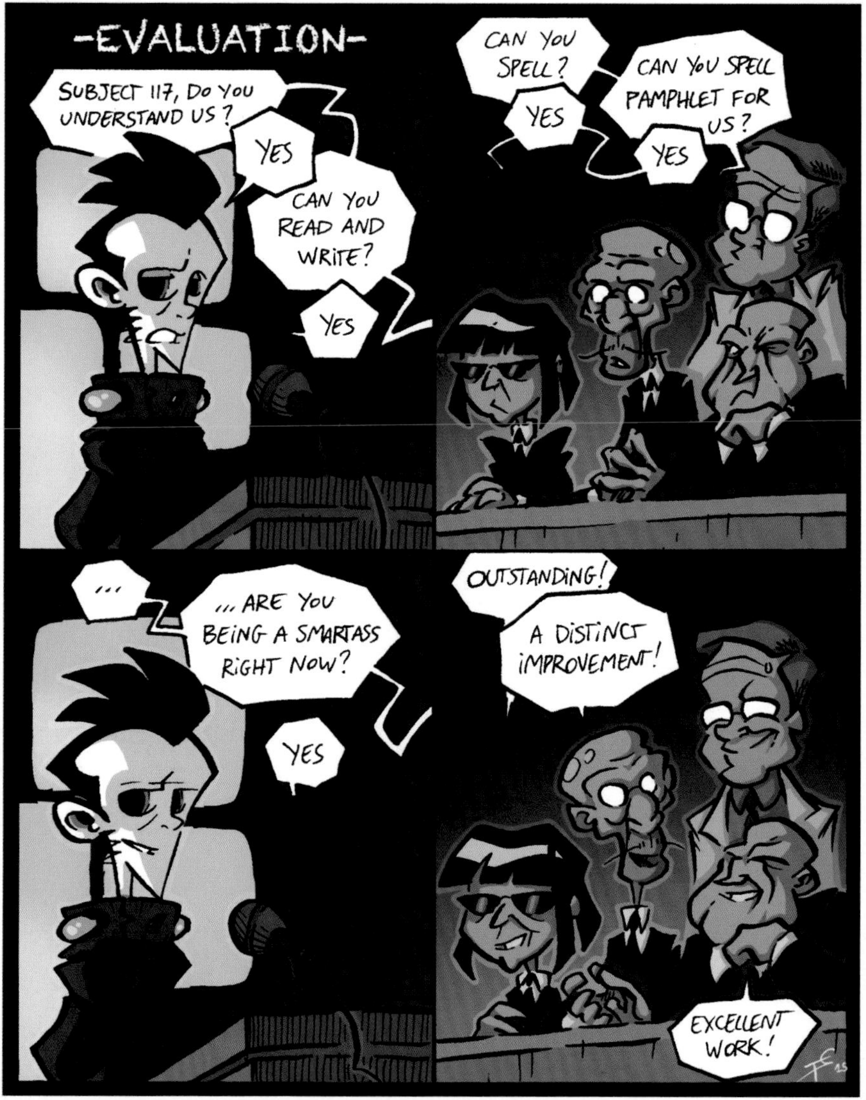
-EVALUATION-
SUBJECT 117, DO YOU UNDERSTAND US?
YES
CAN YOU READ AND WRITE?
YES
CAN YOU SPELL?
YES
CAN YOU SPELL PAMPHLET FOR US?
YES
...
... ARE YOU BEING A SMARTASS RIGHT NOW?
YES
OUTSTANDING!
A DISTINCT IMPROVEMENT!
EXCELLENT WORK!

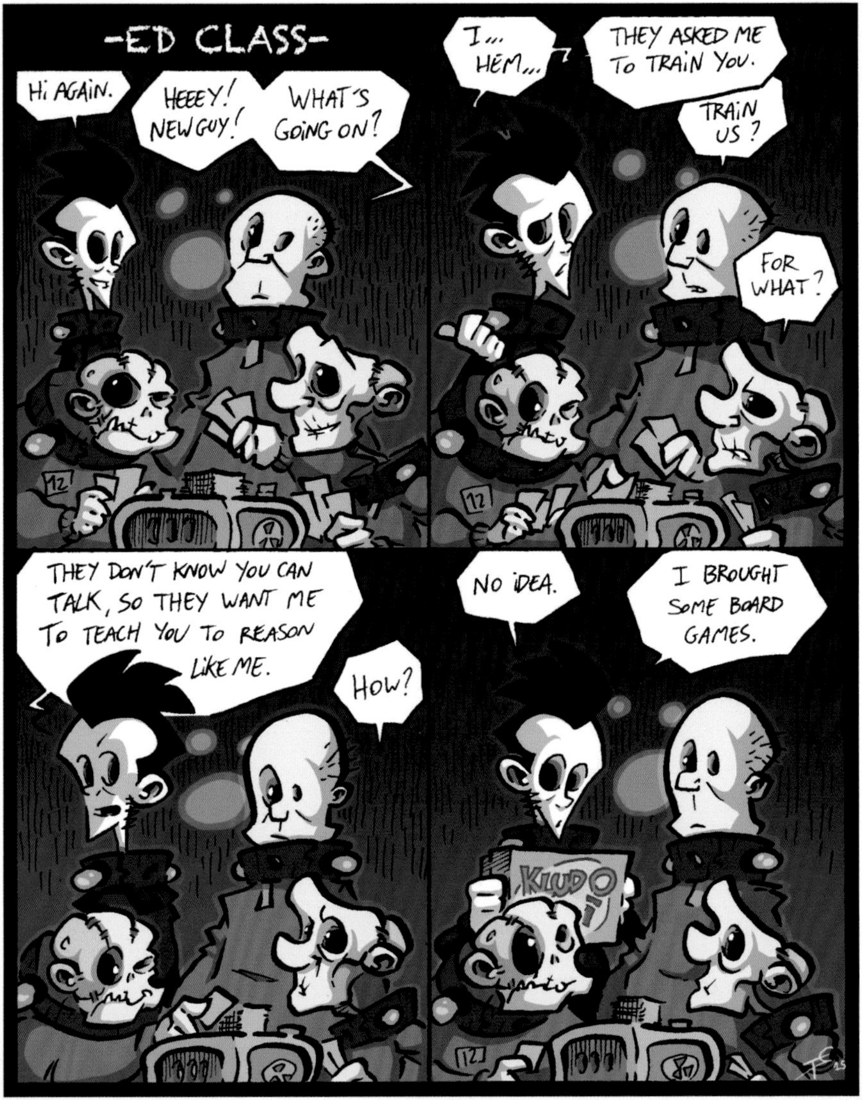
-ED CLASS-
Hi AGAIN.
HEEEY! NEW GUY!
WHAT'S GOING ON?
I... HEM...
THEY ASKED ME TO TRAIN YOU.
TRAIN US?
FOR WHAT?
THEY DON'T KNOW YOU CAN TALK, SO THEY WANT ME TO TEACH YOU TO REASON LIKE ME.
HOW?
NO IDEA.
I BROUGHT SOME BOARD GAMES.
KLUDO

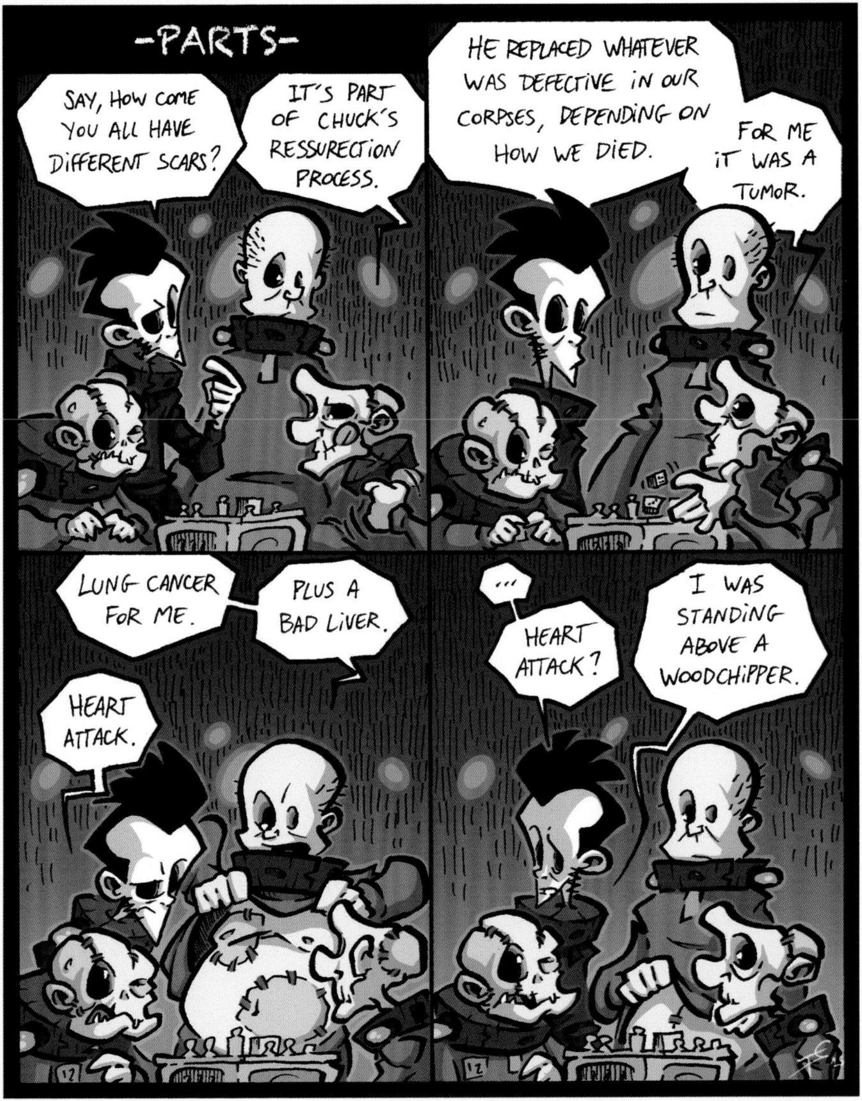
-PARTS-
SAY, HOW COME YOU ALL HAVE DIFFERENT SCARS?
IT'S PART OF CHUCK'S RESSURECTION PROCESS.
HE REPLACED WHATEVER WAS DEFECTIVE IN OUR CORPSES, DEPENDING ON HOW WE DIED.
FOR ME IT WAS A TUMOR.
LUNG CANCER FOR ME.
PLUS A BAD LIVER.
HEART ATTACK.
...
HEART ATTACK?
I WAS STANDING ABOVE A WOODCHIPPER.

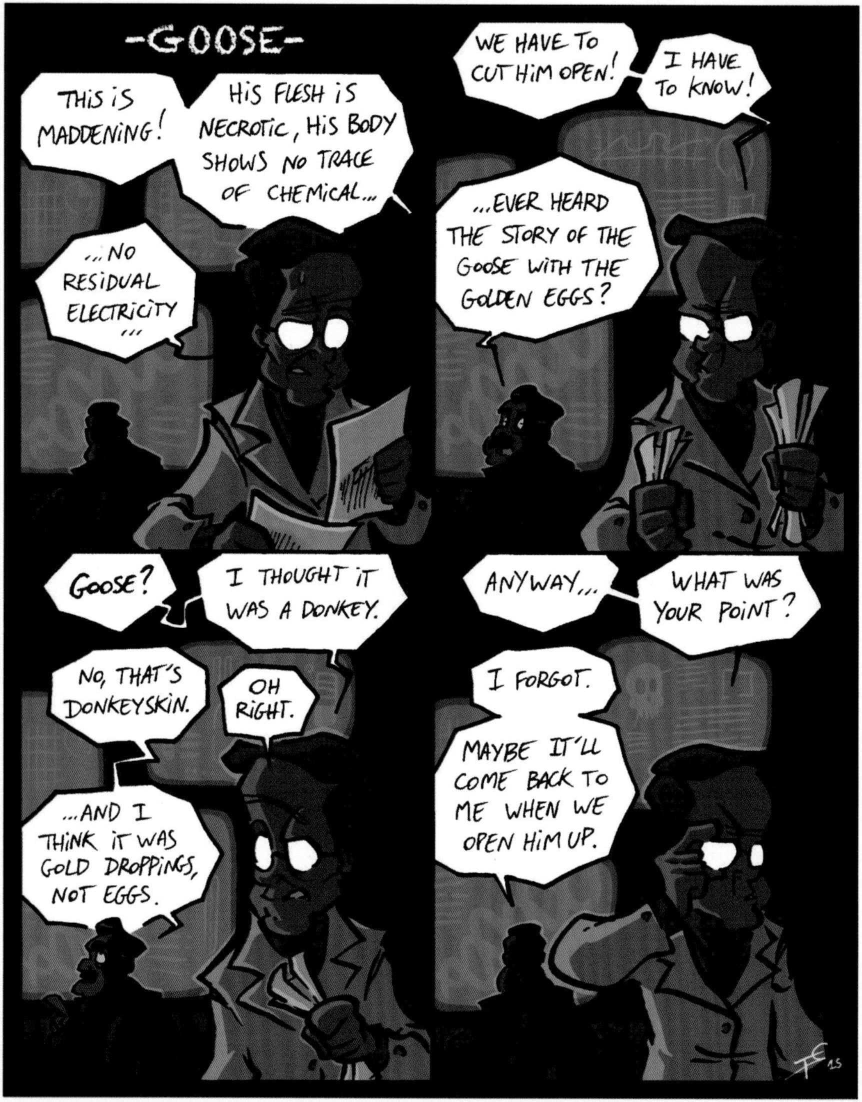
-GOOSE-
THIS IS MADDENING!
HIS FLESH IS NECROTIC, HIS BODY SHOWS NO TRACE OF CHEMICAL...
...NO RESIDUAL ELECTRICITY ...
WE HAVE TO CUT HIM OPEN!
I HAVE TO KNOW!
...EVER HEARD THE STORY OF THE GOOSE WITH THE GOLDEN EGGS?
GOOSE?
I THOUGHT IT WAS A DONKEY.
NO, THAT'S DONKEYSKIN.
OH RIGHT.
...AND I THINK IT WAS GOLD DROPPINGS, NOT EGGS.
ANYWAY...
WHAT WAS YOUR POINT?
I FORGOT.
MAYBE IT'LL COME BACK TO ME WHEN WE OPEN HIM UP.

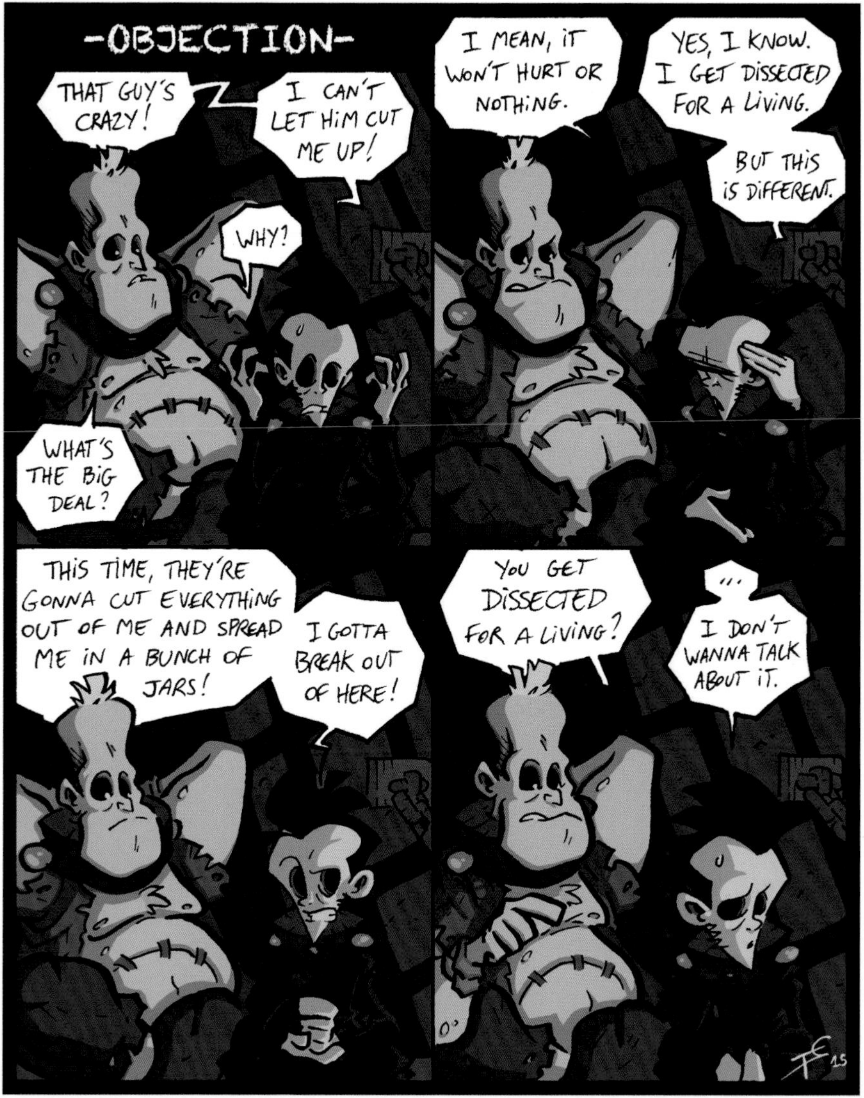
-OBJECTION-
THAT GUY'S CRAZY!
I CAN'T LET HIM CUT ME UP!
WHY?
WHAT'S THE BIG DEAL?
I MEAN, IT WON'T HURT OR NOTHING.
YES, I KNOW. I GET DISSECTED FOR A LIVING.
BUT THIS IS DIFFERENT.
THIS TIME, THEY'RE GONNA CUT EVERYTHING OUT OF ME AND SPREAD ME IN A BUNCH OF JARS!
I GOTTA BREAK OUT OF HERE!
YOU GET DISSECTED FOR A LIVING?
...
I DON'T WANNA TALK ABOUT IT.

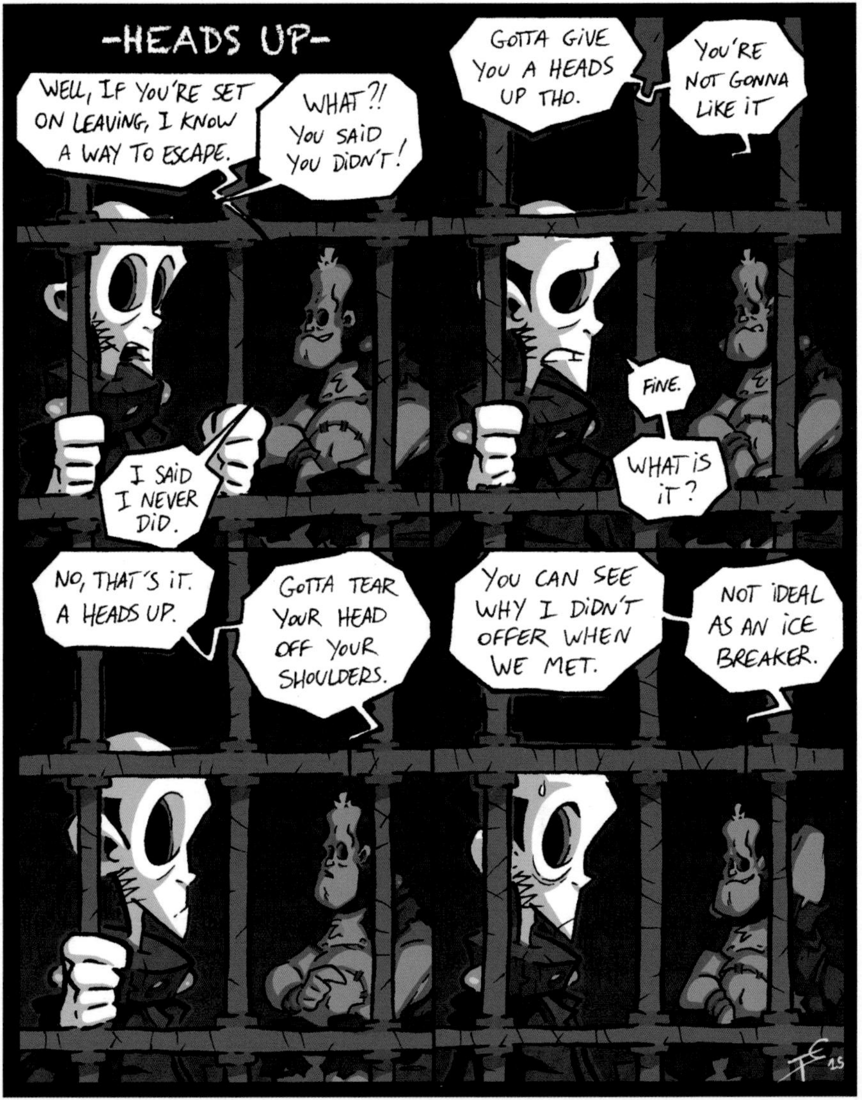
-HEADS UP-
WELL, IF YOU'RE SET ON LEAVING, I KNOW A WAY TO ESCAPE.
WHAT?! YOU SAID YOU DIDN'T!
I SAID I NEVER DID.
GOTTA GIVE YOU A HEADS UP THO.
YOU'RE NOT GONNA LIKE IT
FINE.
WHAT IS IT?
NO, THAT'S IT. A HEADS UP.
GOTTA TEAR YOUR HEAD OFF YOUR SHOULDERS.
YOU CAN SEE WHY I DIDN'T OFFER WHEN WE MET.
NOT IDEAL AS AN ICE BREAKER.

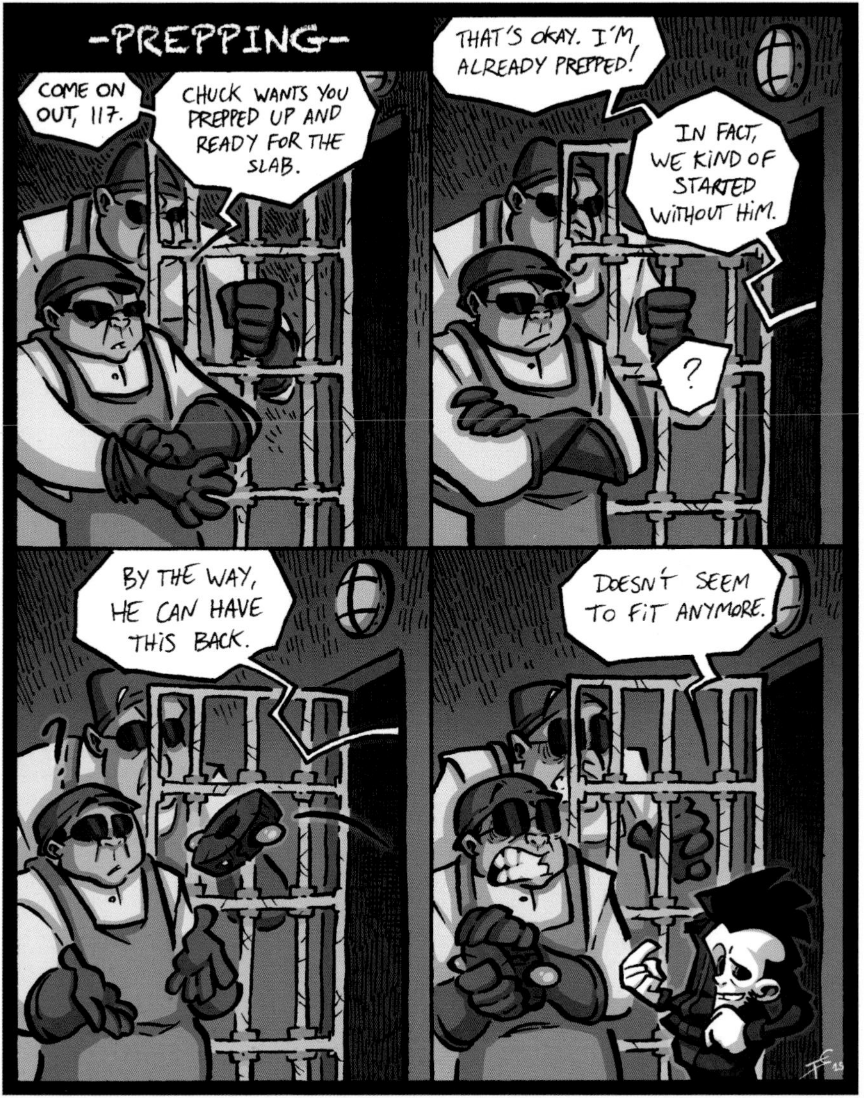
-PREPPING-
COME ON OUT, 117.
CHUCK WANTS YOU PREPPED UP AND READY FOR THE SLAB.
THAT'S OKAY. I'M ALREADY PREPPED!
IN FACT, WE KIND OF STARTED WITHOUT HIM.
?
BY THE WAY, HE CAN HAVE THIS BACK.
?
!
DOESN'T SEEM TO FIT ANYMORE.

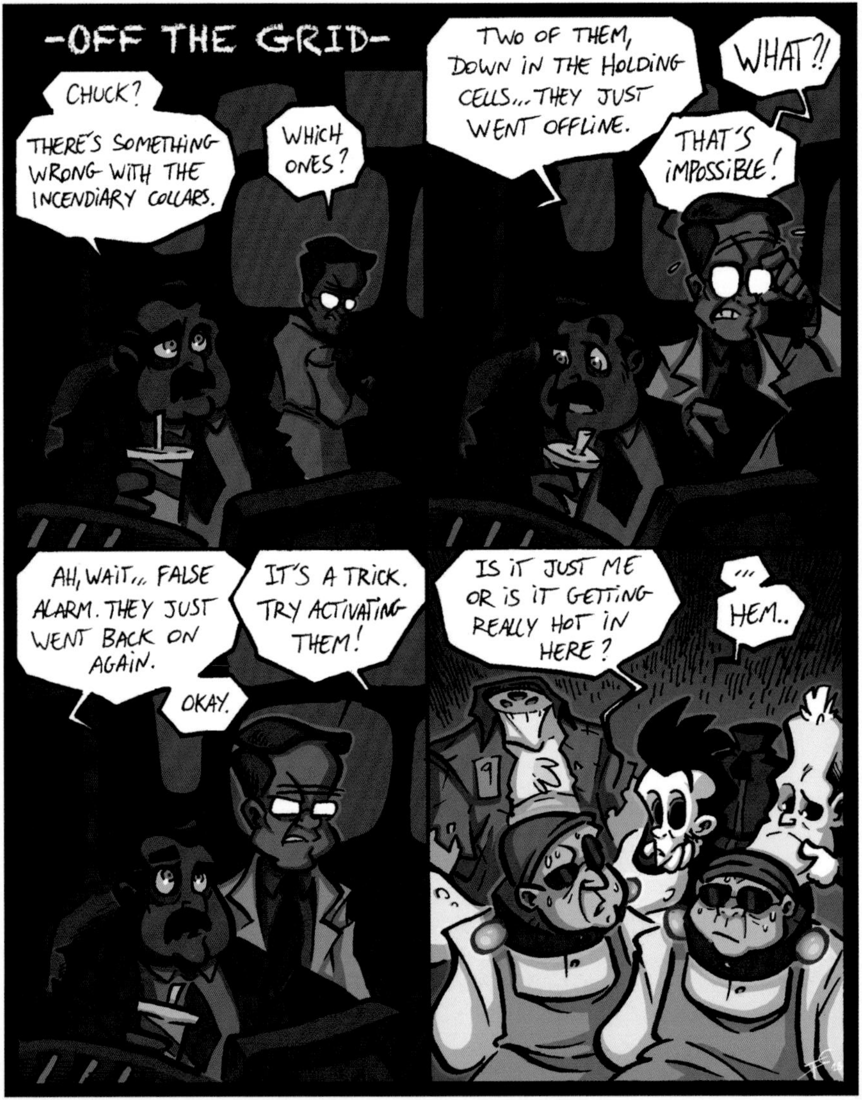
-OFF THE GRID-
CHUCK?
THERE'S SOMETHING WRONG WITH THE INCENDIARY COLLARS.
WHICH ONES?
TWO OF THEM, DOWN IN THE HOLDING CELLS... THEY JUST WENT OFFLINE.
WHAT?!
THAT'S IMPOSSIBLE!
AH, WAIT... FALSE ALARM. THEY JUST WENT BACK ON AGAIN.
IT'S A TRICK. TRY ACTIVATING THEM!
OKAY.
IS IT JUST ME OR IS IT GETTING REALLY HOT IN HERE?
...
HEM..

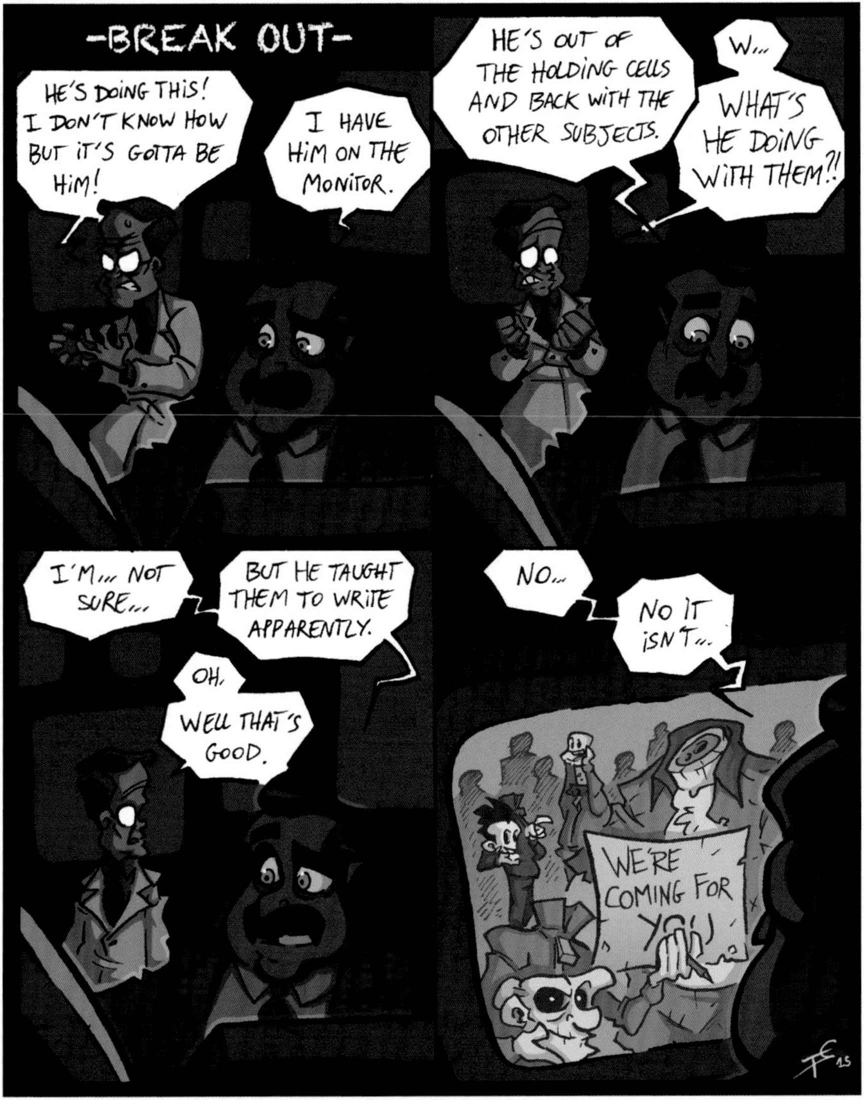
-BREAK OUT-
HE'S DOING THIS! I DON'T KNOW HOW BUT IT'S GOTTA BE HIM!
I HAVE HIM ON THE MONITOR.
HE'S OUT OF THE HOLDING CELLS AND BACK WITH THE OTHER SUBJECTS.
W...
WHAT'S HE DOING WITH THEM?!
I'M... NOT SURE...
BUT HE TAUGHT THEM TO WRITE APPARENTLY.
OH,
WELL THAT'S GOOD.
NO...
NO IT ISN'T...
WE'RE COMING FOR YOU

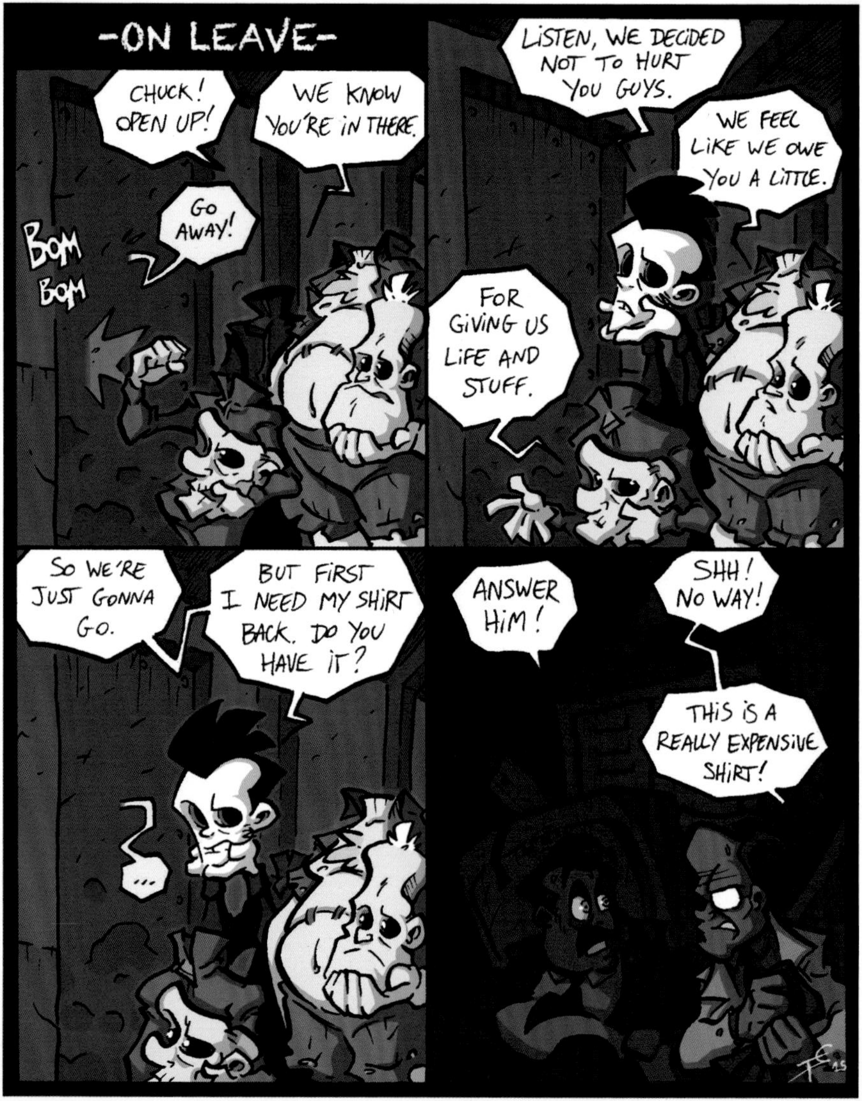
-ON LEAVE-
CHUCK! OPEN UP!
WE KNOW YOU'RE IN THERE.
BOM BOM
GO AWAY!
LISTEN, WE DECIDED NOT TO HURT YOU GUYS.
WE FEEL LIKE WE OWE YOU A LITTLE.
FOR GIVING US LIFE AND STUFF.
SO WE'RE JUST GONNA GO.
BUT FIRST I NEED MY SHIRT BACK. DO YOU HAVE IT?
...
ANSWER HIM!
SHH! NO WAY!
THIS IS A REALLY EXPENSIVE SHIRT!

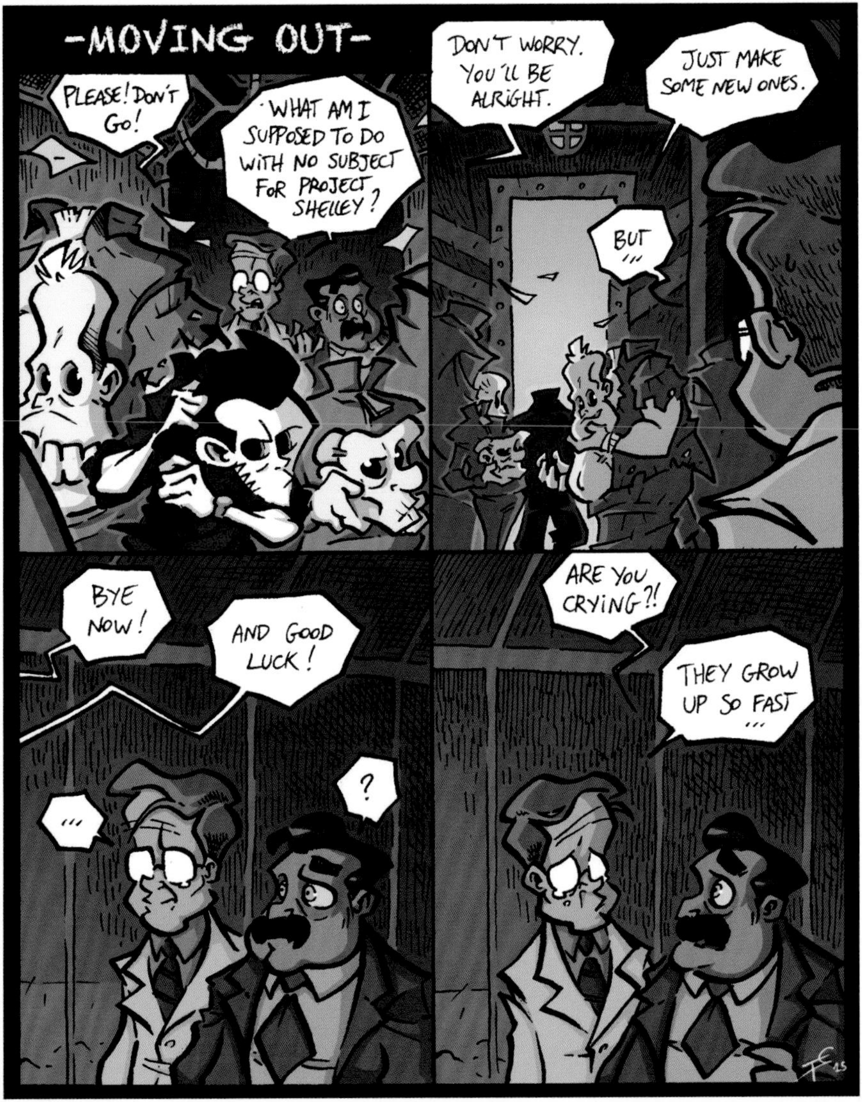
-MOVING OUT-
PLEASE! DON'T GO!
WHAT AM I SUPPOSED TO DO WITH NO SUBJECT FOR PROJECT SHELLEY?
DON'T WORRY. YOU'LL BE ALRIGHT.
JUST MAKE SOME NEW ONES.
BUT ...
BYE NOW!
AND GOOD LUCK!
...
?
ARE YOU CRYING?!
THEY GROW UP SO FAST ...

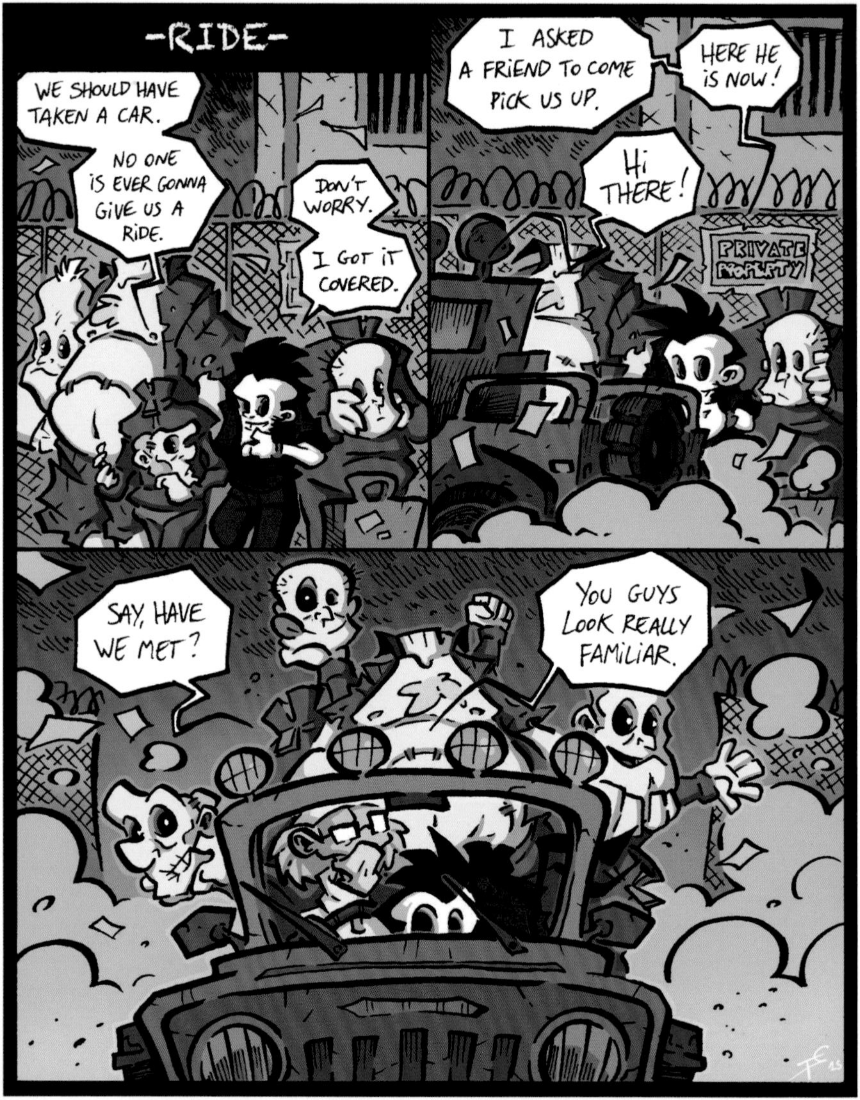
-RIDE-
WE SHOULD HAVE TAKEN A CAR.
NO ONE IS EVER GONNA GIVE US A RIDE.
DON'T WORRY.
I GOT IT COVERED.
I ASKED A FRIEND TO COME PICK US UP.
HERE HE IS NOW!
Hi THERE!
PRIVATE PROPERTY
SAY, HAVE WE MET?
YOU GUYS LOOK REALLY FAMILIAR.

The nice
thing with
being dead:

you can
relate to a lot
of people.

Chapter IV
-Depression-

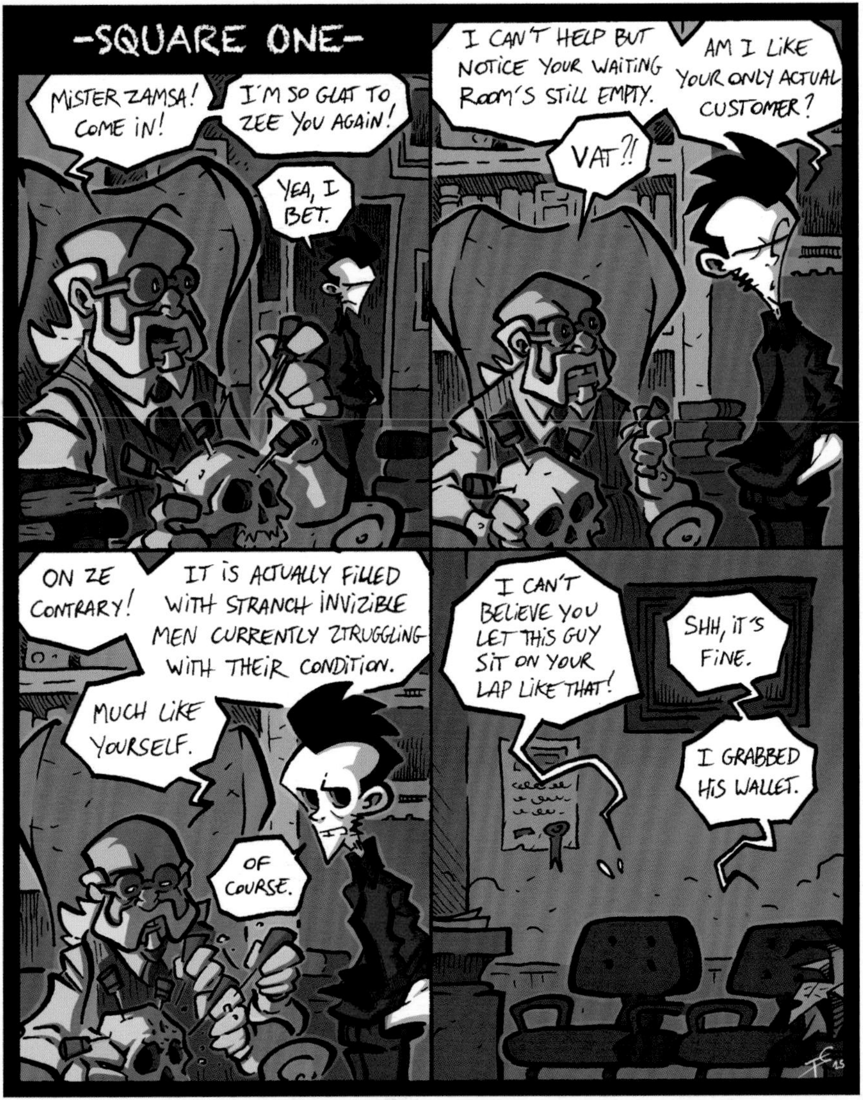
-SQUARE ONE-
MISTER ZAMSA! COME IN!
I'M SO GLAT TO ZEE YOU AGAIN!
YEA, I BET.
I CAN'T HELP BUT NOTICE YOUR WAITING ROOM'S STILL EMPTY.
VAT?!
AM I LIKE YOUR ONLY ACTUAL CUSTOMER?
ON ZE CONTRARY!
IT IS ACTUALLY FILLED WITH STRANCH INVIZIBLE MEN CURRENTLY ZTRUGGLING WITH THEIR CONDITION.
MUCH LIKE YOURSELF.
OF COURSE.
I CAN'T BELIEVE YOU LET THIS GUY SIT ON YOUR LAP LIKE THAT!
SHH, IT'S FINE.
I GRABBED HIS WALLET.

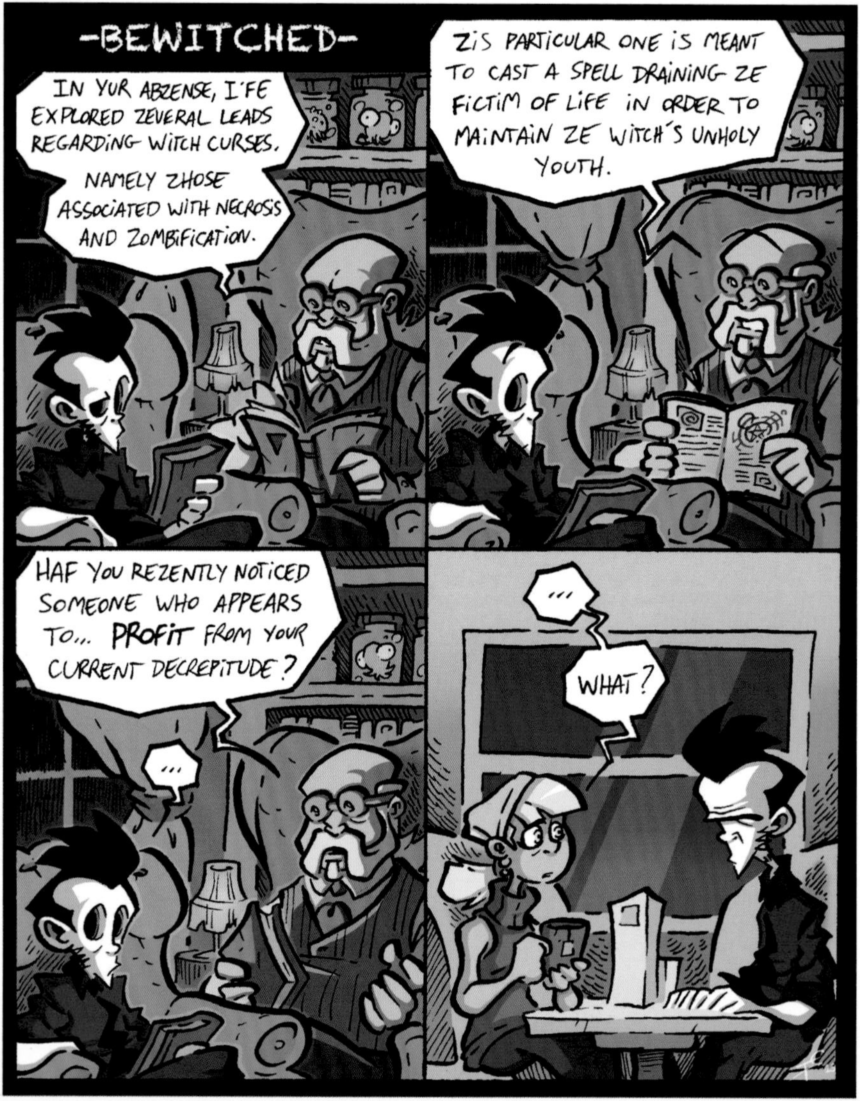
-BEWITCHED-
IN YUR ABZENSE, I'FE EXPLORED ZEVERAL LEADS REGARDING WITCH CURSES.
NAMELY ZHOSE ASSOCIATED WITH NECROSIS AND ZOMBIFICATION.
ZIS PARTICULAR ONE IS MEANT TO CAST A SPELL DRAINING ZE FICTIM OF LIFE IN ORDER TO MAINTAIN ZE WITCH'S UNHOLY YOUTH.
HAF YOU REZENTLY NOTICED SOMEONE WHO APPEARS TO... PROFIT FROM YOUR CURRENT DECREPITUDE?
...
...
WHAT?

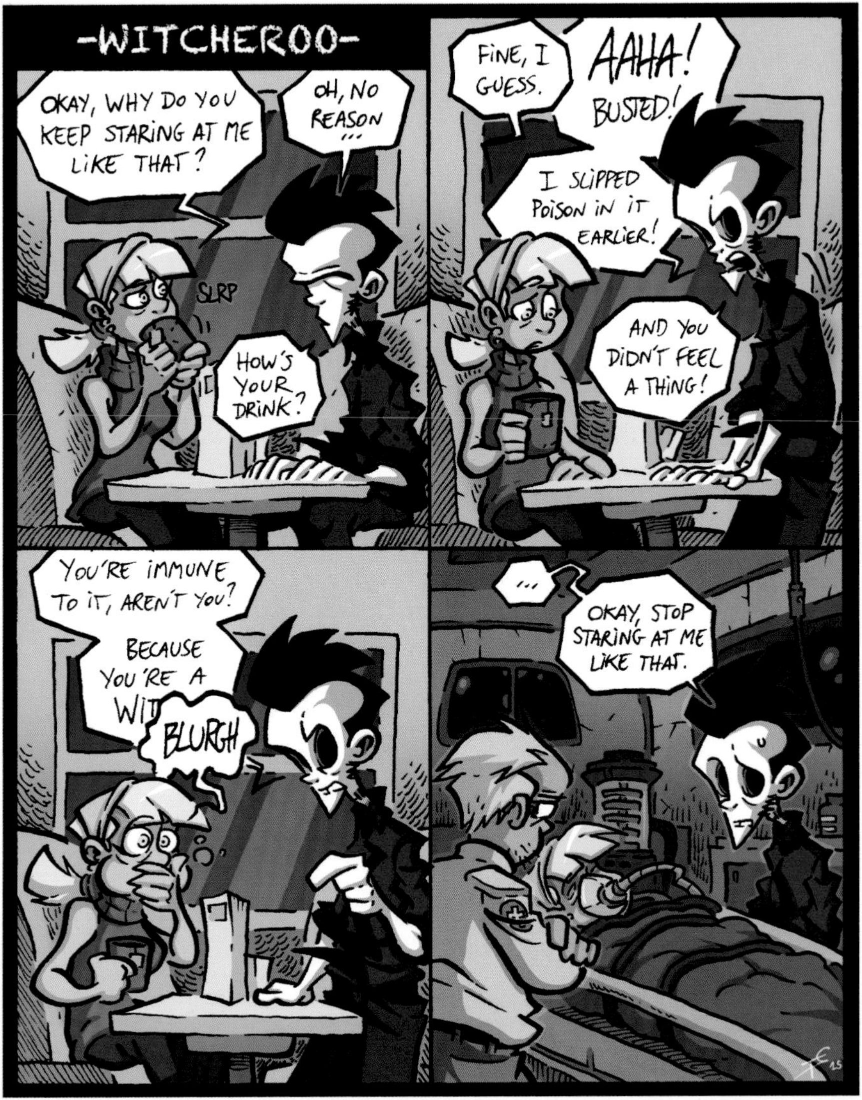
-WITCHEROO-
OKAY, WHY DO YOU KEEP STARING AT ME LIKE THAT?
OH, NO REASON...
SLRP
HOW'S YOUR DRINK?
FINE, I GUESS.
AAHA! BUSTED!
I SLIPPED POISON IN IT EARLIER!
AND YOU DIDN'T FEEL A THING!
YOU'RE IMMUNE TO IT, AREN'T YOU?
BECAUSE YOU'RE A WIT
BLURGH
...
OKAY, STOP STARING AT ME LIKE THAT.

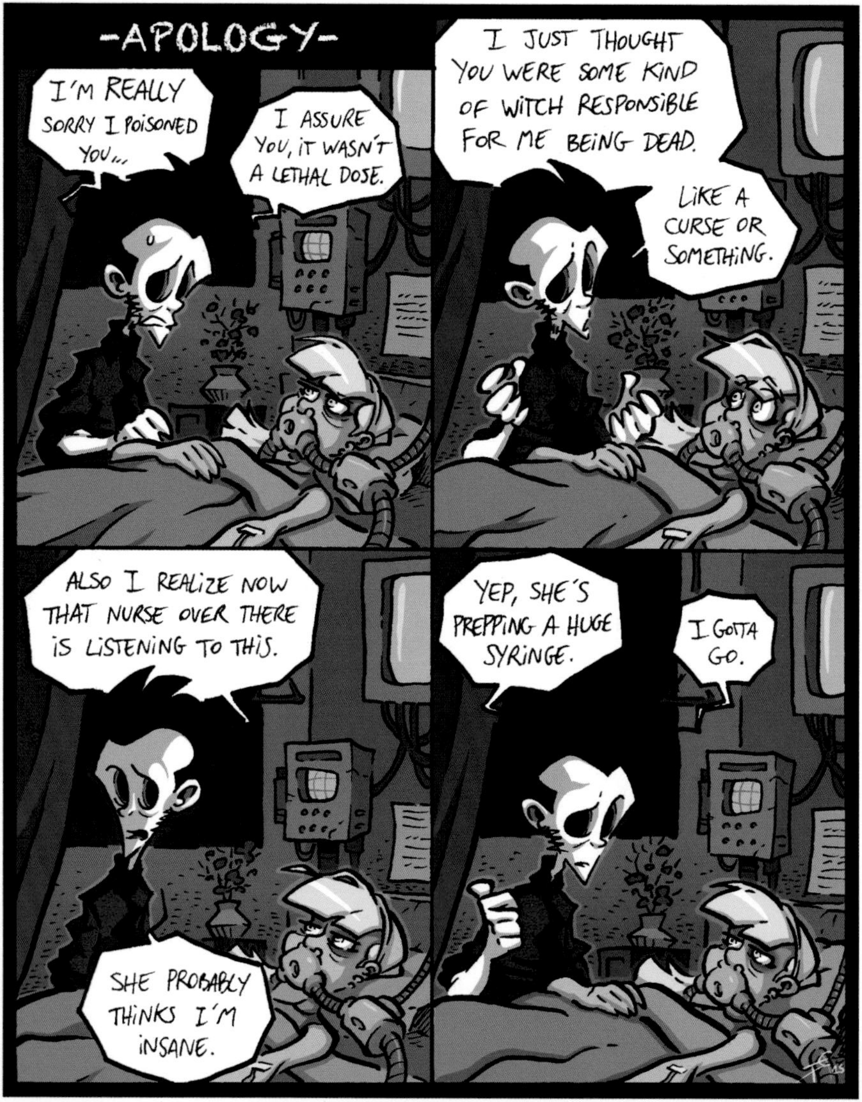
-APOLOGY-
I'M REALLY SORRY I POISONED YOU...
I ASSURE YOU, IT WASN'T A LETHAL DOSE.
I JUST THOUGHT YOU WERE SOME KIND OF WITCH RESPONSIBLE FOR ME BEING DEAD.
LIKE A CURSE OR SOMETHING.
ALSO I REALIZE NOW THAT NURSE OVER THERE IS LISTENING TO THIS.
SHE PROBABLY THINKS I'M INSANE.
YEP, SHE'S PREPPING A HUGE SYRINGE.
I GOTTA GO.

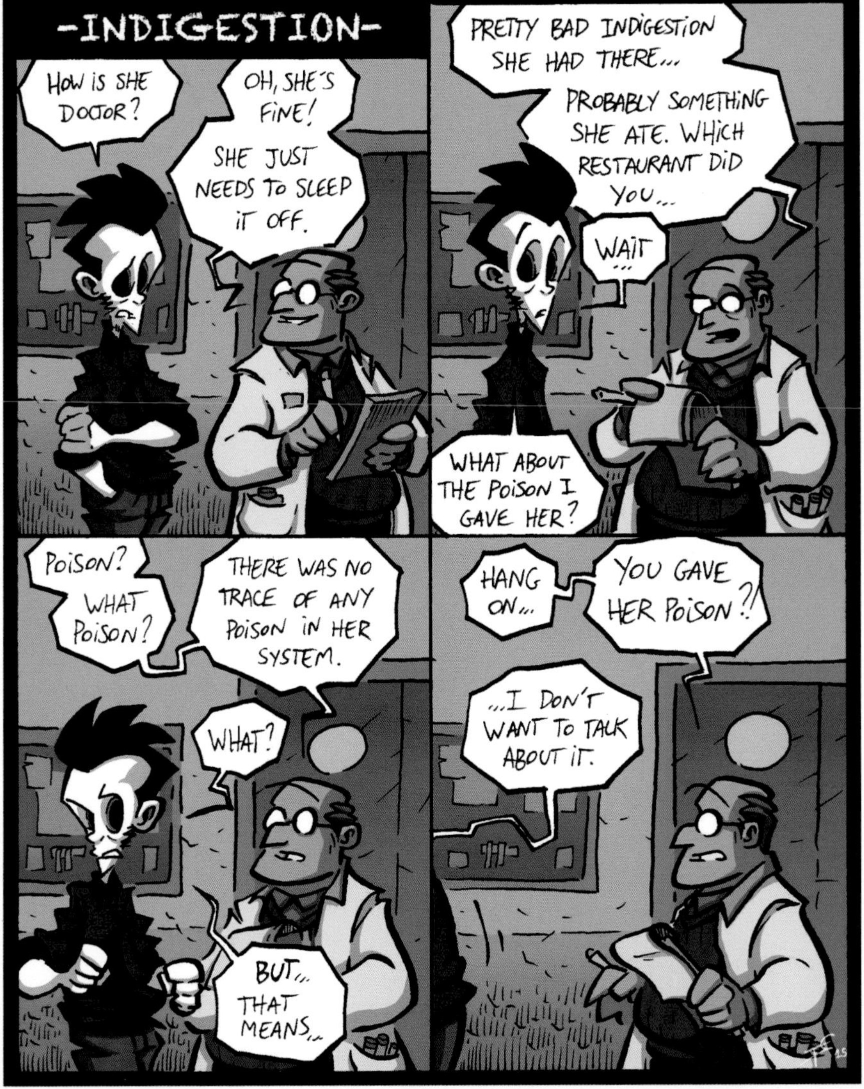
-INDIGESTION-
HOW IS SHE DOCTOR?
OH, SHE'S FINE!
SHE JUST NEEDS TO SLEEP IT OFF.
PRETTY BAD INDIGESTION SHE HAD THERE...
PROBABLY SOMETHING SHE ATE. WHICH RESTAURANT DID YOU...
WAIT...
WHAT ABOUT THE POISON I GAVE HER?
POISON?
WHAT POISON?
THERE WAS NO TRACE OF ANY POISON IN HER SYSTEM.
WHAT?
BUT... THAT MEANS...
HANG ON...
YOU GAVE HER POISON?!
...I DON'T WANT TO TALK ABOUT IT.

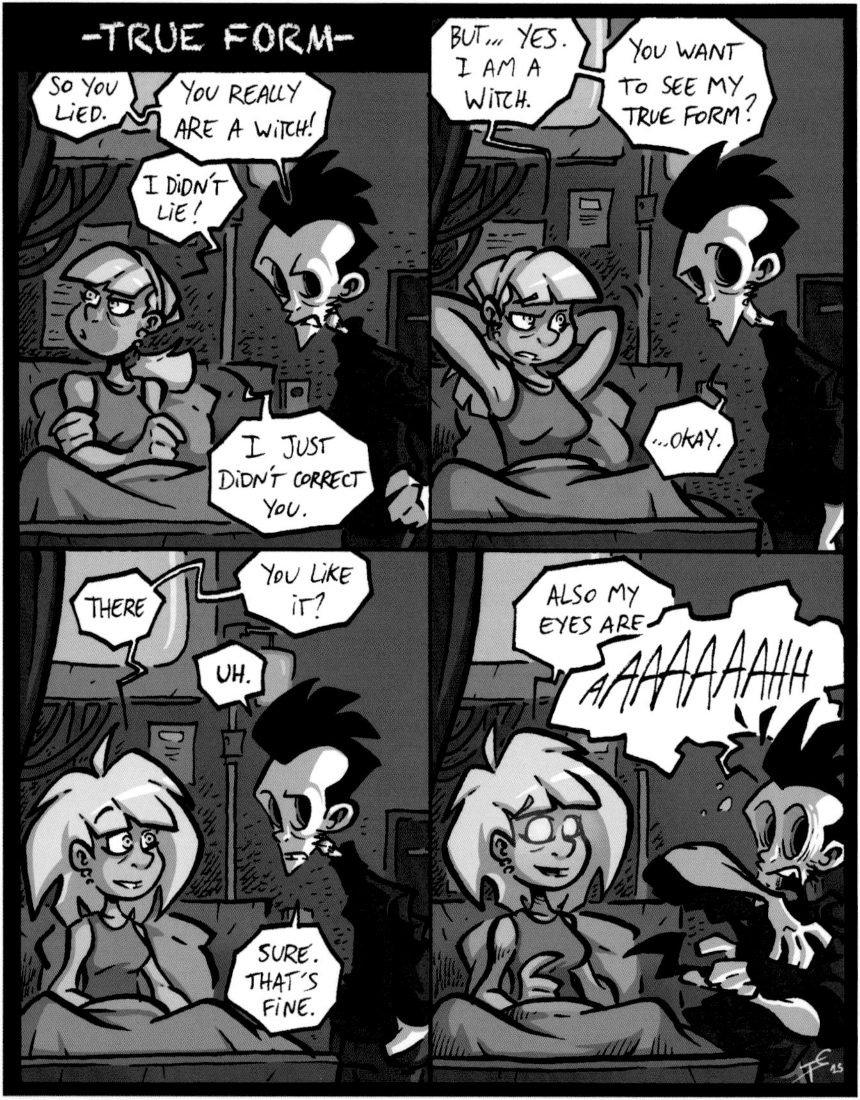
-TRUE FORM-
SO YOU LIED.
YOU REALLY ARE A WITCH!
I DIDN'T LIE!
I JUST DIDN'T CORRECT YOU.
BUT... YES. I AM A WITCH.
YOU WANT TO SEE MY TRUE FORM?
...OKAY.
THERE
YOU LIKE IT?
UH.
SURE. THAT'S FINE.
ALSO MY EYES ARE
AAAAAAAAHH

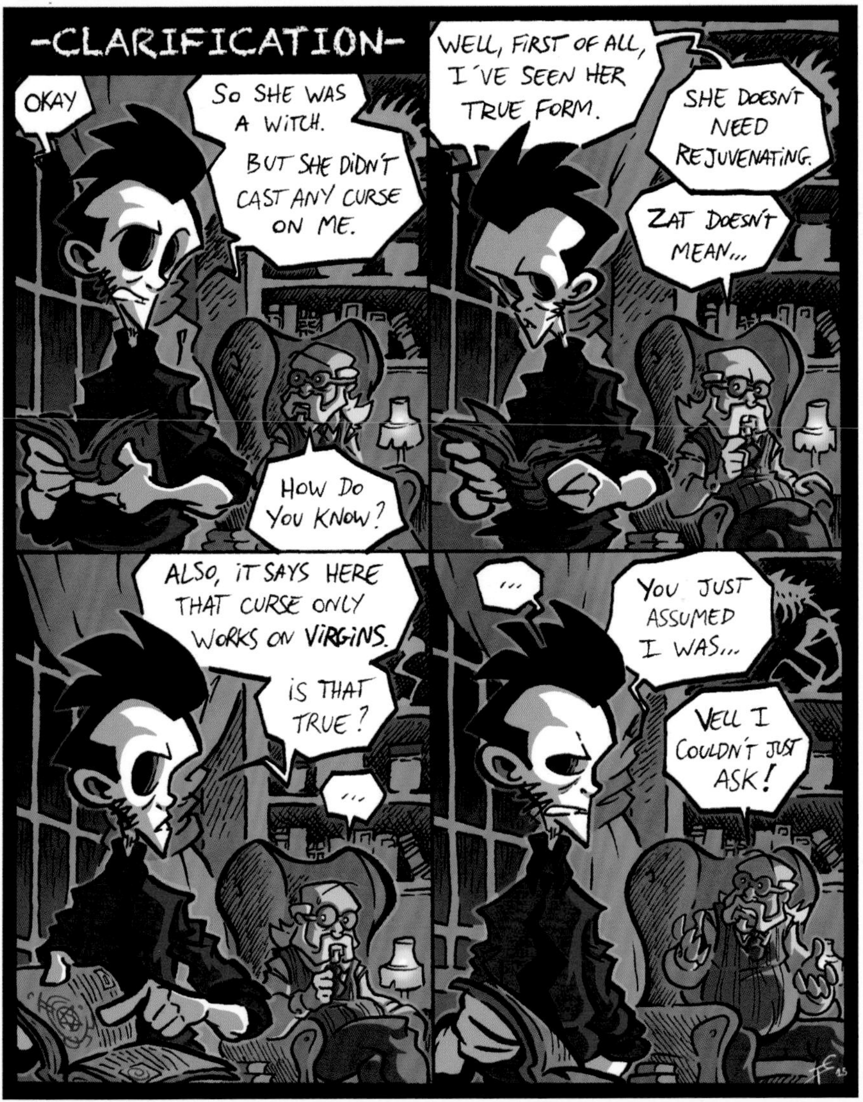
-CLARIFICATION-
OKAY
SO SHE WAS A WITCH.
BUT SHE DIDN'T CAST ANY CURSE ON ME.
HOW DO YOU KNOW?
WELL, FIRST OF ALL, I'VE SEEN HER TRUE FORM.
SHE DOESN'T NEED REJUVENATING.
ZAT DOESN'T JUST MEAN...
ALSO, IT SAYS HERE THAT CURSE ONLY WORKS ON VIRGINS.
IS THAT TRUE?
...
...
YOU JUST ASSUMED I WAS...
VELL I COULDN'T JUST ASK!

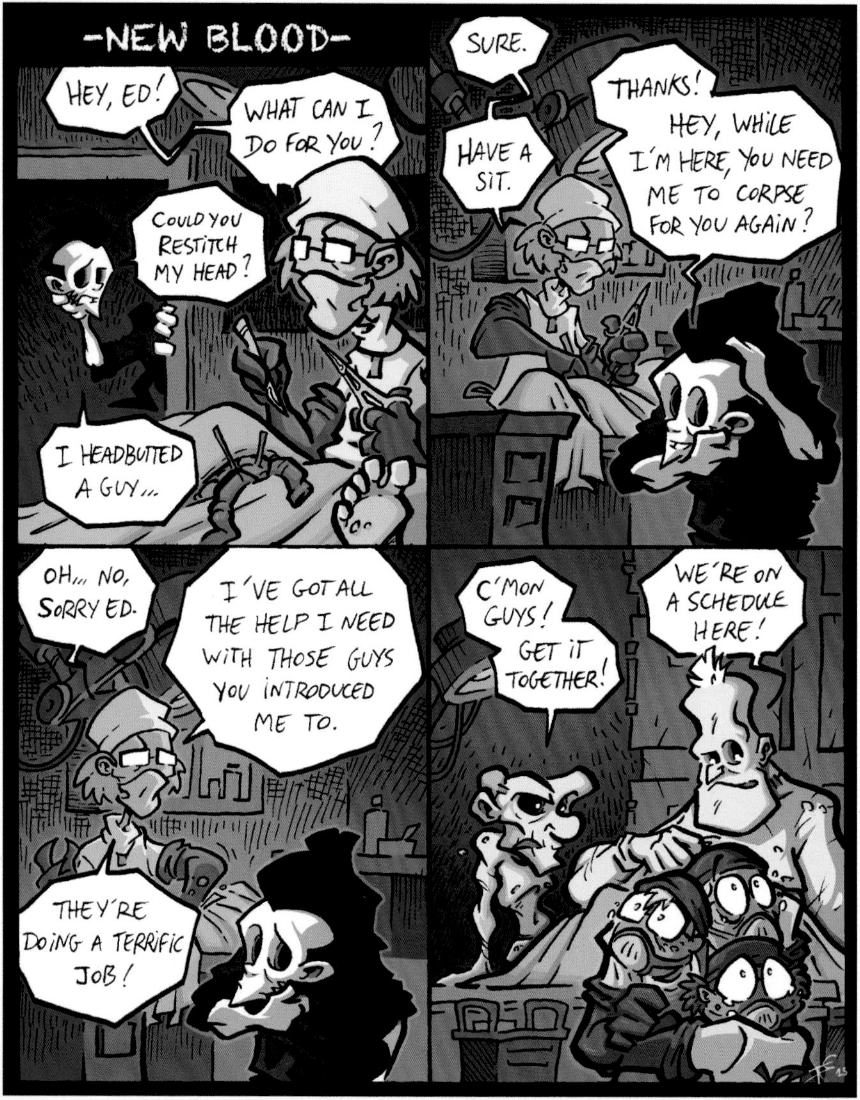
-NEW BLOOD-
HEY, ED!
WHAT CAN I DO FOR YOU?
COULD YOU RESTITCH MY HEAD?
I HEADBUTTED A GUY...
SURE.
HAVE A SIT.
THANKS!
HEY, WHILE I'M HERE, YOU NEED ME TO CORPSE FOR YOU AGAIN?
OH... NO, SORRY ED.
I'VE GOT ALL THE HELP I NEED WITH THOSE GUYS YOU INTRODUCED ME TO.
THEY'RE DOING A TERRIFIC JOB!
C'MON GUYS!
GET IT TOGETHER!
WE'RE ON A SCHEDULE HERE!

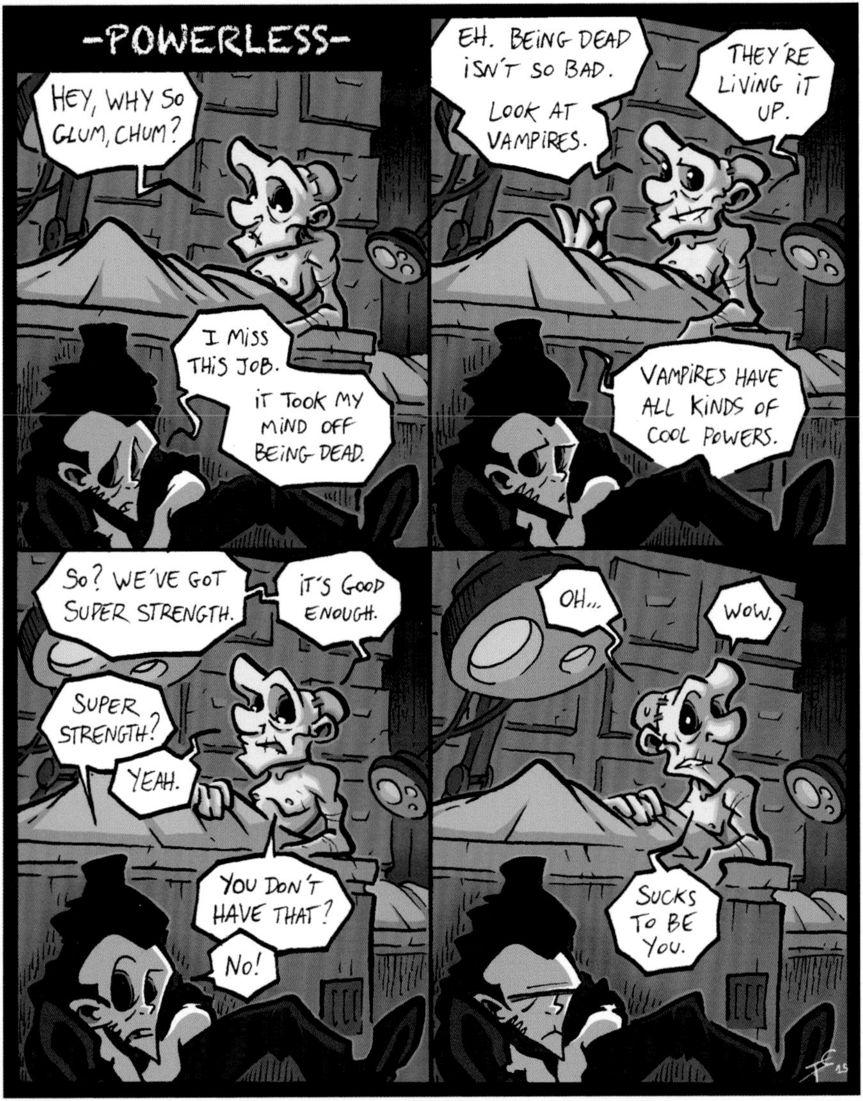
-POWERLESS-
HEY, WHY SO GLUM, CHUM?
I MISS THIS JOB.
IT TOOK MY MIND OFF BEING DEAD.
EH. BEING DEAD ISN'T SO BAD.
LOOK AT VAMPIRES.
THEY'RE LIVING IT UP.
VAMPIRES HAVE ALL KINDS OF COOL POWERS.
SO? WE'VE GOT SUPER STRENGTH.
IT'S GOOD ENOUGH.
SUPER STRENGTH?
YEAH.
YOU DON'T HAVE THAT?
NO!
OH...
WOW.
SUCKS TO BE YOU.

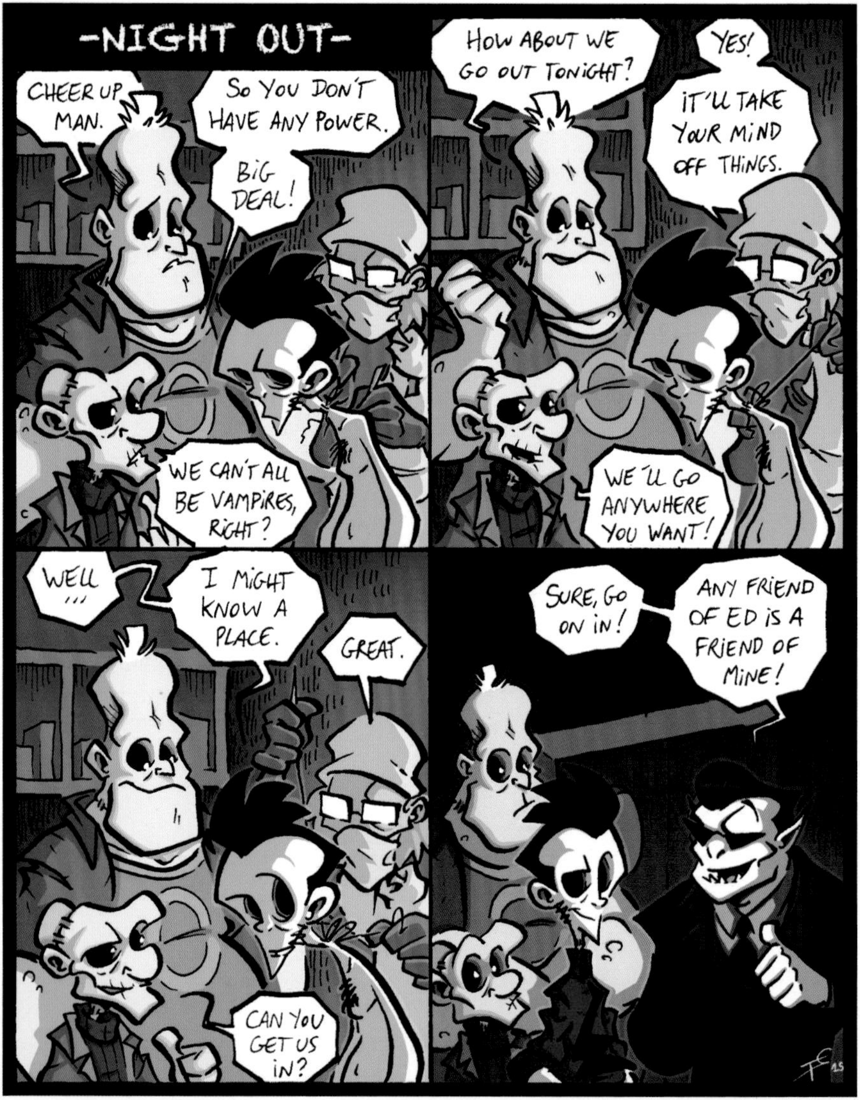
-NIGHT OUT-
CHEER UP MAN.
SO YOU DON'T HAVE ANY POWER.
BIG DEAL!
WE CAN'T ALL BE VAMPIRES, RIGHT?
HOW ABOUT WE GO OUT TONIGHT?
YES!
IT'LL TAKE YOUR MIND OFF THINGS.
WE'LL GO ANYWHERE YOU WANT!
WELL ...
I MIGHT KNOW A PLACE.
GREAT.
CAN YOU GET US IN?
SURE, GO ON IN!
ANY FRIEND OF ED IS A FRIEND OF MINE!

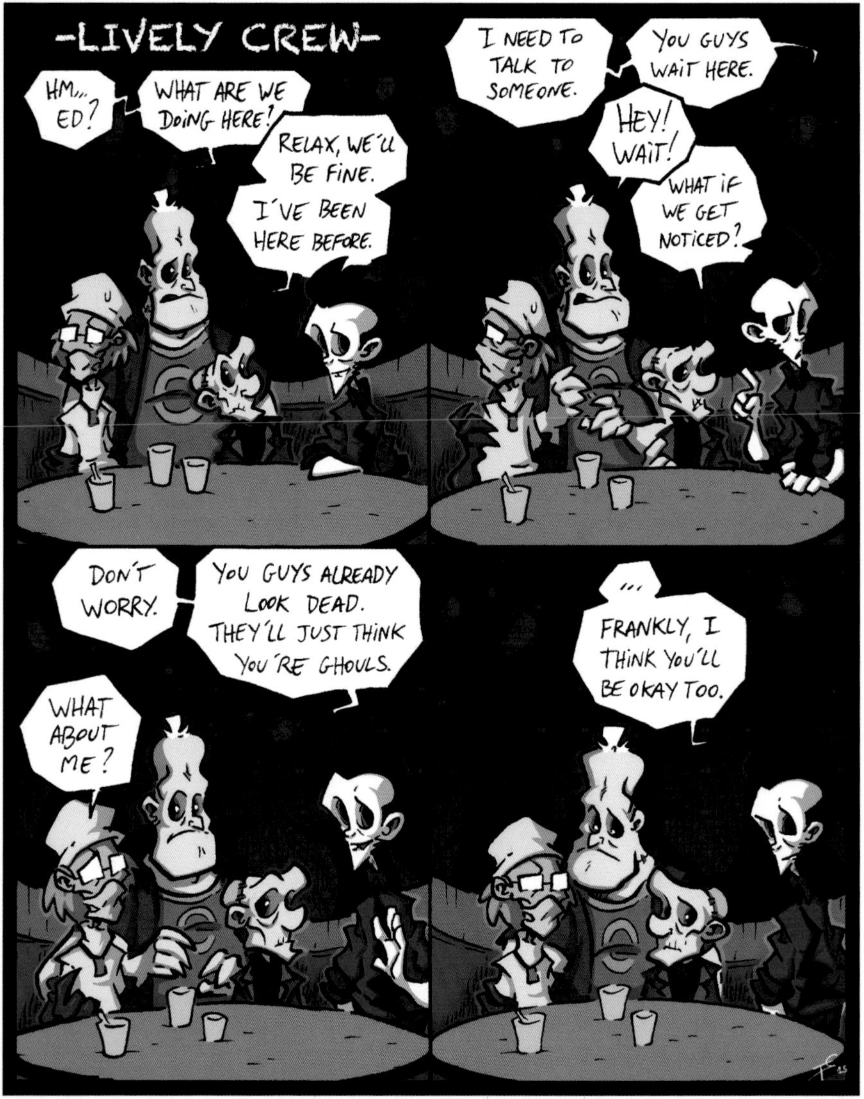
-LIVELY CREW-
HM,,, ED?
WHAT ARE WE DOING HERE?
RELAX, WE'LL BE FINE.
I'VE BEEN HERE BEFORE.
I NEED TO TALK TO SOMEONE.
YOU GUYS WAIT HERE.
HEY! WAIT!
WHAT IF WE GET NOTICED?
DON'T WORRY.
YOU GUYS ALREADY LOOK DEAD. THEY'LL JUST THINK YOU'RE GHOULS.
WHAT ABOUT ME?
,,,
FRANKLY, I THINK YOU'LL BE OKAY TOO.

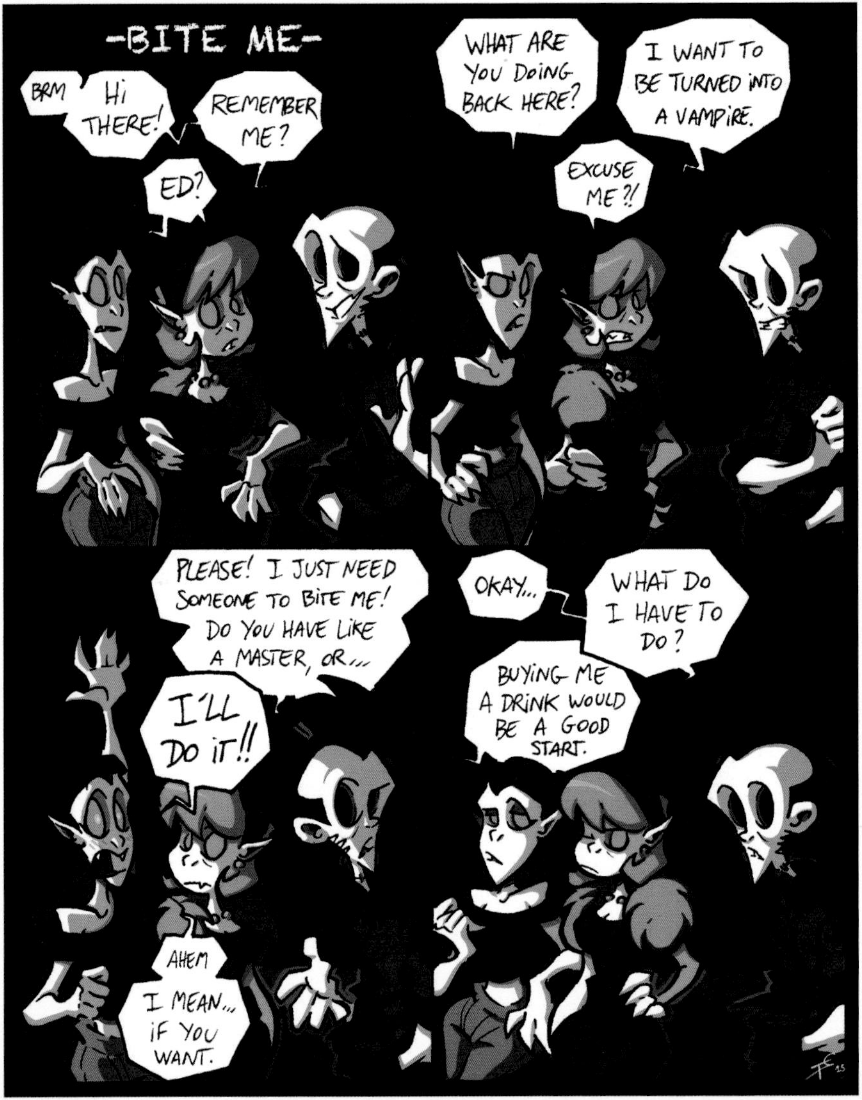
-BITE ME-
BRM
Hi THERE!
REMEMBER ME?
ED?
WHAT ARE YOU DOING BACK HERE?
I WANT TO BE TURNED INTO A VAMPIRE.
EXCUSE ME?!
PLEASE! I JUST NEED SOMEONE TO BITE ME! DO YOU HAVE LIKE A MASTER, OR...
I'LL DO IT!!
AHEM
I MEAN... iF YOU WANT.
OKAY...
WHAT DO I HAVE TO DO?
BUYING ME A DRINK WOULD BE A GOOD START.

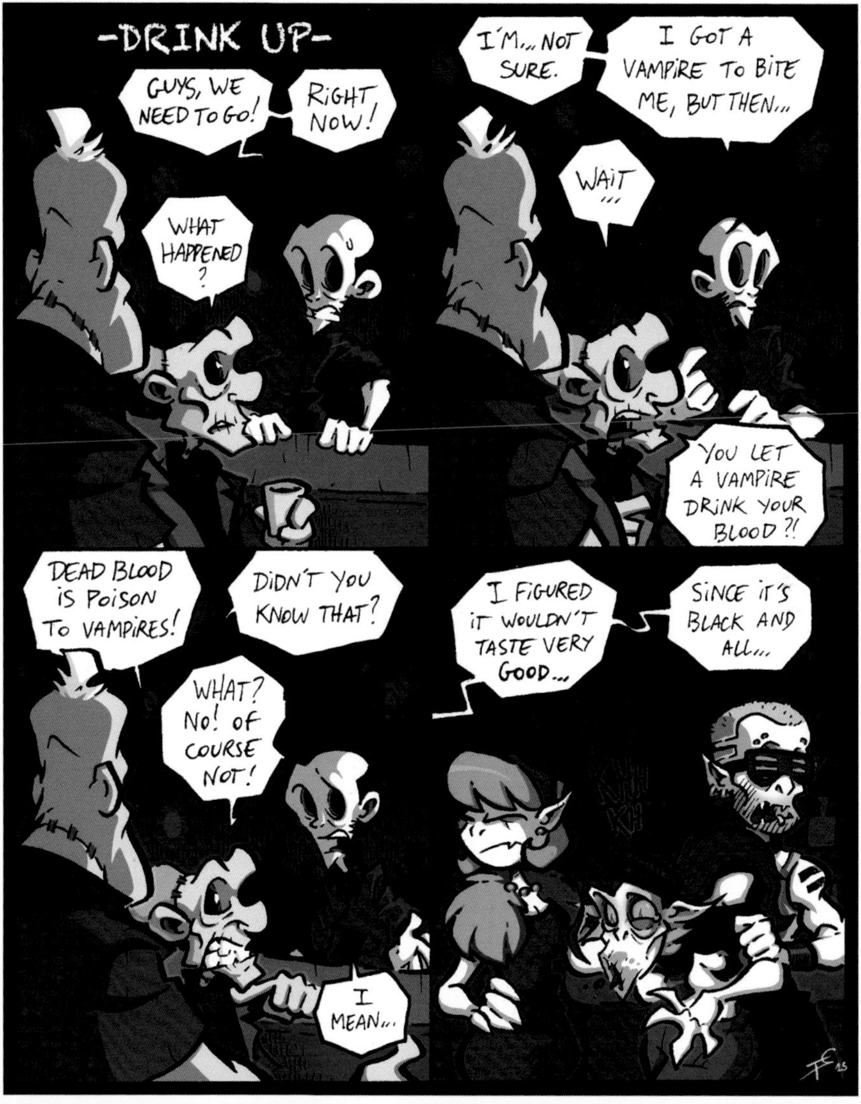
-DRINK UP-
GUYS, WE NEED TO GO!
RIGHT NOW!
WHAT HAPPENED?
I'M... NOT SURE.
I GOT A VAMPIRE TO BITE ME, BUT THEN...
WAIT...
YOU LET A VAMPIRE DRINK YOUR BLOOD?!
DEAD BLOOD IS POISON TO VAMPIRES!
DIDN'T YOU KNOW THAT?
WHAT? NO! OF COURSE NOT!
I MEAN...
I FIGURED IT WOULDN'T TASTE VERY GOOD...
SINCE IT'S BLACK AND ALL...

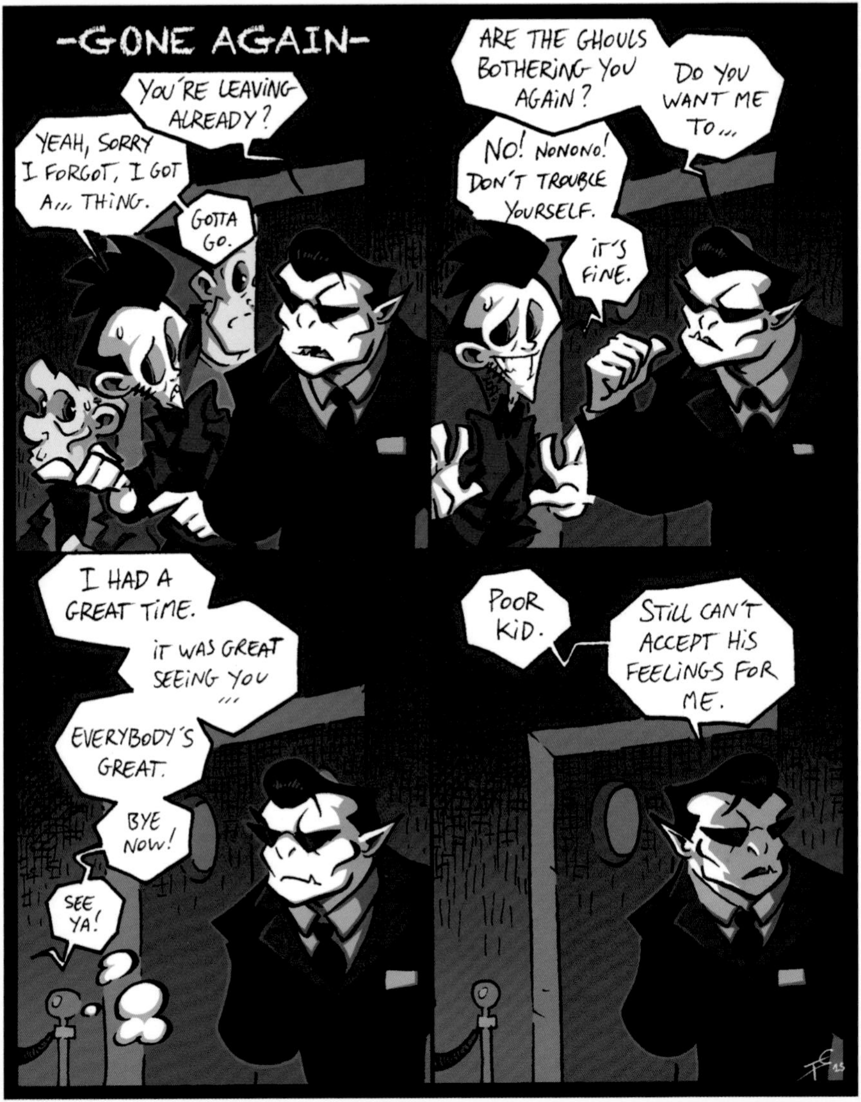
-GONE AGAIN-
YOU'RE LEAVING ALREADY?
YEAH, SORRY I FORGOT, I GOT A... THING.
GOTTA GO.
ARE THE GHOULS BOTHERING YOU AGAIN?
DO YOU WANT ME TO...
NO! NONONO! DON'T TROUBLE YOURSELF.
IT'S FINE.
I HAD A GREAT TIME.
IT WAS GREAT SEEING YOU ...
EVERYBODY'S GREAT.
BYE NOW!
SEE YA!
POOR KID.
STILL CAN'T ACCEPT HIS FEELINGS FOR ME.

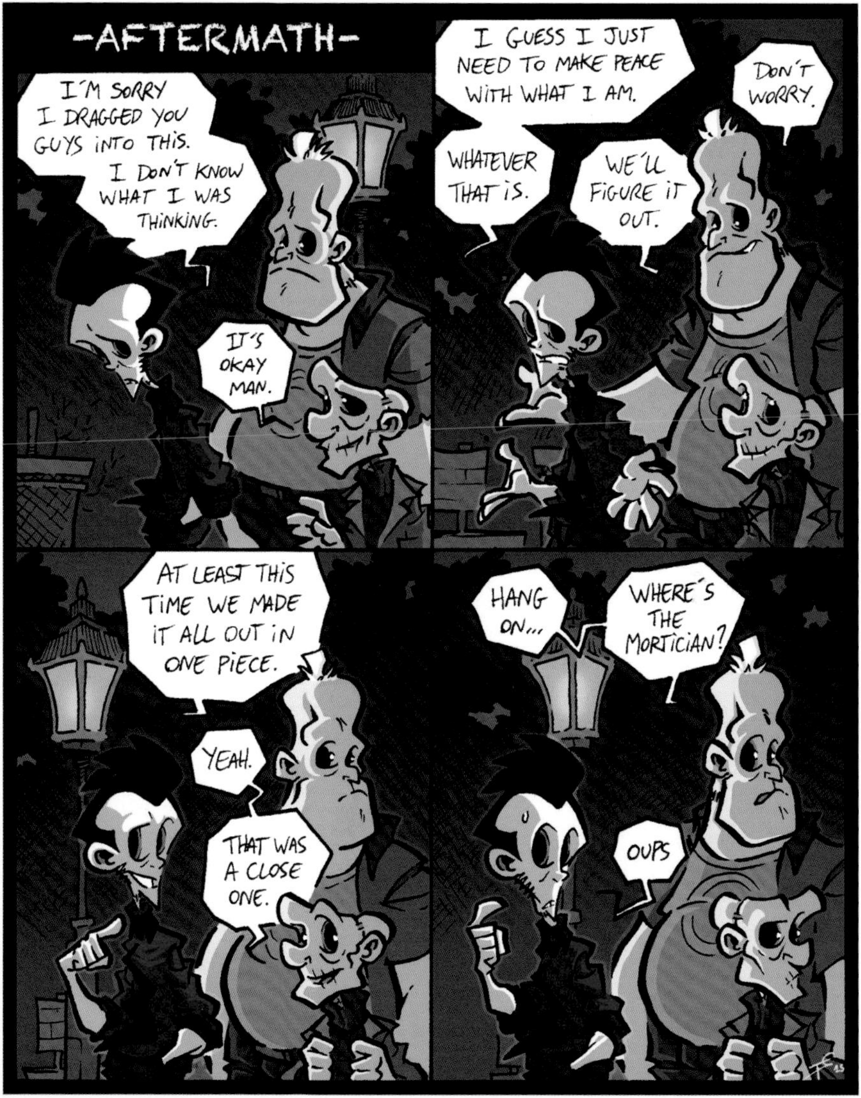
-AFTERMATH-
I'M SORRY I DRAGGED YOU GUYS INTO THIS.
I DON'T KNOW WHAT I WAS THINKING.
IT'S OKAY MAN.
I GUESS I JUST NEED TO MAKE PEACE WITH WHAT I AM.
DON'T WORRY.
WHATEVER THAT IS.
WE'LL FIGURE IT OUT.
AT LEAST THIS TIME WE MADE IT ALL OUT IN ONE PIECE.
YEAH.
THAT WAS A CLOSE ONE.
HANG ON...
WHERE'S THE MORTICIAN?
OUPS

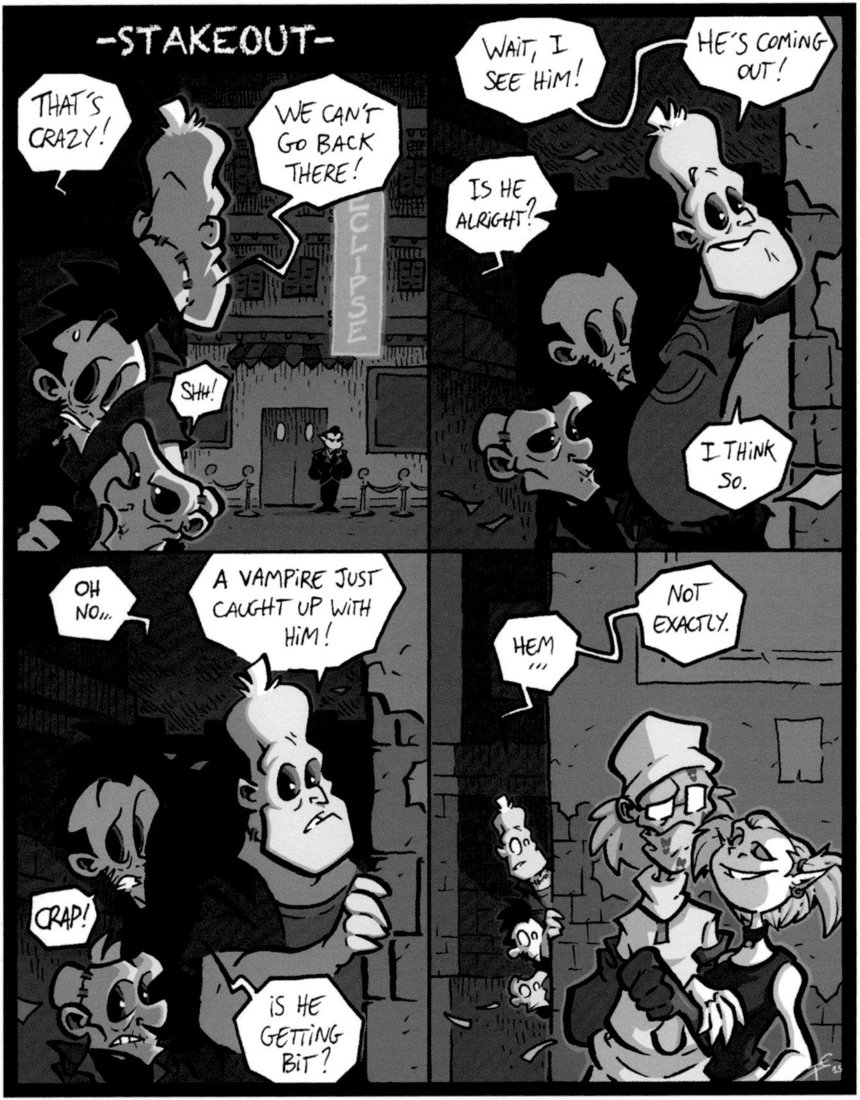
-STAKEOUT-
THAT'S CRAZY!
WE CAN'T GO BACK THERE!
ECLIPSE
SHH!
WAIT, I SEE HIM!
HE'S COMING OUT!
IS HE ALRIGHT?
I THINK SO.
OH NO...
A VAMPIRE JUST CAUGHT UP WITH HIM!
CRAP!
IS HE GETTING BIT?
HEM ...
NOT EXACTLY.

-INTRODUCTION-

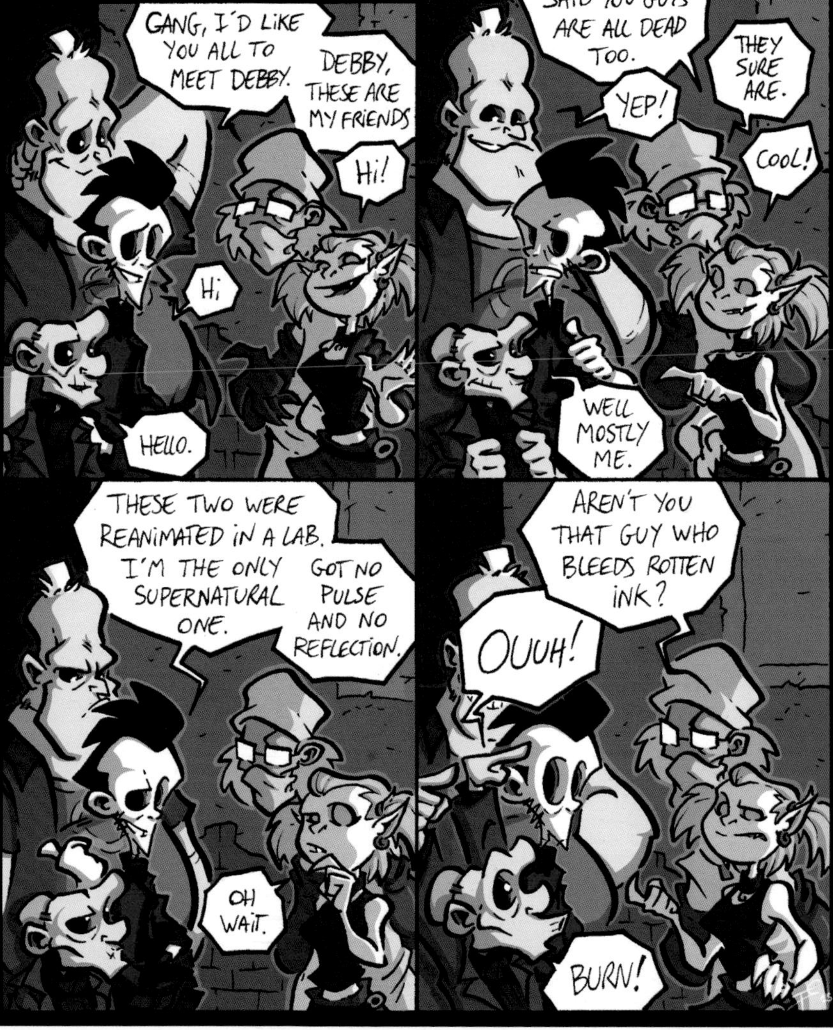

GANG, I'D LIKE YOU ALL TO MEET DEBBY.
DEBBY, THESE ARE MY FRIENDS
Hi!
Hi
HELLO.
SO, MORT SAID YOU GUYS ARE ALL DEAD TOO.
YEP!
THEY SURE ARE.
COOL!
WELL MOSTLY ME.
THESE TWO WERE REANIMATED IN A LAB. I'M THE ONLY SUPERNATURAL ONE.
GOT NO PULSE AND NO REFLECTION.
OH WAIT.
AREN'T YOU THAT GUY WHO BLEEDS ROTTEN INK?
OUUH!
BURN!

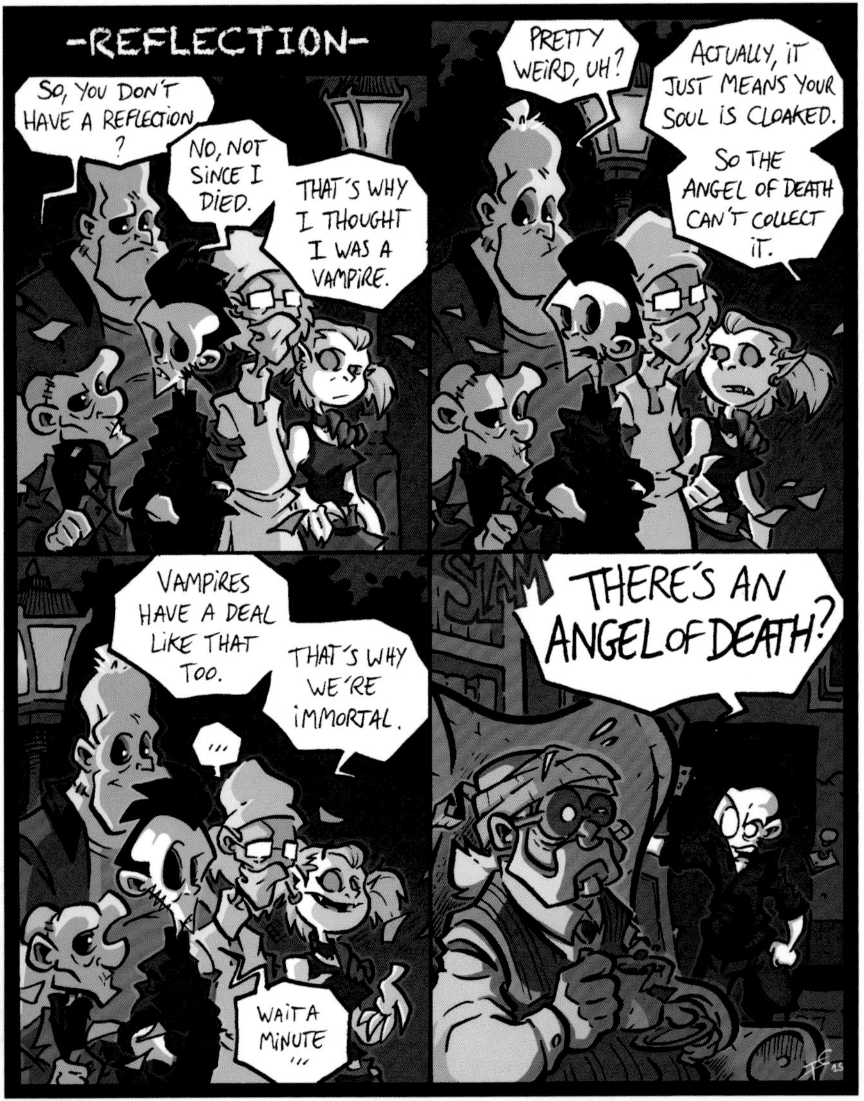

-REFLECTION-
SO, YOU DON'T HAVE A REFLECTION ?
NO, NOT SINCE I DIED.
THAT'S WHY I THOUGHT I WAS A VAMPIRE.
PRETTY WEIRD, UH?
ACTUALLY, IT JUST MEANS YOUR SOUL IS CLOAKED.
SO THE ANGEL OF DEATH CAN'T COLLECT IT.
VAMPIRES HAVE A DEAL LIKE THAT TOO.
THAT'S WHY WE'RE IMMORTAL.
...
WAIT A MINUTE ...
SLAM
THERE'S AN ANGEL OF DEATH?

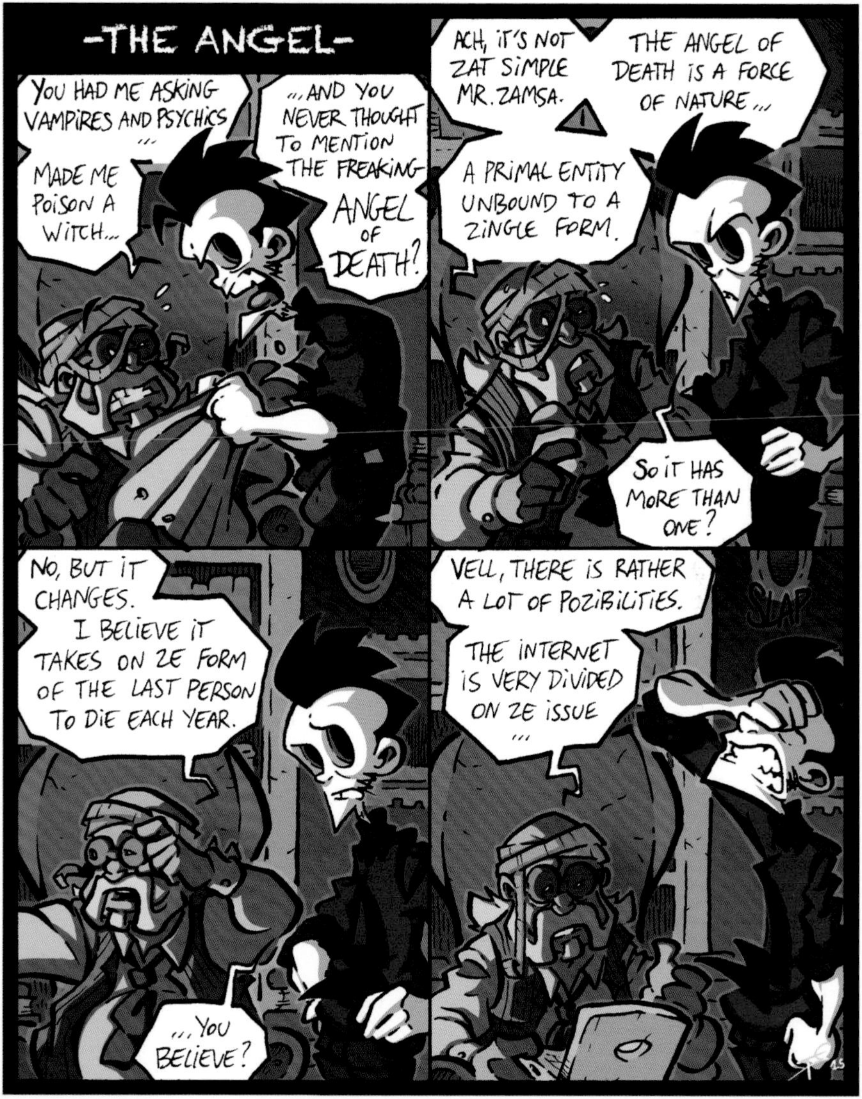
-THE ANGEL-
YOU HAD ME ASKING VAMPIRES AND PSYCHICS ...
MADE ME POISON A WITCH...
...AND YOU NEVER THOUGHT TO MENTION THE FREAKING-
ANGEL OF DEATH?
ACH, IT'S NOT ZAT SIMPLE MR. ZAMSA.
THE ANGEL OF DEATH IS A FORCE OF NATURE...
A PRIMAL ENTITY UNBOUND TO A ZINGLE FORM.
SO IT HAS MORE THAN ONE?
NO, BUT IT CHANGES.
I BELIEVE IT TAKES ON ZE FORM OF THE LAST PERSON TO DIE EACH YEAR.
...YOU BELIEVE?
VELL, THERE IS RATHER A LOT OF POZIBILITIES.
THE INTERNET IS VERY DIVIDED ON ZE ISSUE ...
SLAP
15

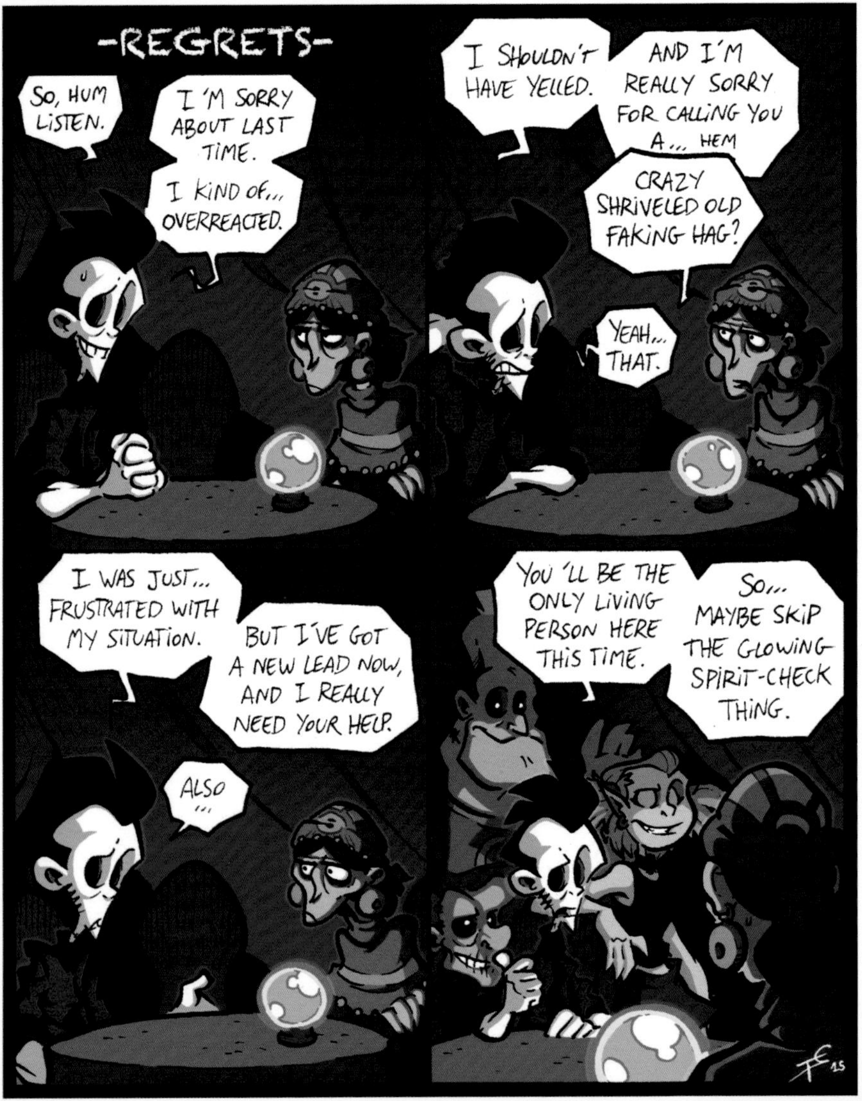
-REGRETS-
SO, HUM LISTEN.
I'M SORRY ABOUT LAST TIME.
I KIND OF... OVERREACTED.
I SHOULDN'T HAVE YELLED.
AND I'M REALLY SORRY FOR CALLING YOU A... HEM
CRAZY SHRIVELED OLD FAKING HAG?
YEAH... THAT.
I WAS JUST... FRUSTRATED WITH MY SITUATION.
BUT I'VE GOT A NEW LEAD NOW, AND I REALLY NEED YOUR HELP.
ALSO ...
YOU'LL BE THE ONLY LIVING PERSON HERE THIS TIME.
SO... MAYBE SKIP THE GLOWING SPIRIT-CHECK THING.

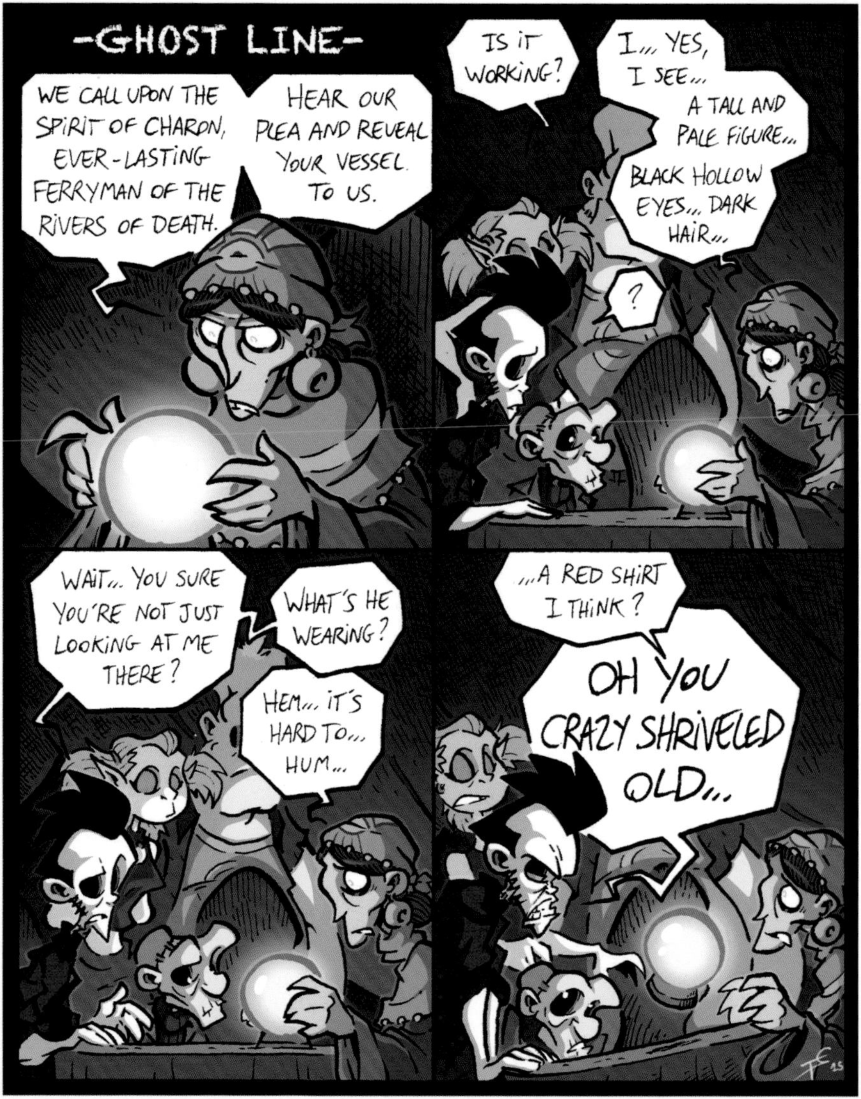
-GHOST LINE-
WE CALL UPON THE SPIRIT OF CHARON, EVER-LASTING FERRYMAN OF THE RIVERS OF DEATH.
HEAR OUR PLEA AND REVEAL YOUR VESSEL TO US.
IS IT WORKING?
I... YES, I SEE...
A TALL AND PALE FIGURE...
BLACK HOLLOW EYES... DARK HAIR...
?
WAIT... YOU SURE YOU'RE NOT JUST LOOKING AT ME THERE?
WHAT'S HE WEARING?
HEM... IT'S HARD TO... HUM...
...A RED SHIRT I THINK?
OH YOU CRAZY SHRIVELED OLD...

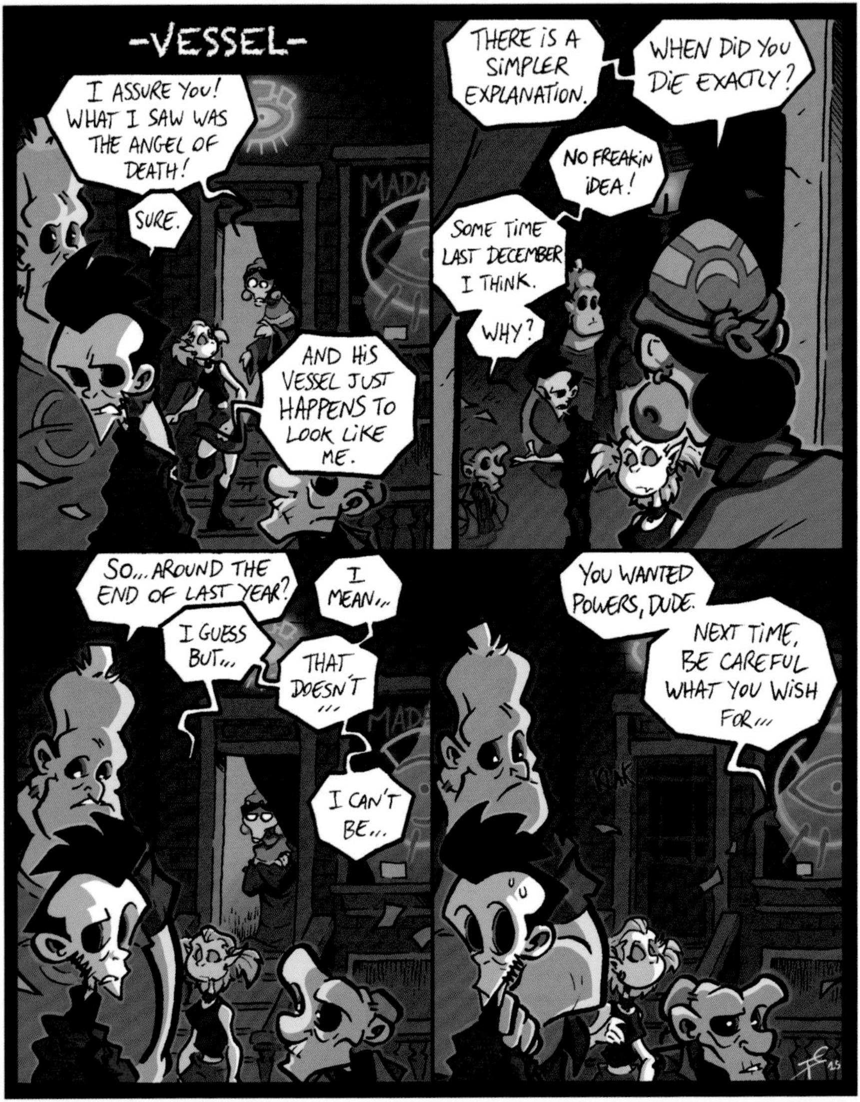
-VESSEL-
I ASSURE YOU! WHAT I SAW WAS THE ANGEL OF DEATH!
SURE.
AND HIS VESSEL JUST HAPPENS TO LOOK LIKE ME.
THERE IS A SIMPLER EXPLANATION.
WHEN DID YOU DIE EXACTLY?
SOME TIME LAST DECEMBER I THINK.
WHY?
NO FREAKIN IDEA!
SO... AROUND THE END OF LAST YEAR?
I GUESS BUT...
I MEAN...
THAT DOESN'T ...
I CAN'T BE...
YOU WANTED POWERS, DUDE.
NEXT TIME, BE CAREFUL WHAT YOU WISH FOR...

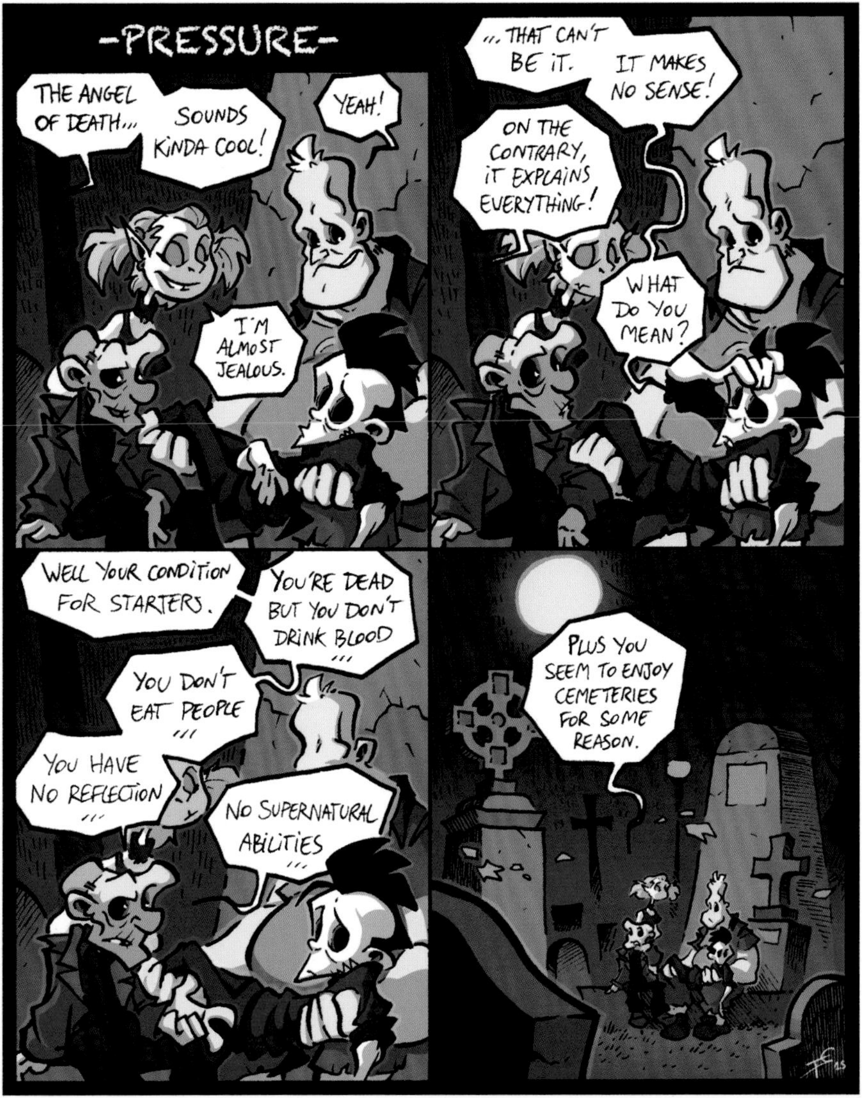

-PRESSURE-
THE ANGEL OF DEATH...
SOUNDS KINDA COOL!
YEAH!
I'M ALMOST JEALOUS.
...THAT CAN'T BE IT.
IT MAKES NO SENSE!
ON THE CONTRARY, IT EXPLAINS EVERYTHING!
WHAT DO YOU MEAN?
WELL YOUR CONDITION FOR STARTERS.
YOU'RE DEAD BUT YOU DON'T DRINK BLOOD...
YOU DON'T EAT PEOPLE...
YOU HAVE NO REFLECTION...
NO SUPERNATURAL ABILITIES...
PLUS YOU SEEM TO ENJOY CEMETERIES FOR SOME REASON.

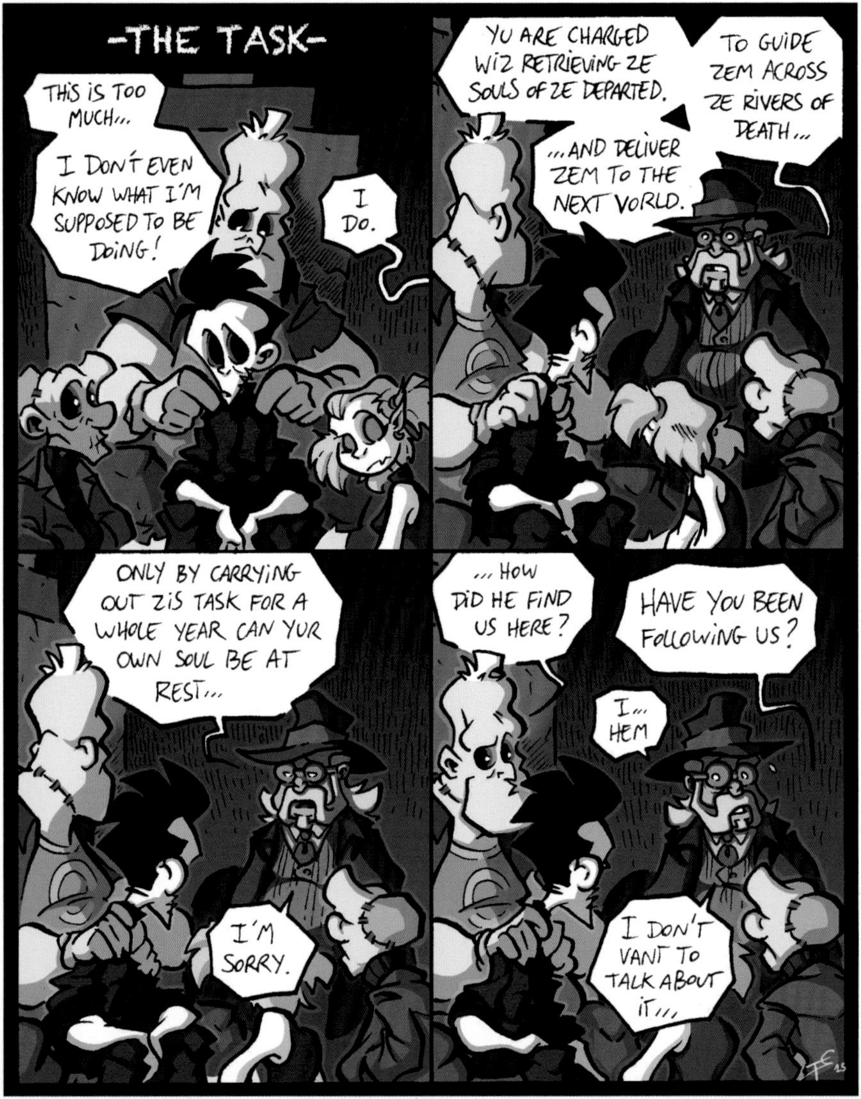
-THE TASK-
THIS IS TOO MUCH...
I DON'T EVEN KNOW WHAT I'M SUPPOSED TO BE DOING!
I DO.
YU ARE CHARGED WIZ RETRIEVING ZE SOULS OF ZE DEPARTED.
TO GUIDE ZEM ACROSS ZE RIVERS OF DEATH...
...AND DELIVER ZEM TO THE NEXT VORLD.
ONLY BY CARRYING OUT ZIS TASK FOR A WHOLE YEAR CAN YUR OWN SOUL BE AT REST...
I'M SORRY.
...HOW DID HE FIND US HERE?
HAVE YOU BEEN FOLLOWING US?
I... HEM
I DON'T VANT TO TALK ABOUT IT...

So
what if i'm
dead ?

Life goes
on.

Chapter V

-Acceptance-

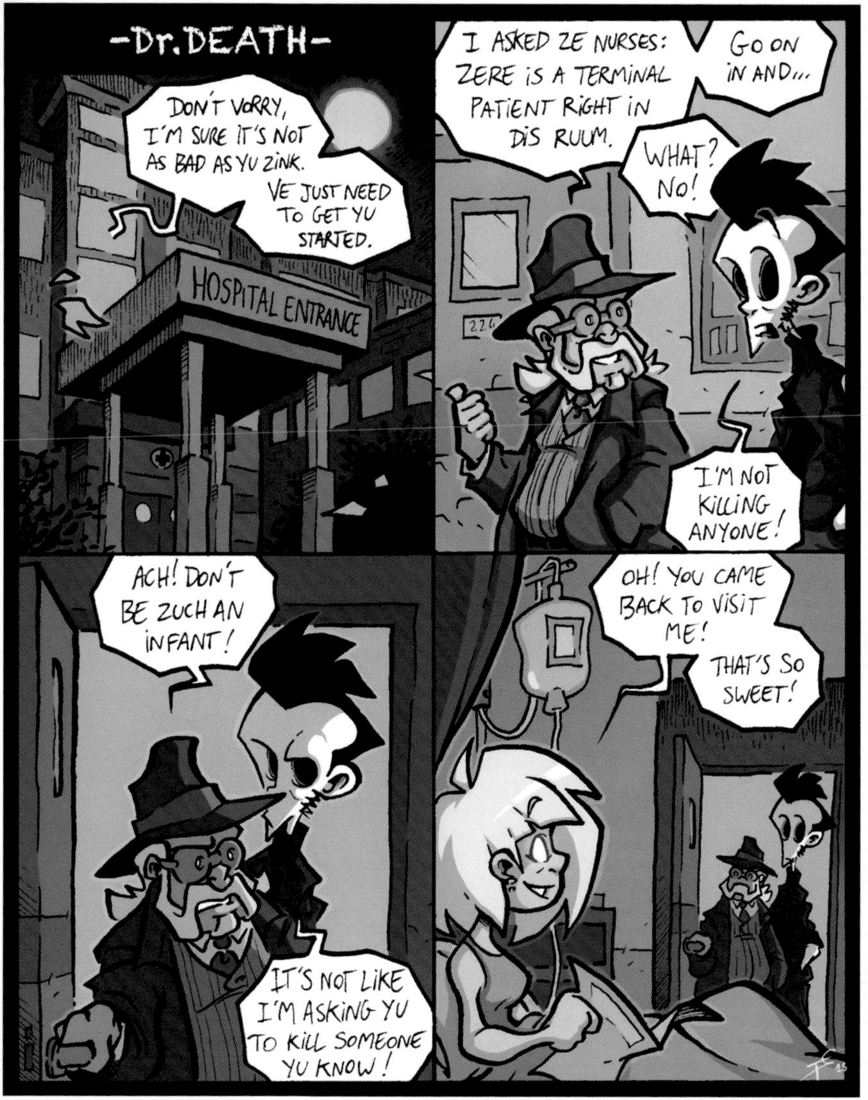
-Dr. DEATH-
DON'T VORRY, I'M SURE IT'S NOT AS BAD AS YU ZINK.
VE JUST NEED TO GET YU STARTED.
HOSPITAL ENTRANCE
I ASKED ZE NURSES: ZERE IS A TERMINAL PATIENT RIGHT IN DIS RUUM.
GO ON IN AND...
WHAT? NO!
226
I'M NOT KILLING ANYONE!
ACH! DON'T BE ZUCH AN INFANT!
IT'S NOT LIKE I'M ASKING YU TO KILL SOMEONE YU KNOW!
OH! YOU CAME BACK TO VISIT ME!
THAT'S SO SWEET!

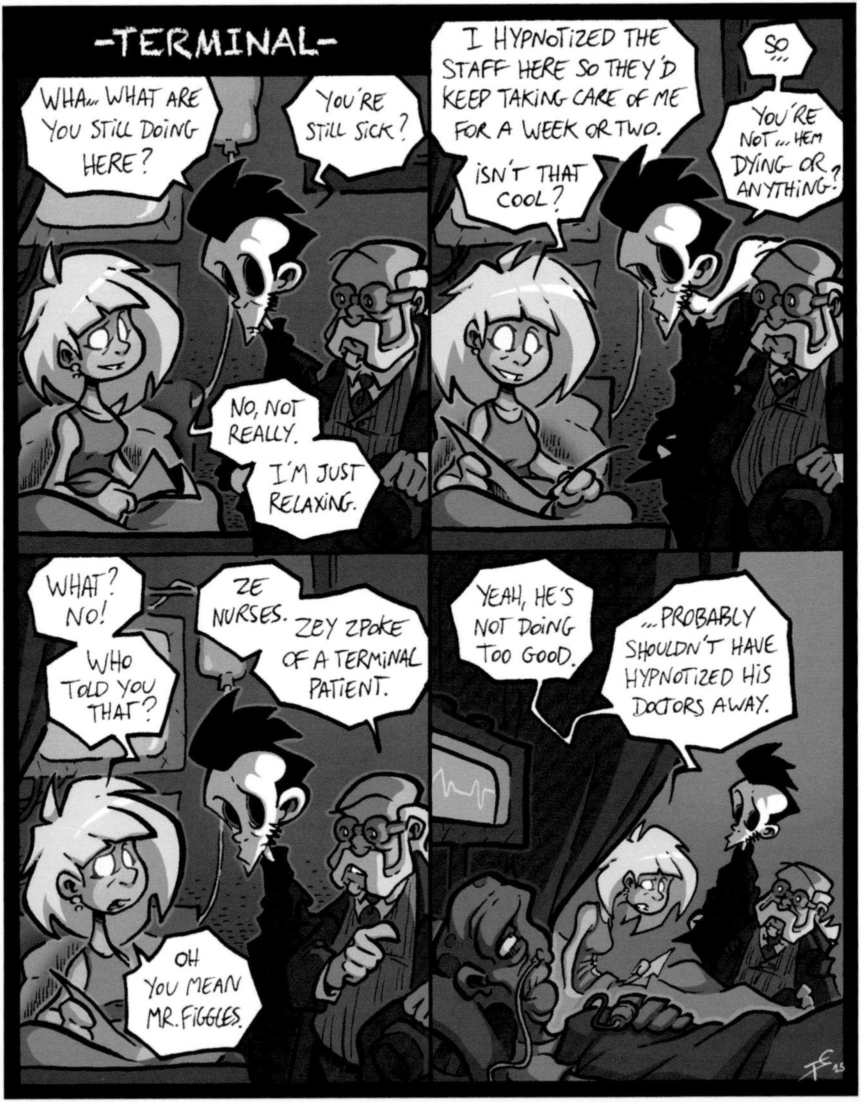
-TERMINAL-
WHA... WHAT ARE YOU STILL DOING HERE?
YOU'RE STILL SICK?
NO, NOT REALLY.
I'M JUST RELAXING.
I HYPNOTIZED THE STAFF HERE SO THEY'D KEEP TAKING CARE OF ME FOR A WEEK OR TWO.
ISN'T THAT COOL?
SO...
YOU'RE NOT... HEM DYING OR ANYTHING?
WHAT? NO!
WHO TOLD YOU THAT?
ZE NURSES.
ZEY ZPOKE OF A TERMINAL PATIENT.
OH YOU MEAN MR. FIGGLES.
YEAH, HE'S NOT DOING TOO GOOD.
...PROBABLY SHOULDN'T HAVE HYPNOTIZED HIS DOCTORS AWAY.

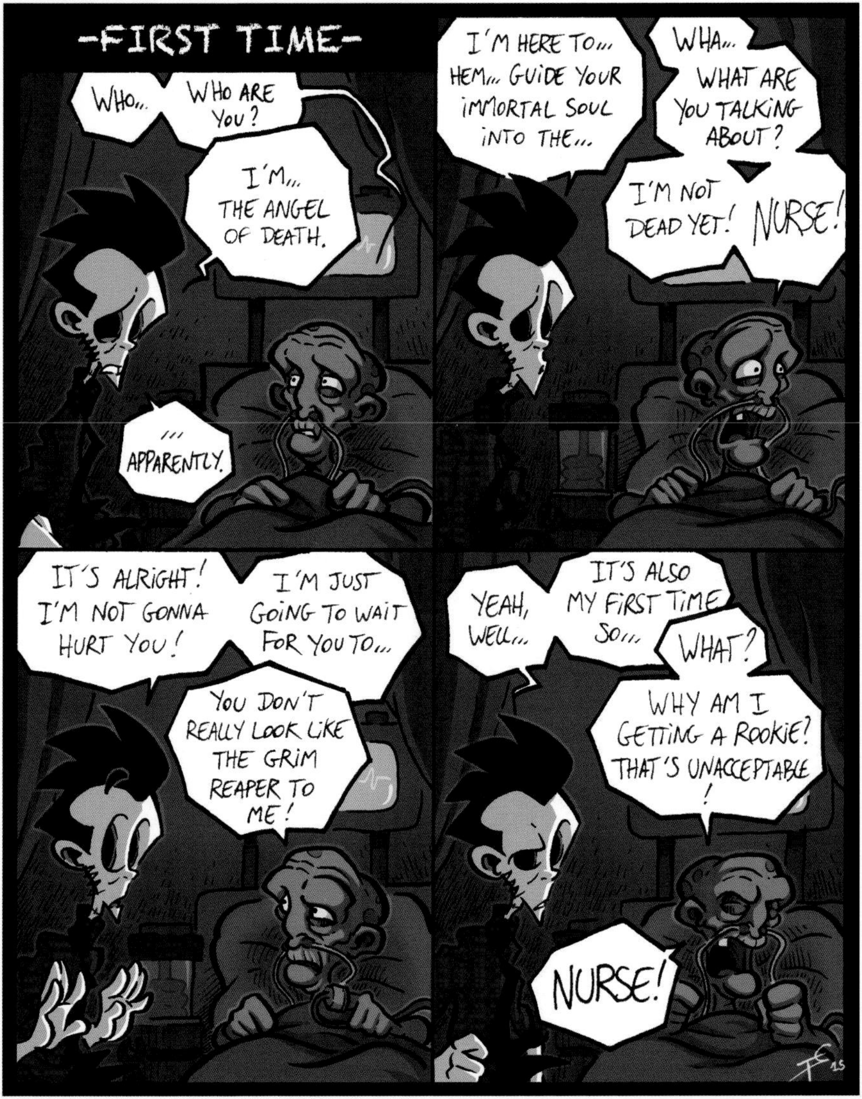
-FIRST TIME-
WHO...
WHO ARE YOU?
I'M... THE ANGEL OF DEATH.
... APPARENTLY.
I'M HERE TO... HEM... GUIDE YOUR IMMORTAL SOUL INTO THE...
WHA... WHAT ARE YOU TALKING ABOUT?
I'M NOT DEAD YET!
NURSE!
IT'S ALRIGHT! I'M NOT GONNA HURT YOU!
I'M JUST GOING TO WAIT FOR YOU TO...
YOU DON'T REALLY LOOK LIKE THE GRIM REAPER TO ME!
YEAH, WELL...
IT'S ALSO MY FIRST TIME SO...
WHAT?
WHY AM I GETTING A ROOKIE? THAT'S UNACCEPTABLE!
NURSE!

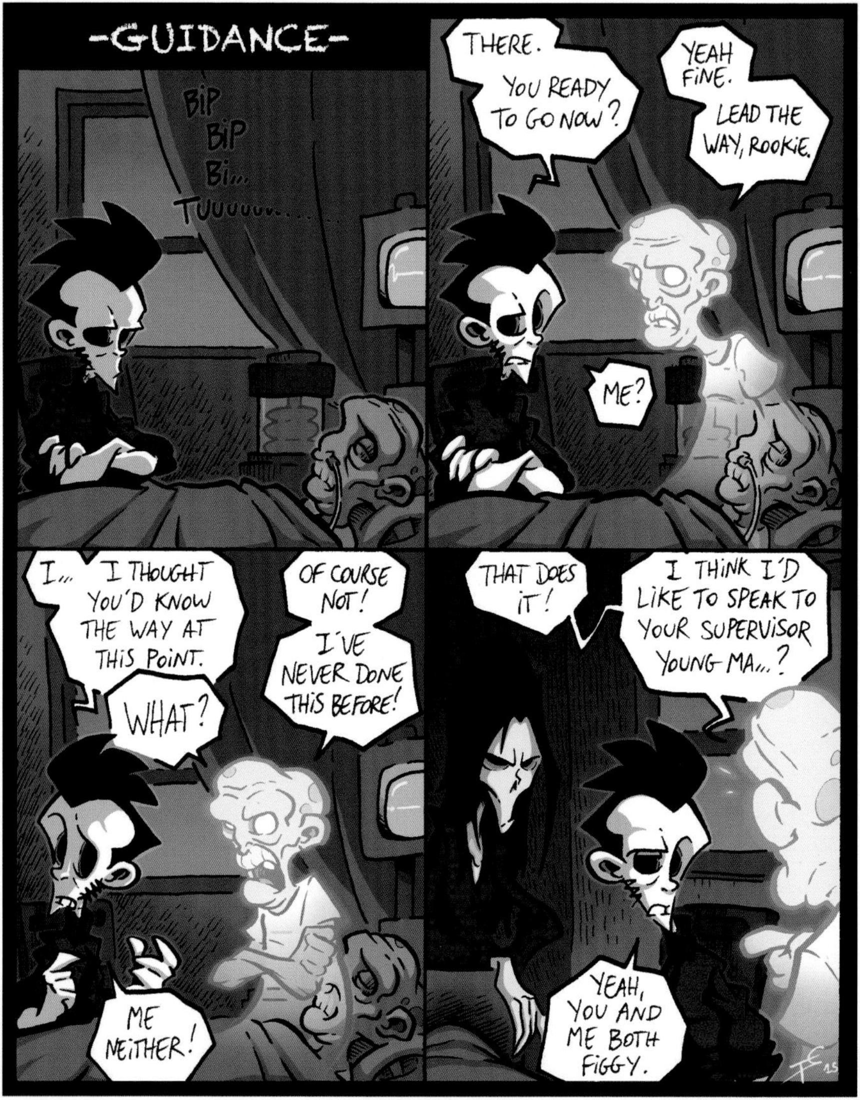
-GUIDANCE-
BIP
BIP
BI...
TUUUUUU.......
THERE.
YOU READY TO GO NOW?
YEAH FINE.
LEAD THE WAY, ROOKIE.
ME?
I... I THOUGHT YOU'D KNOW THE WAY AT THIS POINT.
WHAT?
OF COURSE NOT!
I'VE NEVER DONE THIS BEFORE!
ME NEITHER!
THAT DOES IT!
I THINK I'D LIKE TO SPEAK TO YOUR SUPERVISOR YOUNG MA...?
YEAH, YOU AND ME BOTH FIGGY.

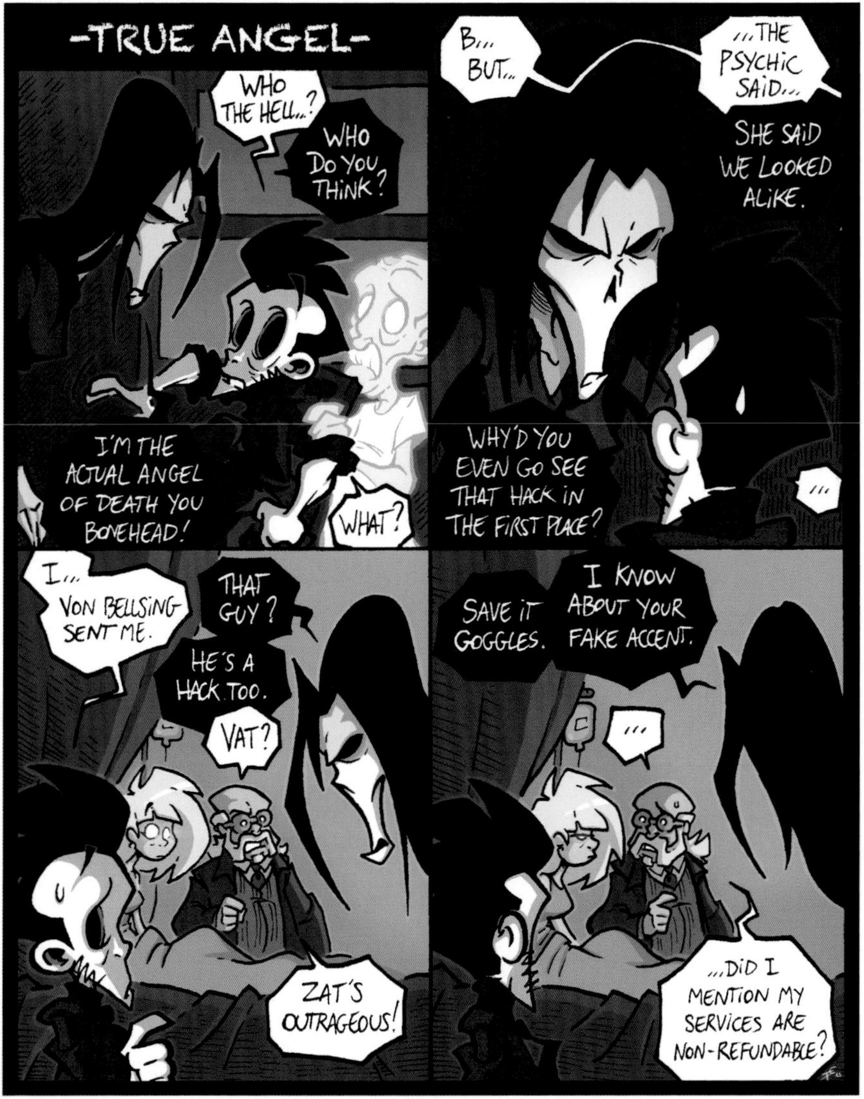
-TRUE ANGEL-
WHO THE HELL...?
WHO DO YOU THINK?
I'M THE ACTUAL ANGEL OF DEATH YOU BONEHEAD!
WHAT?
B... BUT...
...THE PSYCHIC SAID...
SHE SAID WE LOOKED ALIKE.
WHY'D YOU EVEN GO SEE THAT HACK IN THE FIRST PLACE?
...
I... VON BELLSING SENT ME.
THAT GUY?
HE'S A HACK TOO.
VAT?
ZAT'S OUTRAGEOUS!
SAVE IT GOGGLES.
I KNOW ABOUT YOUR FAKE ACCENT.
...
...DID I MENTION MY SERVICES ARE NON-REFUNDABLE?

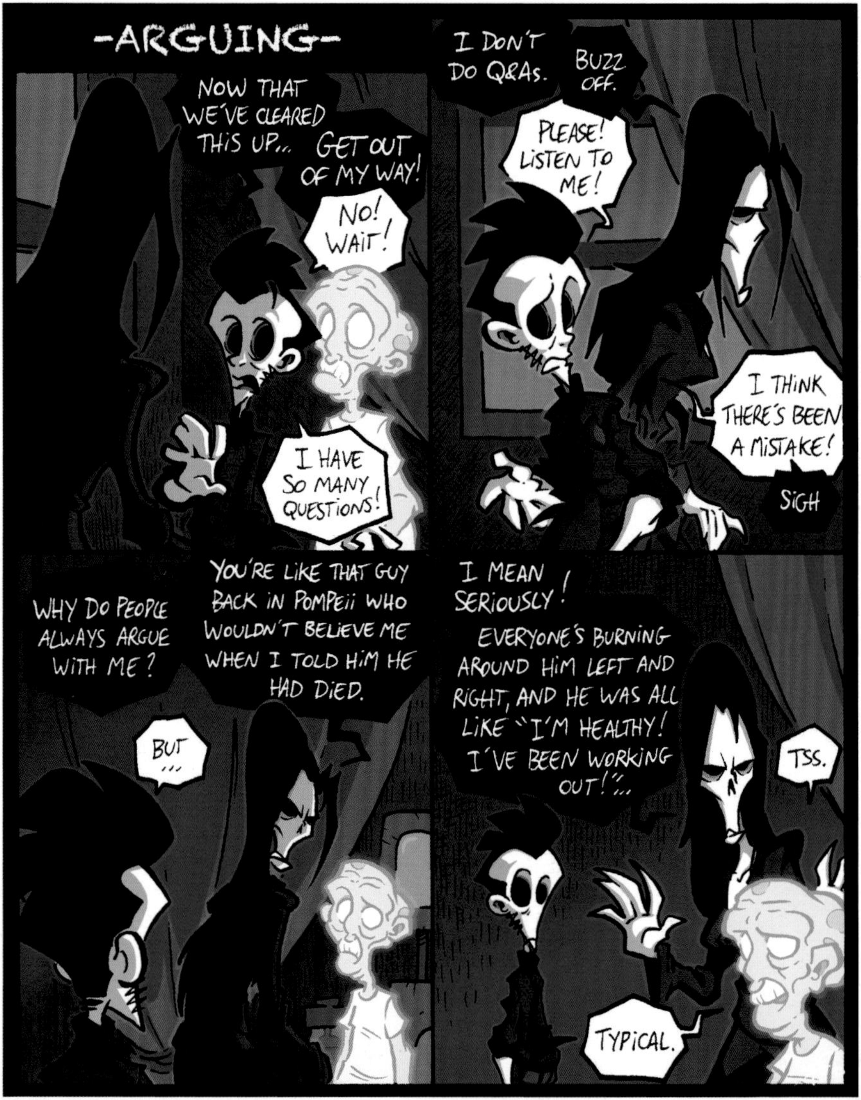
-ARGUING-
NOW THAT WE'VE CLEARED THIS UP... GET OUT OF MY WAY!
NO! WAIT!
I HAVE SO MANY QUESTIONS!
I DON'T DO Q&As.
BUZZ OFF.
PLEASE! LISTEN TO ME!
I THINK THERE'S BEEN A MISTAKE!
SIGH
WHY DO PEOPLE ALWAYS ARGUE WITH ME?
YOU'RE LIKE THAT GUY BACK IN POMPEII WHO WOULDN'T BELIEVE ME WHEN I TOLD HIM HE HAD DIED.
BUT ...
I MEAN SERIOUSLY!
EVERYONE'S BURNING AROUND HIM LEFT AND RIGHT, AND HE WAS ALL LIKE "I'M HEALTHY! I'VE BEEN WORKING OUT!"...
TSS.
TYPICAL.

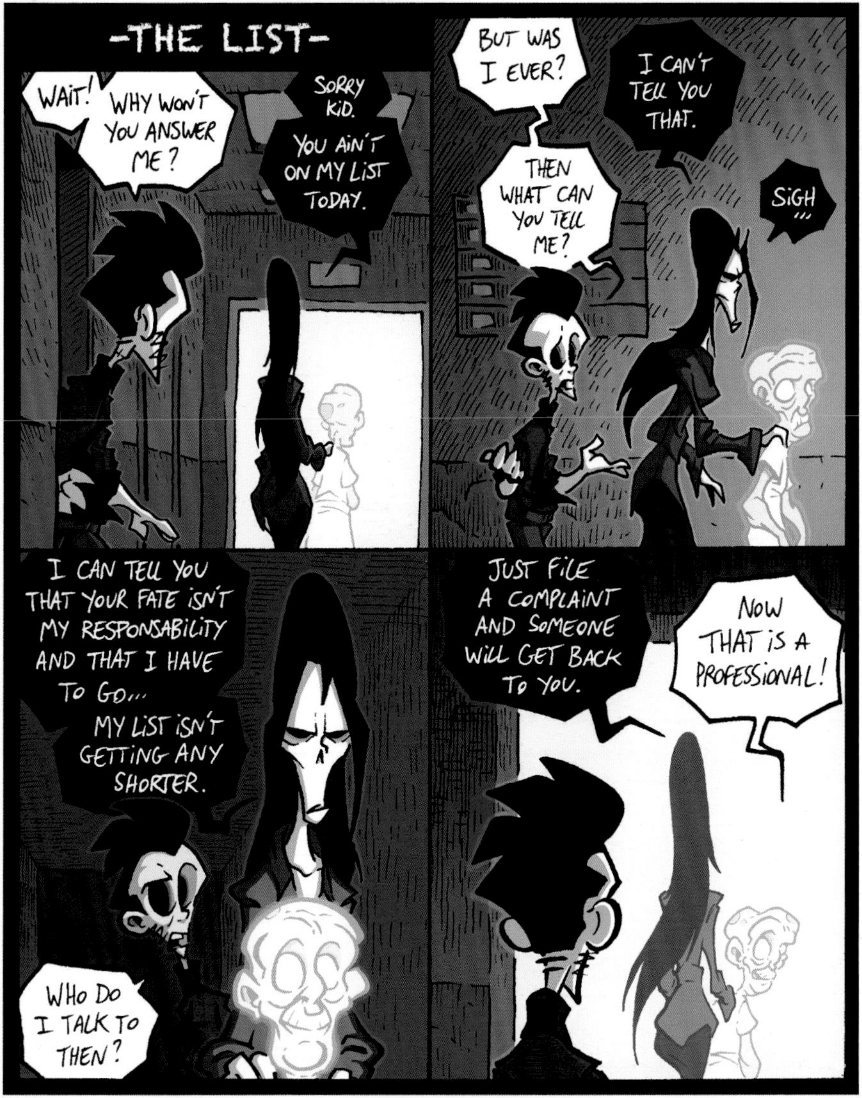
-THE LIST-
WAIT!
WHY WON'T YOU ANSWER ME?
SORRY KID.
YOU AIN'T ON MY LIST TODAY.
BUT WAS I EVER?
I CAN'T TELL YOU THAT.
THEN WHAT CAN YOU TELL ME?
SIGH...
I CAN TELL YOU THAT YOUR FATE ISN'T MY RESPONSABILITY AND THAT I HAVE TO GO...
MY LIST ISN'T GETTING ANY SHORTER.
WHO DO I TALK TO THEN?
JUST FILE A COMPLAINT AND SOMEONE WILL GET BACK TO YOU.
NOW THAT IS A PROFESSIONAL!

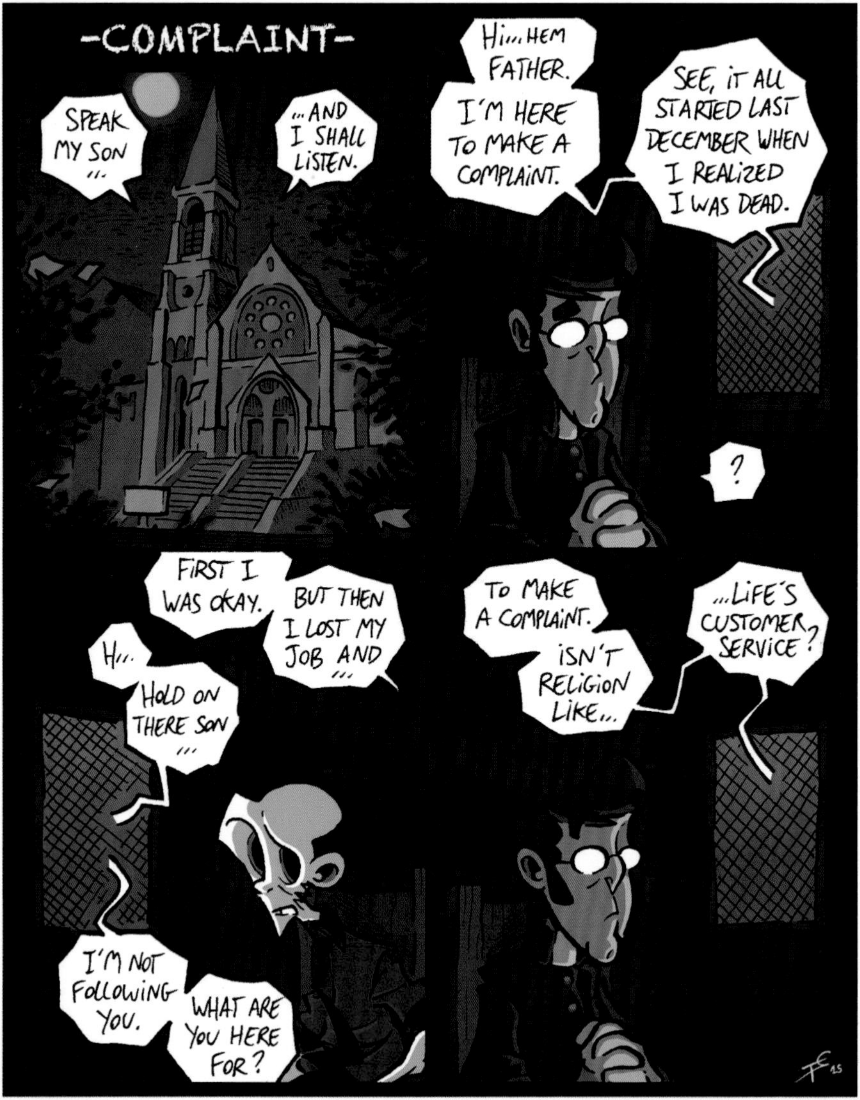
-COMPLAINT-
SPEAK MY SON ...
... AND I SHALL LISTEN.
HI... HEM FATHER.
I'M HERE TO MAKE A COMPLAINT.
SEE, IT ALL STARTED LAST DECEMBER WHEN I REALIZED I WAS DEAD.
?
FIRST I WAS OKAY.
BUT THEN I LOST MY JOB AND ...
H...
HOLD ON THERE SON ...
I'M NOT FOLLOWING YOU.
WHAT ARE YOU HERE FOR?
TO MAKE A COMPLAINT.
ISN'T RELIGION LIKE...
...LIFE'S CUSTOMER SERVICE?

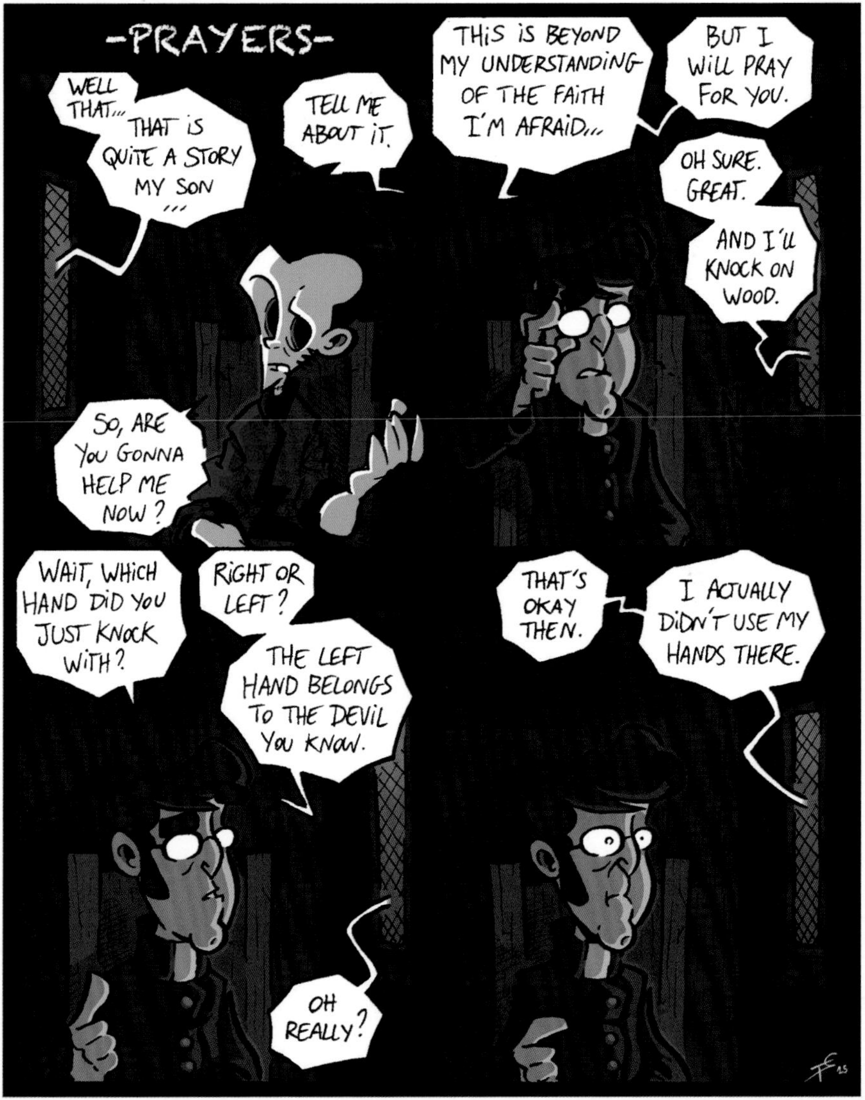
-PRAYERS-
WELL THAT...
THAT IS QUITE A STORY MY SON ...
TELL ME ABOUT IT.
THIS IS BEYOND MY UNDERSTANDING OF THE FAITH I'M AFRAID...
BUT I WILL PRAY FOR YOU.
OH SURE. GREAT.
AND I'LL KNOCK ON WOOD.
SO, ARE YOU GONNA HELP ME NOW?
WAIT, WHICH HAND DID YOU JUST KNOCK WITH?
RIGHT OR LEFT?
THE LEFT HAND BELONGS TO THE DEVIL YOU KNOW.
OH REALLY?
THAT'S OKAY THEN.
I ACTUALLY DIDN'T USE MY HANDS THERE.

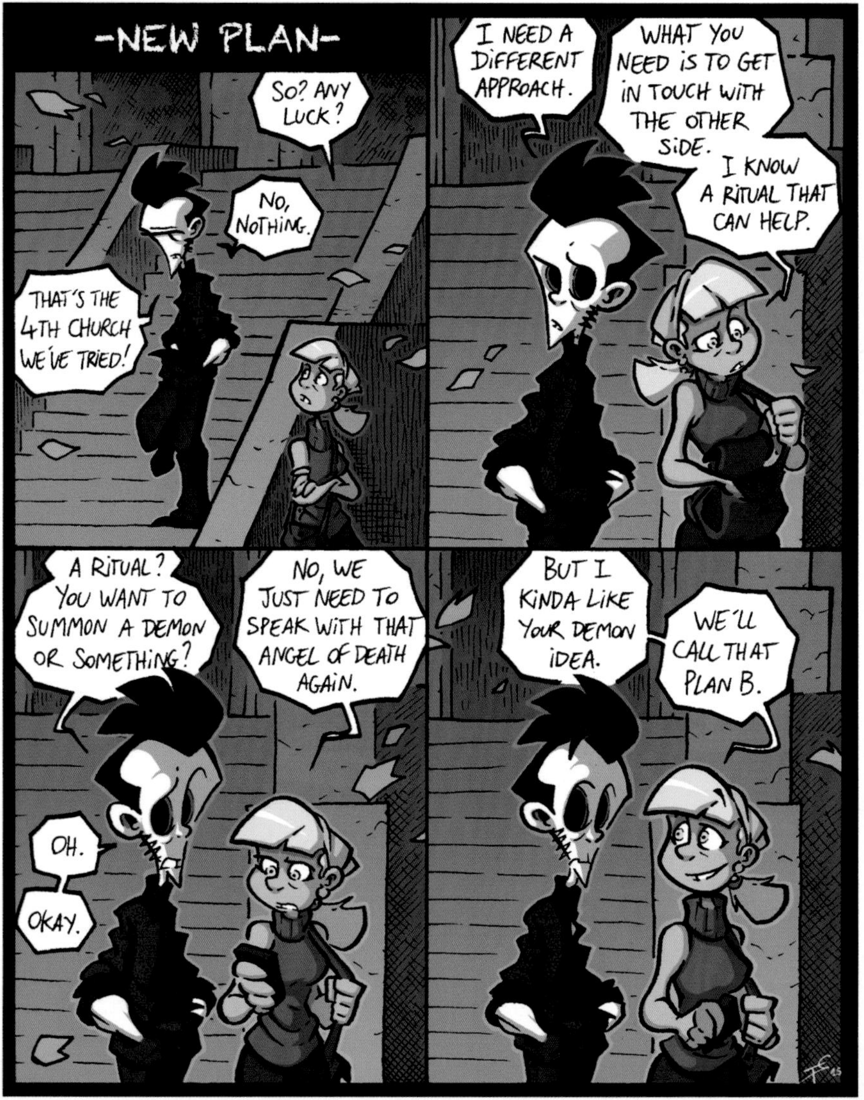
-NEW PLAN-
SO? ANY LUCK?
NO, NOTHING.
THAT'S THE 4TH CHURCH WE'VE TRIED!
I NEED A DIFFERENT APPROACH.
WHAT YOU NEED IS TO GET IN TOUCH WITH THE OTHER SIDE.
I KNOW A RITUAL THAT CAN HELP.
A RITUAL? YOU WANT TO SUMMON A DEMON OR SOMETHING?
NO, WE JUST NEED TO SPEAK WITH THAT ANGEL OF DEATH AGAIN.
OH.
OKAY.
BUT I KINDA LIKE YOUR DEMON IDEA.
WE'LL CALL THAT PLAN B.

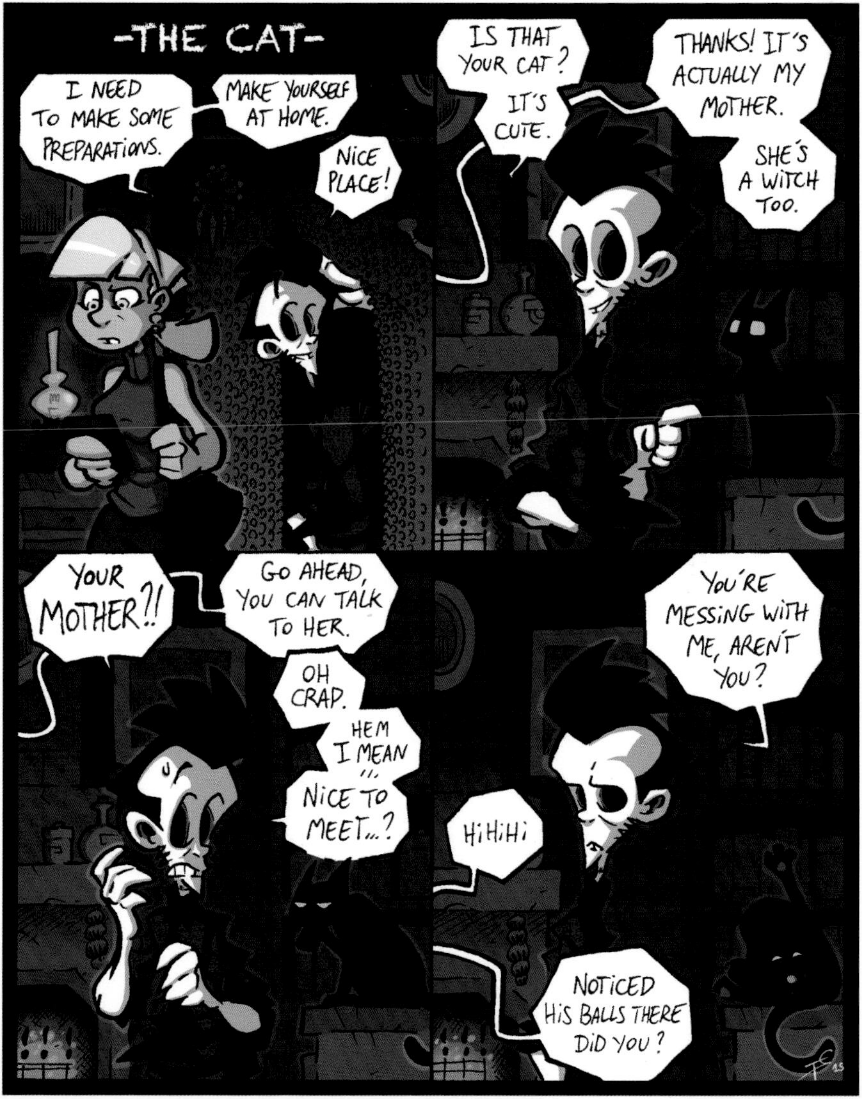
-THE CAT-
I NEED TO MAKE SOME PREPARATIONS.
MAKE YOURSELF AT HOME.
NICE PLACE!
IS THAT YOUR CAT?
IT'S CUTE.
THANKS! IT'S ACTUALLY MY MOTHER.
SHE'S A WITCH TOO.
YOUR MOTHER?!
GO AHEAD, YOU CAN TALK TO HER.
OH CRAP.
HEM I MEAN ...
NICE TO MEET...?
YOU'RE MESSING WITH ME, AREN'T YOU?
HIHIHI
NOTICED HIS BALLS THERE DID YOU?

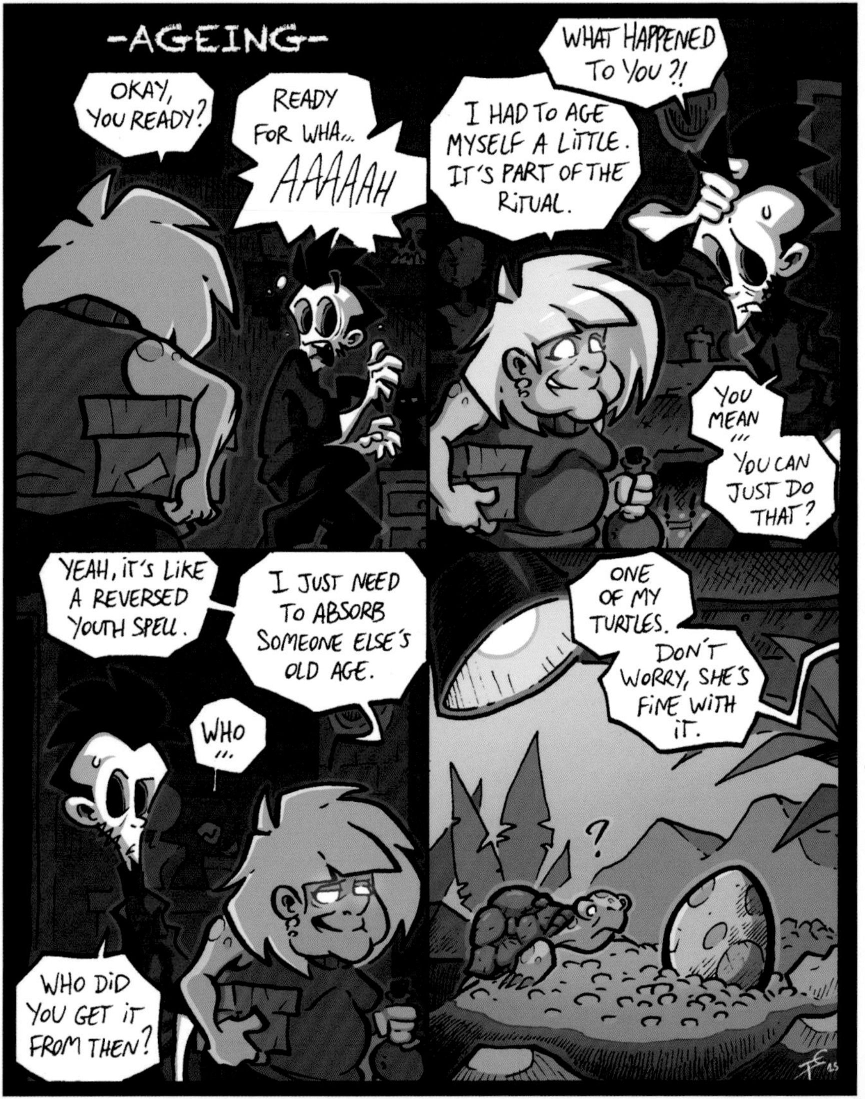

-AGEING-
OKAY, YOU READY?
READY FOR WHA...
AAAAAH
WHAT HAPPENED TO YOU?!
I HAD TO AGE MYSELF A LITTLE. IT'S PART OF THE RITUAL.
YOU MEAN...
YOU CAN JUST DO THAT?
YEAH, IT'S LIKE A REVERSED YOUTH SPELL.
I JUST NEED TO ABSORB SOMEONE ELSE'S OLD AGE.
WHO...
WHO DID YOU GET IT FROM THEN?
ONE OF MY TURTLES.
DON'T WORRY, SHE'S FINE WITH IT.
?

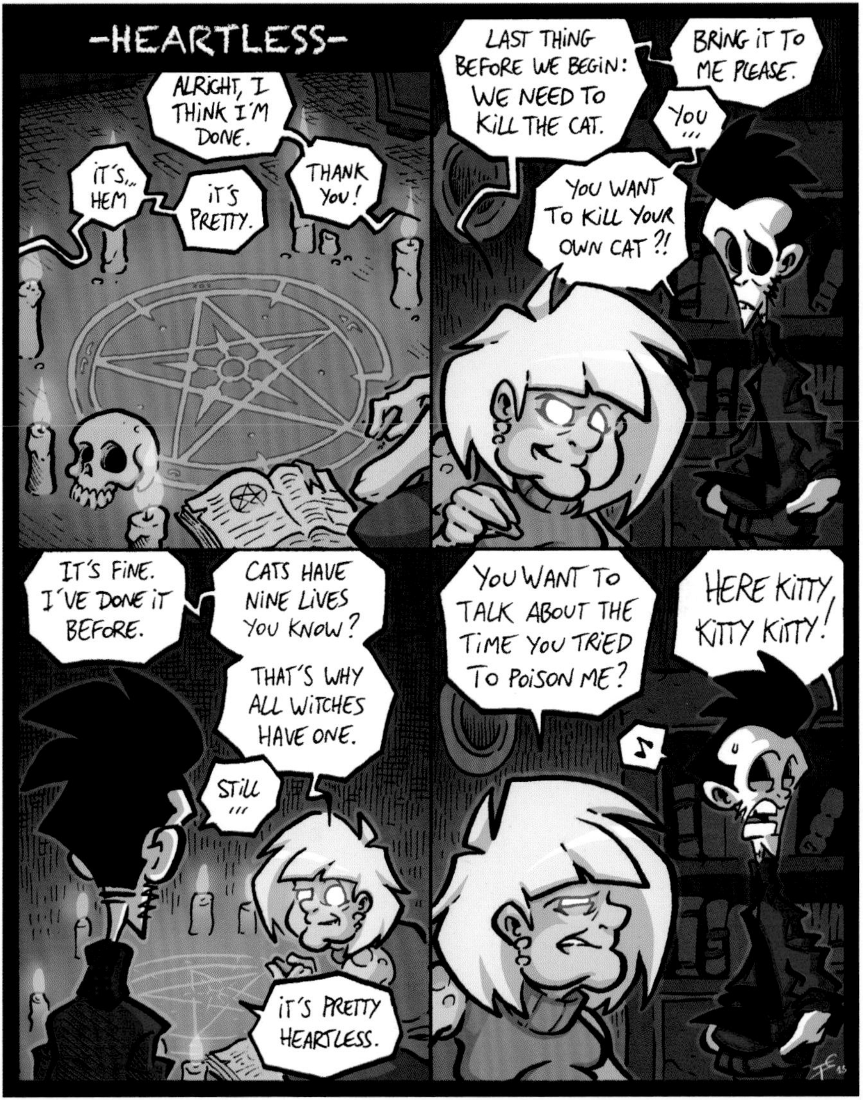
-HEARTLESS-
ALRIGHT, I THINK I'M DONE.
THANK YOU!
IT'S... HEM
IT'S PRETTY.
LAST THING BEFORE WE BEGIN: WE NEED TO KILL THE CAT.
BRING IT TO ME PLEASE.
YOU...
YOU WANT TO KILL YOUR OWN CAT?!
IT'S FINE. I'VE DONE IT BEFORE.
CATS HAVE NINE LIVES YOU KNOW?
THAT'S WHY ALL WITCHES HAVE ONE.
STILL...
IT'S PRETTY HEARTLESS.
YOU WANT TO TALK ABOUT THE TIME YOU TRIED TO POISON ME?
HERE KITTY, KITTY KITTY!

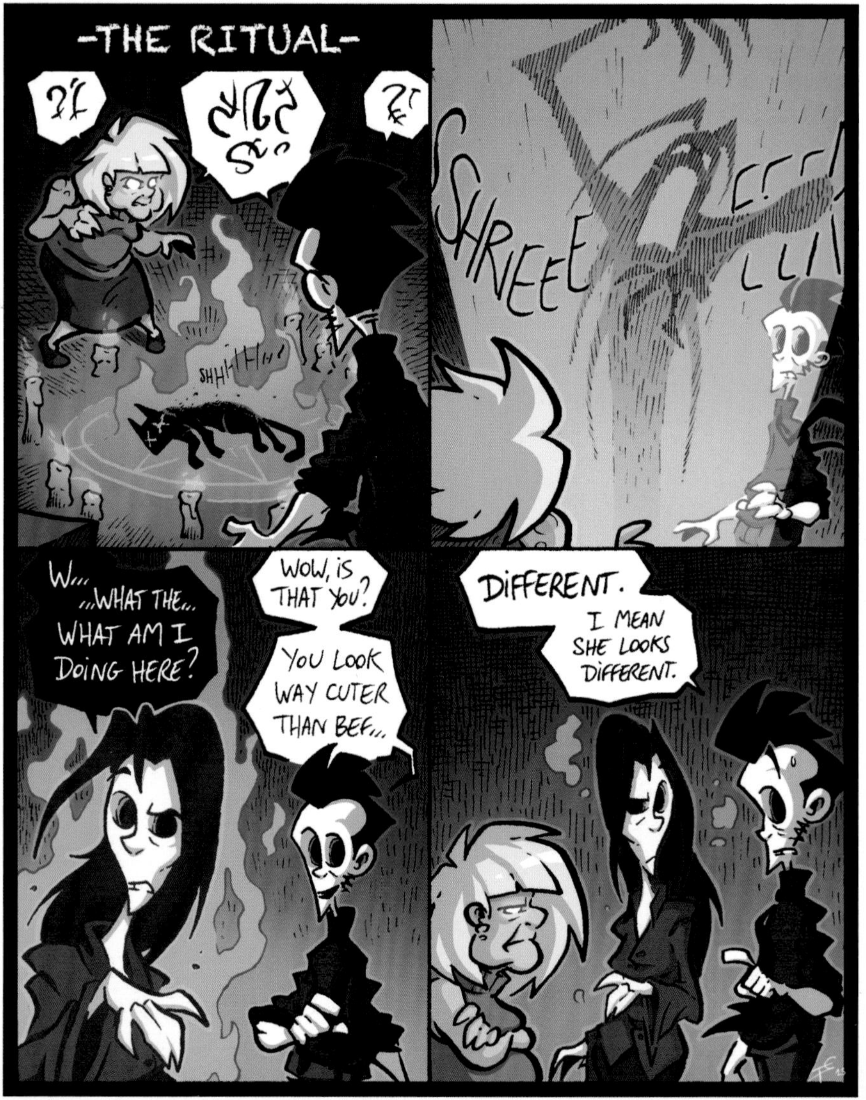
-THE RITUAL-
SHH
SHRIEEE
W... ...WHAT THE... WHAT AM I DOING HERE?
WOW, IS THAT YOU?
YOU LOOK WAY CUTER THAN BEF...
DIFFERENT.
I MEAN SHE LOOKS DIFFERENT.

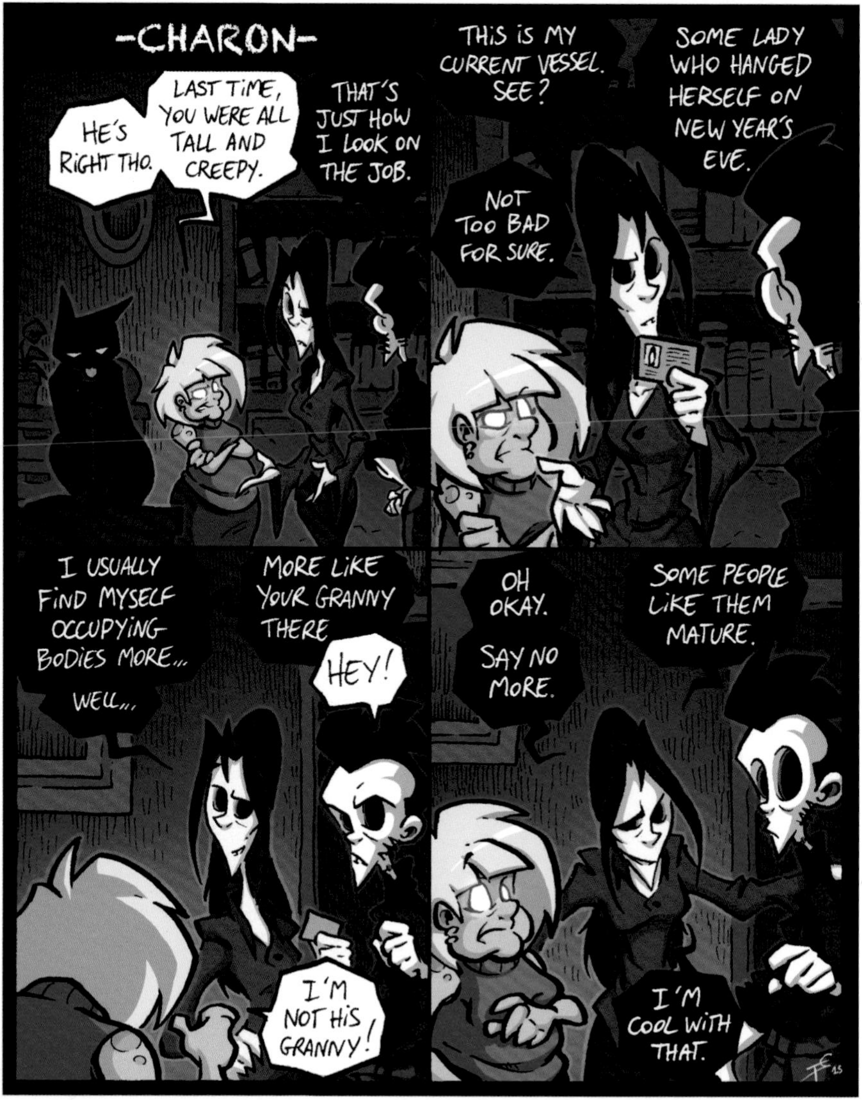
-CHARON-
HE'S RIGHT THO.
LAST TIME, YOU WERE ALL TALL AND CREEPY.
THAT'S JUST HOW I LOOK ON THE JOB.
THIS IS MY CURRENT VESSEL. SEE?
SOME LADY WHO HANGED HERSELF ON NEW YEAR'S EVE.
NOT TOO BAD FOR SURE.
I USUALLY FIND MYSELF OCCUPYING BODIES MORE...
WELL...
MORE LIKE YOUR GRANNY THERE
HEY!
I'M NOT HIS GRANNY!
OH OKAY.
SAY NO MORE.
SOME PEOPLE LIKE THEM MATURE.
I'M COOL WITH THAT.

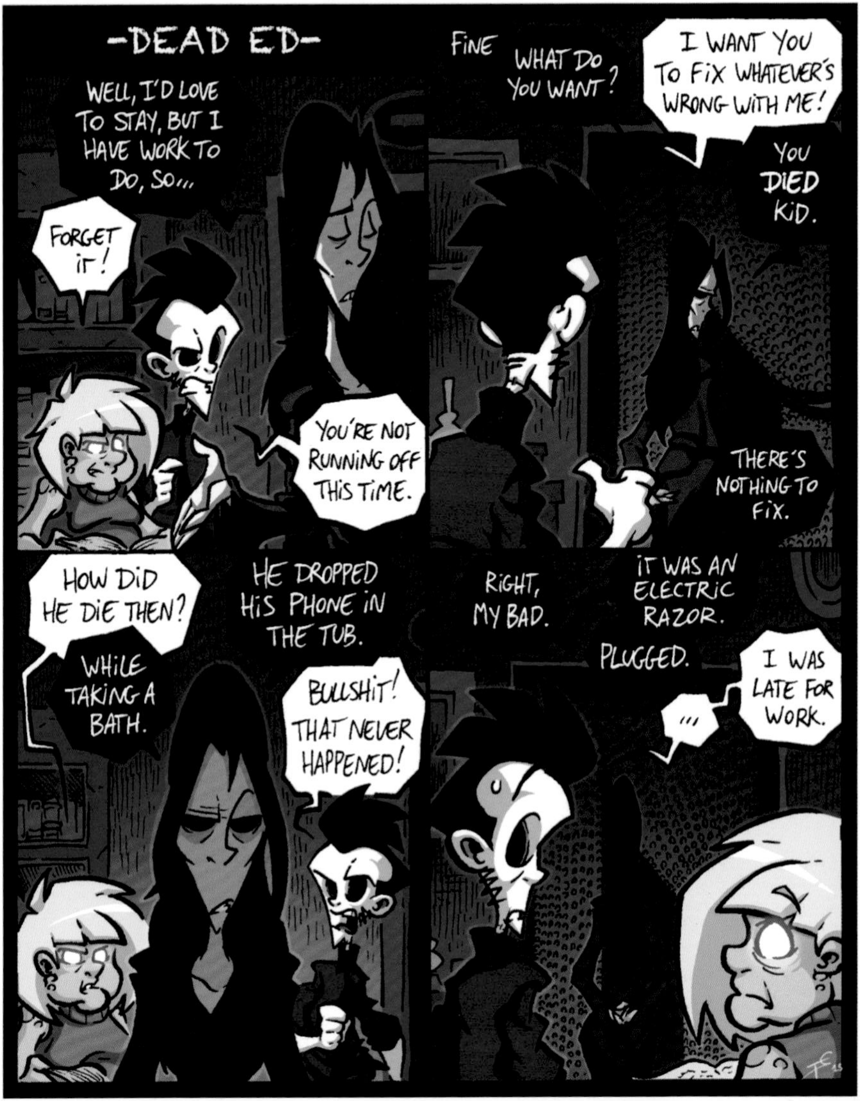
-DEAD ED-
WELL, I'D LOVE TO STAY, BUT I HAVE WORK TO DO, SO...
FORGET IT!
YOU'RE NOT RUNNING OFF THIS TIME.
FINE
WHAT DO YOU WANT?
I WANT YOU TO FIX WHATEVER'S WRONG WITH ME!
YOU DIED KID.
THERE'S NOTHING TO FIX.
HOW DID HE DIE THEN?
WHILE TAKING A BATH.
HE DROPPED HIS PHONE IN THE TUB.
BULLSHIT! THAT NEVER HAPPENED!
RIGHT, MY BAD.
IT WAS AN ELECTRIC RAZOR.
PLUGGED.
...
I WAS LATE FOR WORK.

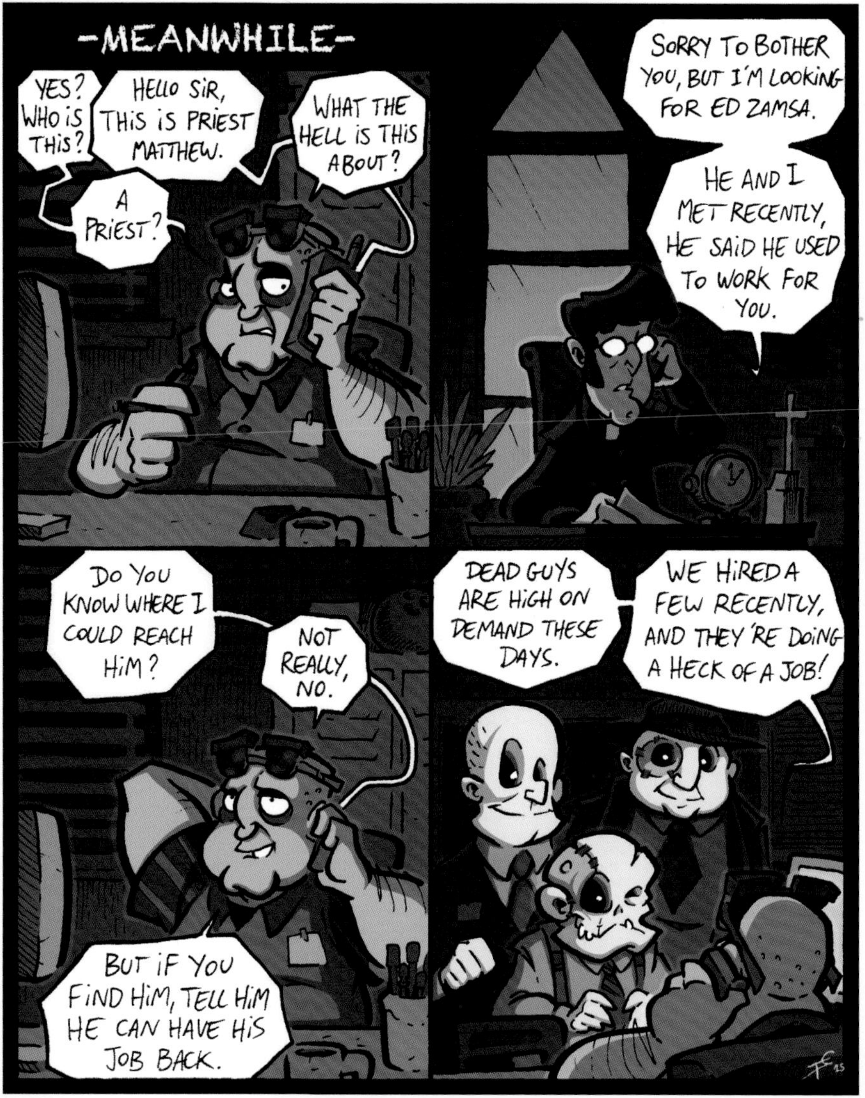
-MEANWHILE-
YES? WHO IS THIS?
HELLO SIR, THIS IS PRIEST MATTHEW.
A PRIEST?
WHAT THE HELL IS THIS ABOUT?
SORRY TO BOTHER YOU, BUT I'M LOOKING FOR ED ZAMSA.
HE AND I MET RECENTLY, HE SAID HE USED TO WORK FOR YOU.
DO YOU KNOW WHERE I COULD REACH HIM?
NOT REALLY, NO.
BUT IF YOU FIND HIM, TELL HIM HE CAN HAVE HIS JOB BACK.
DEAD GUYS ARE HIGH ON DEMAND THESE DAYS.
WE HIRED A FEW RECENTLY, AND THEY'RE DOING A HECK OF A JOB!

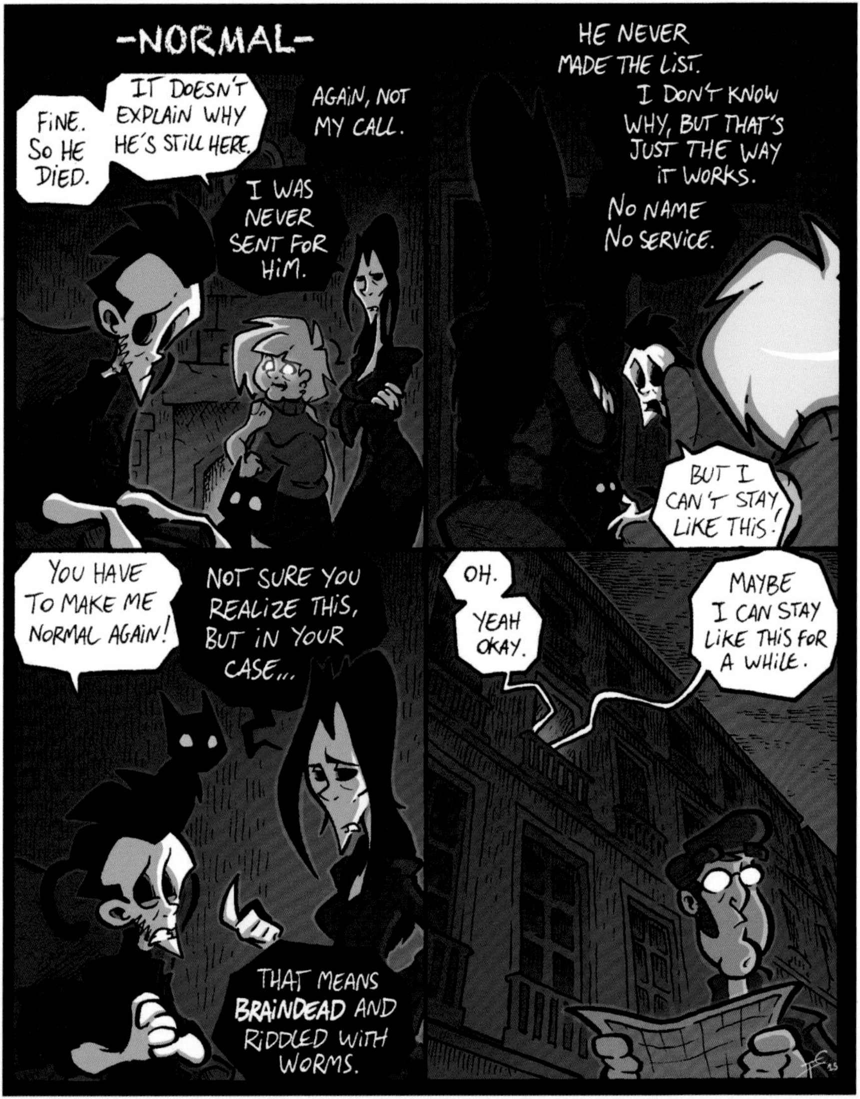
-NORMAL-
FINE. SO HE DIED.
IT DOESN'T EXPLAIN WHY HE'S STILL HERE.
AGAIN, NOT MY CALL.
I WAS NEVER SENT FOR HIM.
HE NEVER MADE THE LIST.
I DON'T KNOW WHY, BUT THAT'S JUST THE WAY IT WORKS.
NO NAME NO SERVICE.
BUT I CAN'T STAY LIKE THIS!
YOU HAVE TO MAKE ME NORMAL AGAIN!
NOT SURE YOU REALIZE THIS, BUT IN YOUR CASE...
THAT MEANS **BRAINDEAD** AND RIDDLED WITH WORMS.
OH.
YEAH OKAY.
MAYBE I CAN STAY LIKE THIS FOR A WHILE.

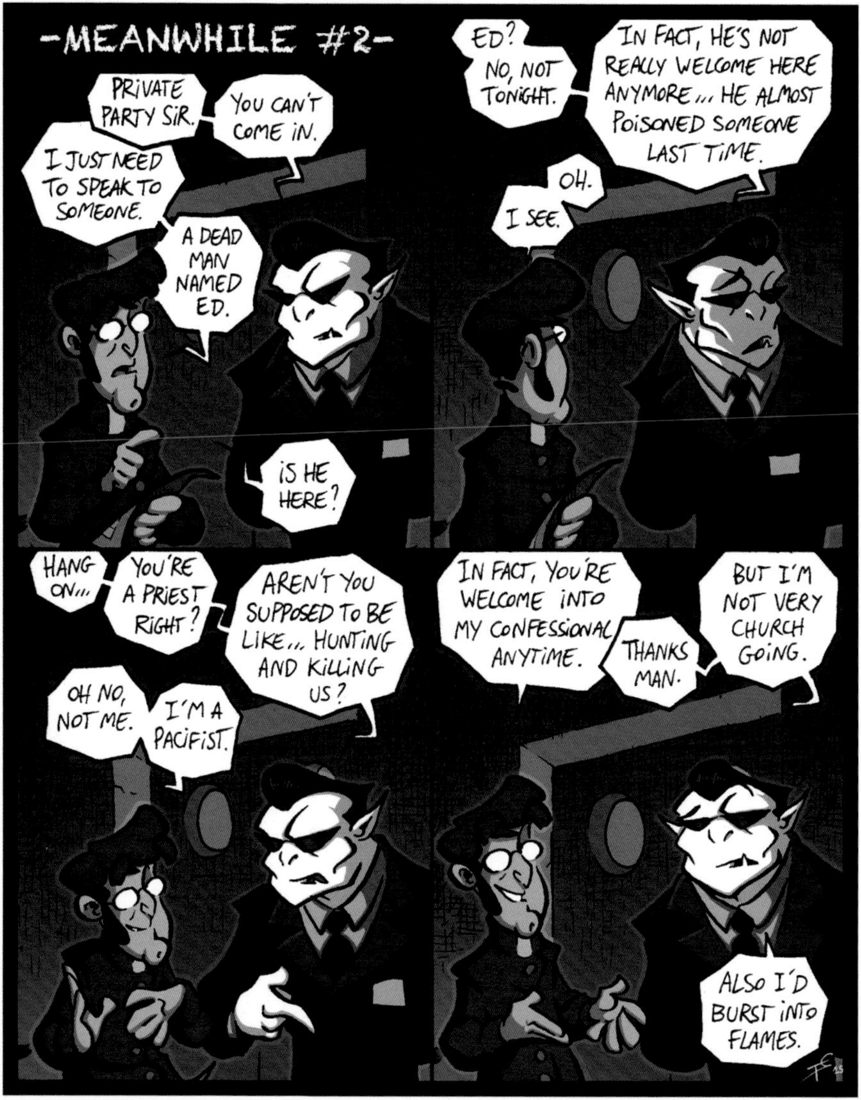
-MEANWHILE #2-
PRIVATE PARTY SIR.
YOU CAN'T COME IN.
I JUST NEED TO SPEAK TO SOMEONE.
A DEAD MAN NAMED ED.
IS HE HERE?
ED?
NO, NOT TONIGHT.
IN FACT, HE'S NOT REALLY WELCOME HERE ANYMORE... HE ALMOST POISONED SOMEONE LAST TIME.
OH.
I SEE.
HANG ON...
YOU'RE A PRIEST RIGHT?
AREN'T YOU SUPPOSED TO BE LIKE... HUNTING AND KILLING US?
OH NO, NOT ME.
I'M A PACIFIST.
IN FACT, YOU'RE WELCOME INTO MY CONFESSIONAL ANYTIME.
THANKS MAN.
BUT I'M NOT VERY CHURCH GOING.
ALSO I'D BURST INTO FLAMES.

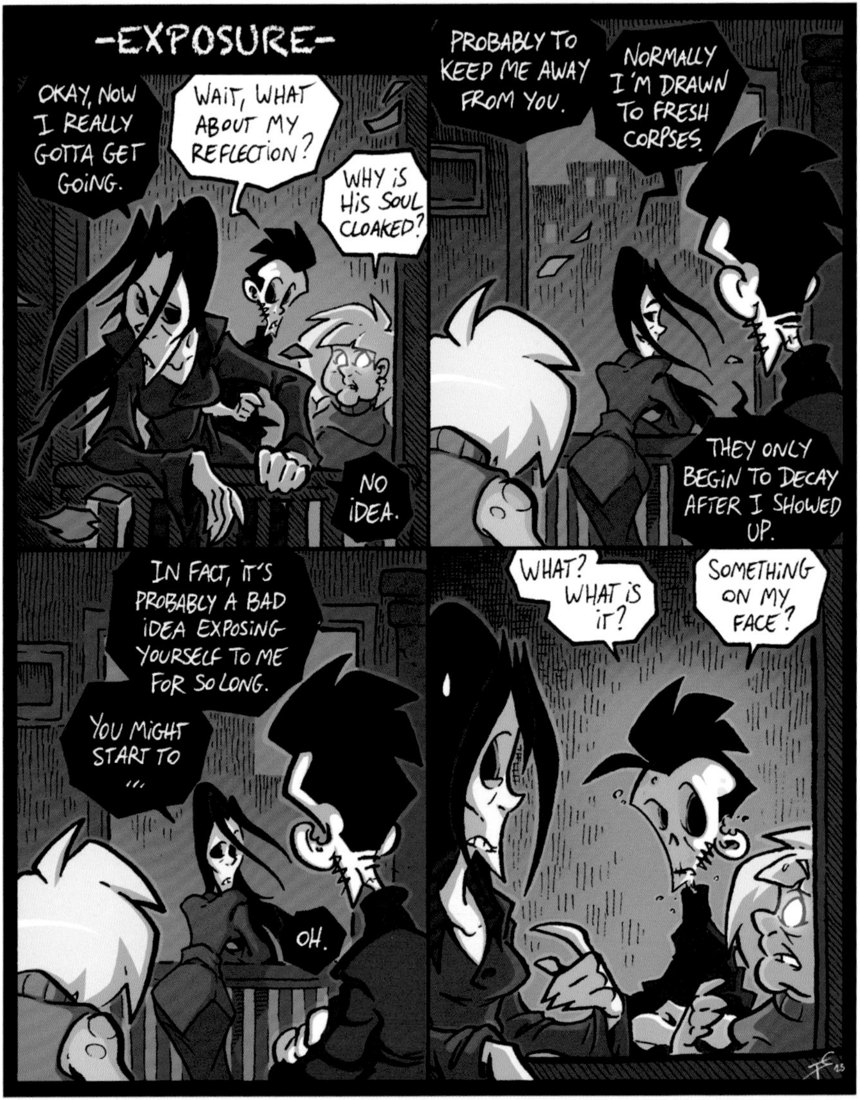
-EXPOSURE-
OKAY, NOW I REALLY GOTTA GET GOING.
WAIT, WHAT ABOUT MY REFLECTION?
WHY IS HIS SOUL CLOAKED?
NO IDEA.
PROBABLY TO KEEP ME AWAY FROM YOU.
NORMALLY I'M DRAWN TO FRESH CORPSES.
THEY ONLY BEGIN TO DECAY AFTER I SHOWED UP.
IN FACT, IT'S PROBABLY A BAD IDEA EXPOSING YOURSELF TO ME FOR SO LONG.
YOU MIGHT START TO ...
OH.
WHAT? WHAT IS IT?
SOMETHING ON MY FACE?

I'm already
dead.

What's the worst
that could
happen?

Chapter VI
-Conclusion-

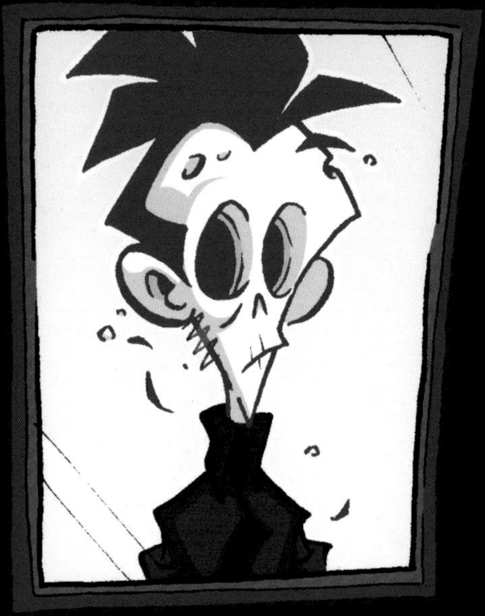

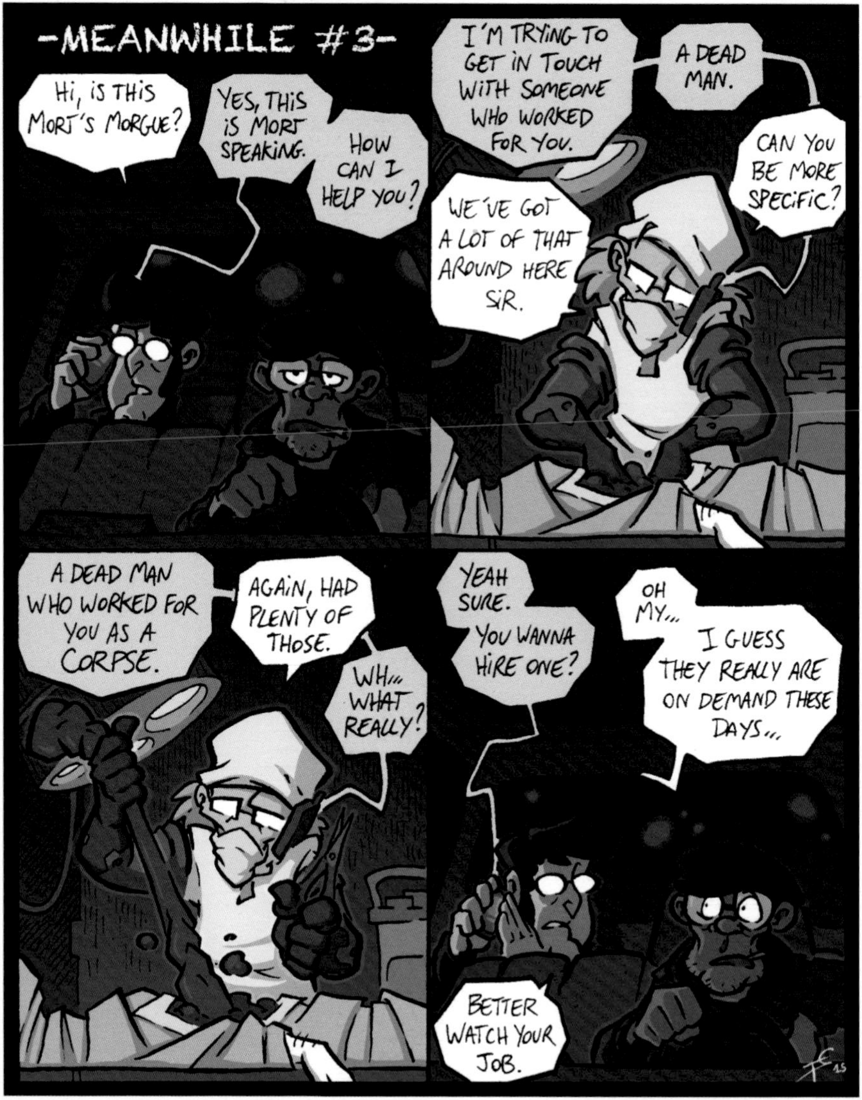
-MEANWHILE #3-
Hi, is THIS MORT'S MORGUE?
YES, THIS iS MORT SPEAKiNG.
HOW CAN I HELP YOU?
I'M TRYiNG TO GET iN TOUCH WiTH SOMEONE WHO WORKED FOR YOU.
A DEAD MAN.
CAN YOU BE MORE SPECiFiC?
WE'VE GOT A LOT OF THAT AROUND HERE SiR.
A DEAD MAN WHO WORKED FOR YOU AS A CORPSE.
AGAiN, HAD PLENTY OF THOSE.
WH... WHAT REALLY?
YEAH SURE.
YOU WANNA HiRE ONE?
OH MY...
I GUESS THEY REALLY ARE ON DEMAND THESE DAYS...
BETTER WATCH YOUR JOB.

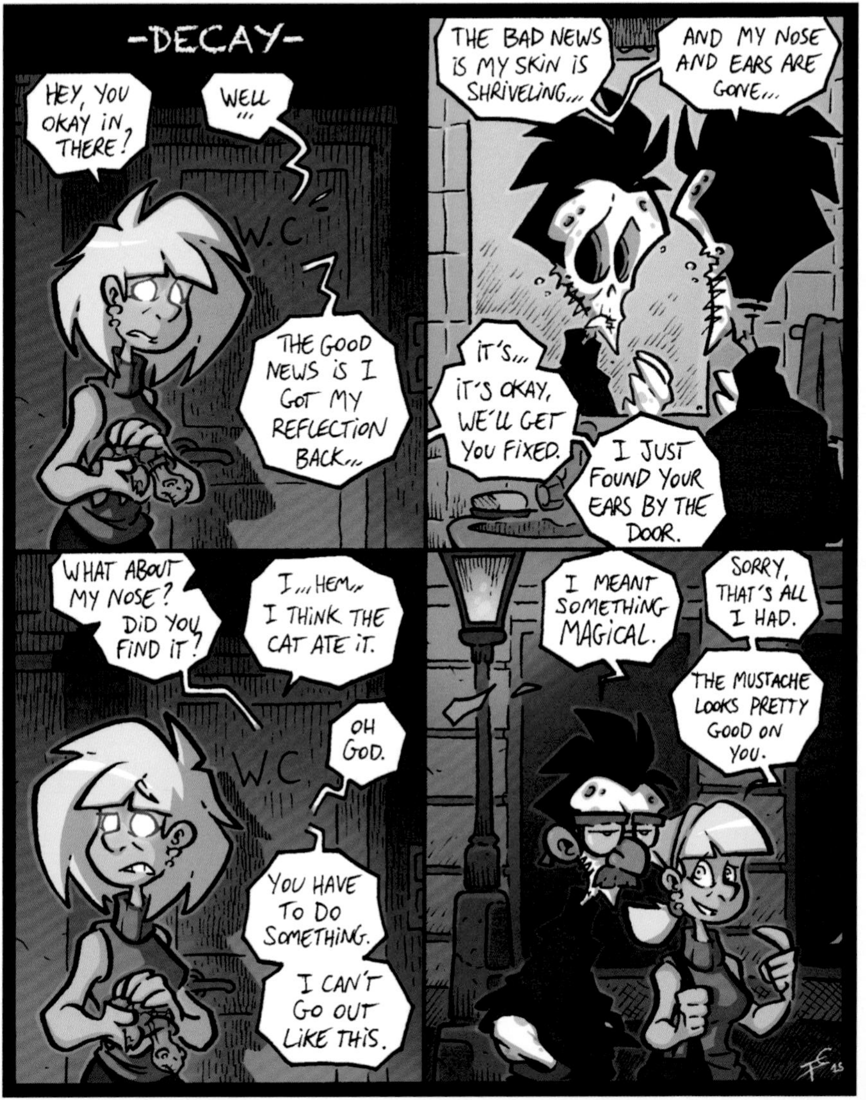
-DECAY-
HEY, YOU OKAY IN THERE?
WELL ...
THE GOOD NEWS IS I GOT MY REFLECTION BACK...
W.C.
THE BAD NEWS IS MY SKIN IS SHRIVELING...
AND MY NOSE AND EARS ARE GONE...
IT'S...
IT'S OKAY, WE'LL GET YOU FIXED.
I JUST FOUND YOUR EARS BY THE DOOR.
WHAT ABOUT MY NOSE? DID YOU FIND IT?
I... HEM.. I THINK THE CAT ATE IT.
OH GOD.
W.C.
YOU HAVE TO DO SOMETHING.
I CAN'T GO OUT LIKE THIS.
I MEANT SOMETHING MAGICAL.
SORRY, THAT'S ALL I HAD.
THE MUSTACHE LOOKS PRETTY GOOD ON YOU.

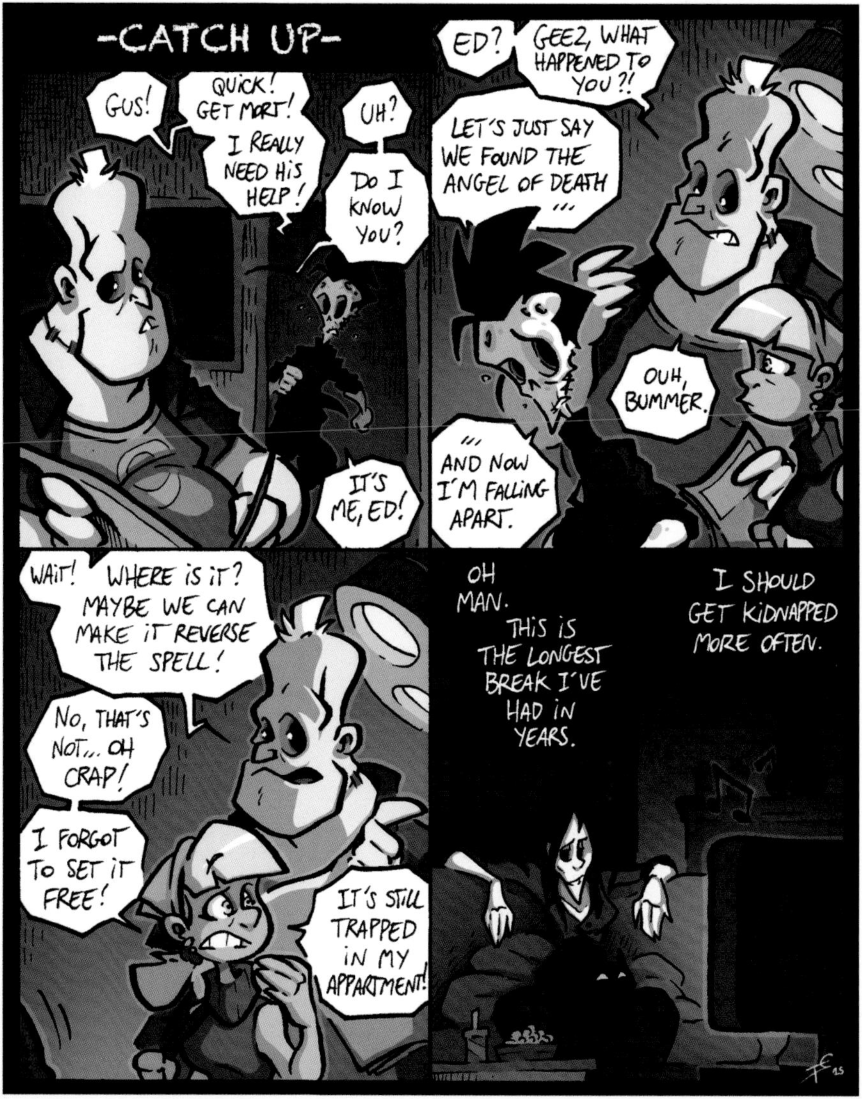
-CATCH UP-
GUS!
QUICK! GET MORT!
I REALLY NEED HIS HELP!
UH?
DO I KNOW YOU?
IT'S ME, ED!
ED?
GEEZ, WHAT HAPPENED TO YOU?!
LET'S JUST SAY WE FOUND THE ANGEL OF DEATH ...
OUH, BUMMER.
... AND NOW I'M FALLING APART.
WAIT!
WHERE IS IT? MAYBE WE CAN MAKE IT REVERSE THE SPELL!
NO, THAT'S NOT... OH CRAP!
I FORGOT TO SET IT FREE!
IT'S STILL TRAPPED IN MY APPARTMENT!
OH MAN.
THIS IS THE LONGEST BREAK I'VE HAD IN YEARS.
I SHOULD GET KIDNAPPED MORE OFTEN.

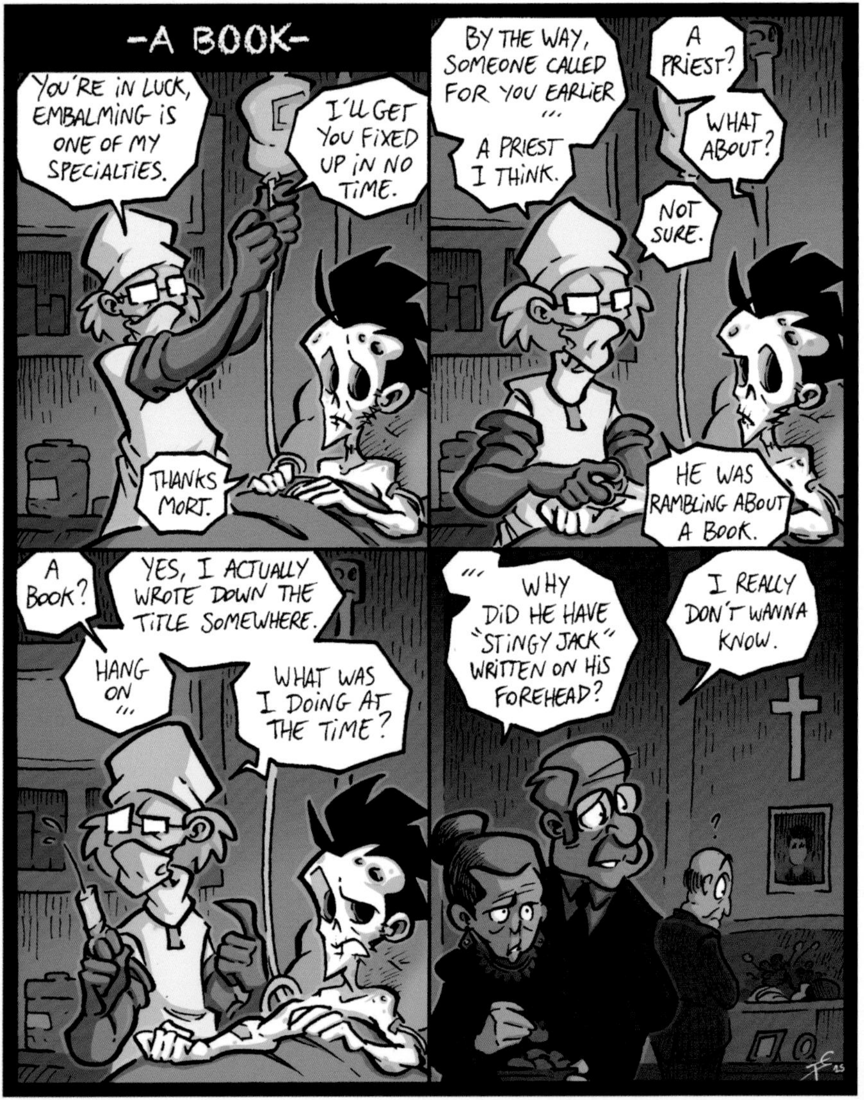
-A BOOK-
YOU'RE IN LUCK, EMBALMING IS ONE OF MY SPECIALTIES.
I'LL GET YOU FIXED UP IN NO TIME.
THANKS MORT.
BY THE WAY, SOMEONE CALLED FOR YOU EARLIER ...
A PRIEST I THINK.
A PRIEST?
WHAT ABOUT?
NOT SURE.
HE WAS RAMBLING ABOUT A BOOK.
A BOOK?
YES, I ACTUALLY WROTE DOWN THE TITLE SOMEWHERE.
HANG ON ...
WHAT WAS I DOING AT THE TIME?
... WHY DID HE HAVE "STINGY JACK" WRITTEN ON HIS FOREHEAD?
I REALLY DON'T WANNA KNOW.

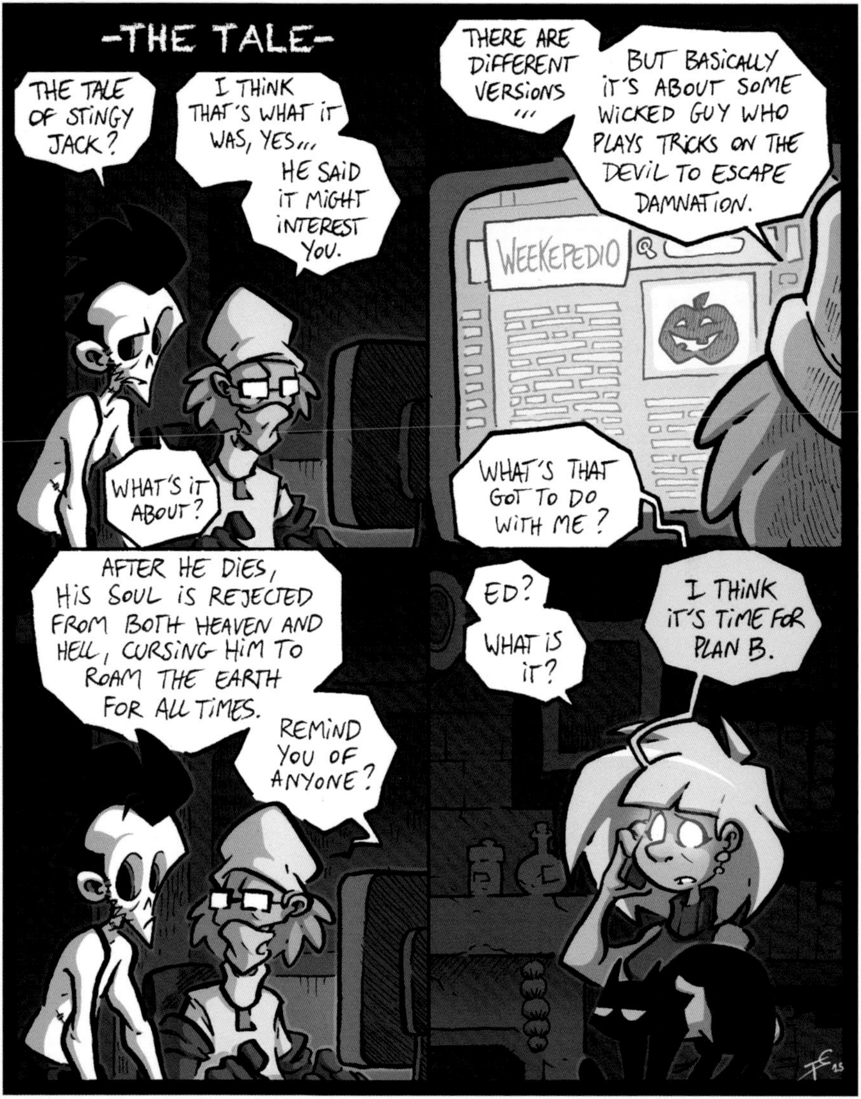
-THE TALE-
THE TALE OF STINGY JACK?
I THINK THAT'S WHAT IT WAS, YES...
HE SAID IT MIGHT INTEREST YOU.
WHAT'S IT ABOUT?
THERE ARE DIFFERENT VERSIONS ...
BUT BASICALLY IT'S ABOUT SOME WICKED GUY WHO PLAYS TRICKS ON THE DEVIL TO ESCAPE DAMNATION.
WEEKEPEDIO
WHAT'S THAT GOT TO DO WITH ME?
AFTER HE DIES, HIS SOUL IS REJECTED FROM BOTH HEAVEN AND HELL, CURSING HIM TO ROAM THE EARTH FOR ALL TIMES.
REMIND YOU OF ANYONE?
ED?
WHAT IS IT?
I THINK IT'S TIME FOR PLAN B.

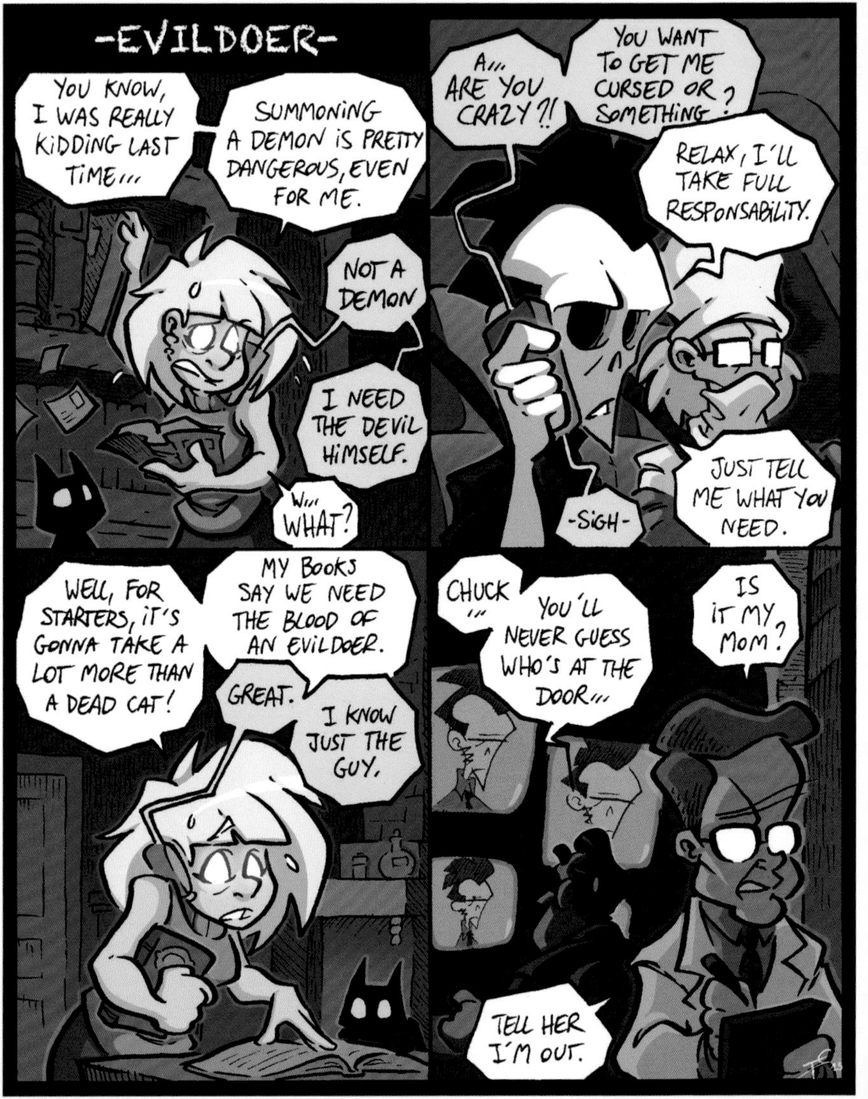
-EVILDOER-
YOU KNOW, I WAS REALLY KIDDING LAST TIME...
SUMMONING A DEMON IS PRETTY DANGEROUS, EVEN FOR ME.
NOT A DEMON
I NEED THE DEVIL HIMSELF.
W... WHAT?
A... ARE YOU CRAZY?!
YOU WANT TO GET ME CURSED OR SOMETHING?
RELAX, I'LL TAKE FULL RESPONSABILITY.
-SIGH-
JUST TELL ME WHAT YOU NEED.
WELL, FOR STARTERS, IT'S GONNA TAKE A LOT MORE THAN A DEAD CAT!
MY BOOKS SAY WE NEED THE BLOOD OF AN EVILDOER.
GREAT.
I KNOW JUST THE GUY.
CHUCK...
YOU'LL NEVER GUESS WHO'S AT THE DOOR...
IS IT MY MOM?
TELL HER I'M OUT.

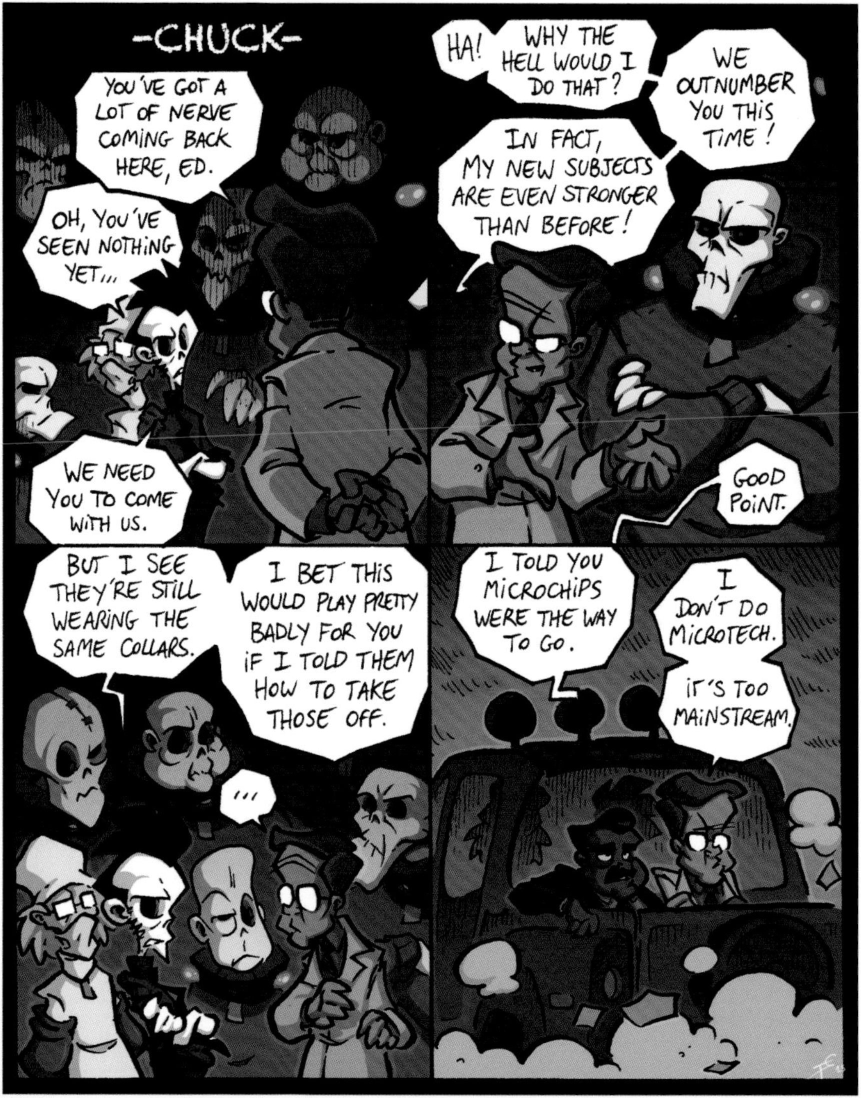
-CHUCK-
YOU'VE GOT A LOT OF NERVE COMING BACK HERE, ED.
OH, YOU'VE SEEN NOTHING YET...
WE NEED YOU TO COME WITH US.
HA!
WHY THE HELL WOULD I DO THAT?
WE OUTNUMBER YOU THIS TIME!
IN FACT, MY NEW SUBJECTS ARE EVEN STRONGER THAN BEFORE!
GOOD POINT.
BUT I SEE THEY'RE STILL WEARING THE SAME COLLARS.
I BET THIS WOULD PLAY PRETTY BADLY FOR YOU IF I TOLD THEM HOW TO TAKE THOSE OFF.
...
I TOLD YOU MICROCHIPS WERE THE WAY TO GO.
I DON'T DO MICROTECH.
IT'S TOO MAINSTREAM.

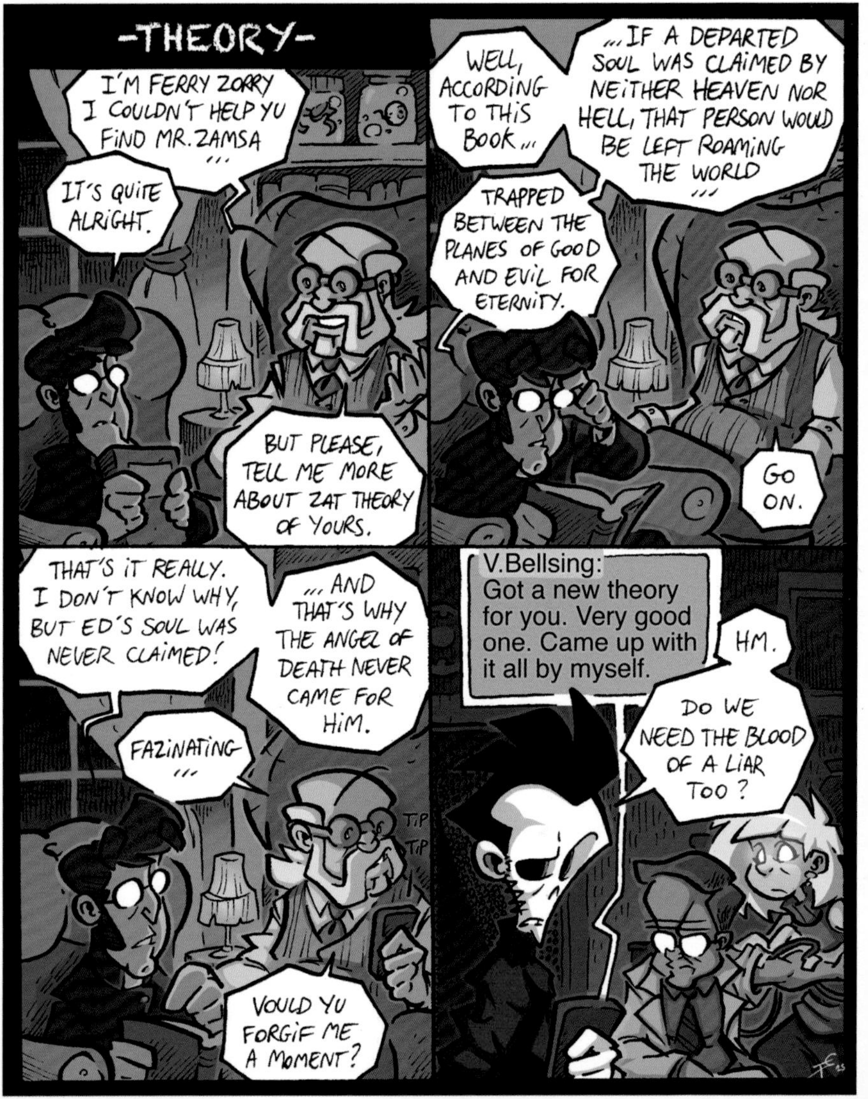
-THEORY-
I'M FERRY ZORRY I COULDN'T HELP YU FIND MR. ZAMSA ...
IT'S QUITE ALRIGHT.
BUT PLEASE, TELL ME MORE ABOUT ZAT THEORY OF YOURS.
WELL, ACCORDING TO THIS BOOK...
...IF A DEPARTED SOUL WAS CLAIMED BY NEITHER HEAVEN NOR HELL, THAT PERSON WOULD BE LEFT ROAMING THE WORLD ...
TRAPPED BETWEEN THE PLANES OF GOOD AND EVIL FOR ETERNITY.
GO ON.
THAT'S IT REALLY. I DON'T KNOW WHY, BUT ED'S SOUL WAS NEVER CLAIMED!
...AND THAT'S WHY THE ANGEL OF DEATH NEVER CAME FOR HIM.
FAZINATING ...
TIP
TIP
VOULD YU FORGIF ME A MOMENT?
V.Bellsing:
Got a new theory for you. Very good one. Came up with it all by myself.
HM.
DO WE NEED THE BLOOD OF A LIAR TOO?

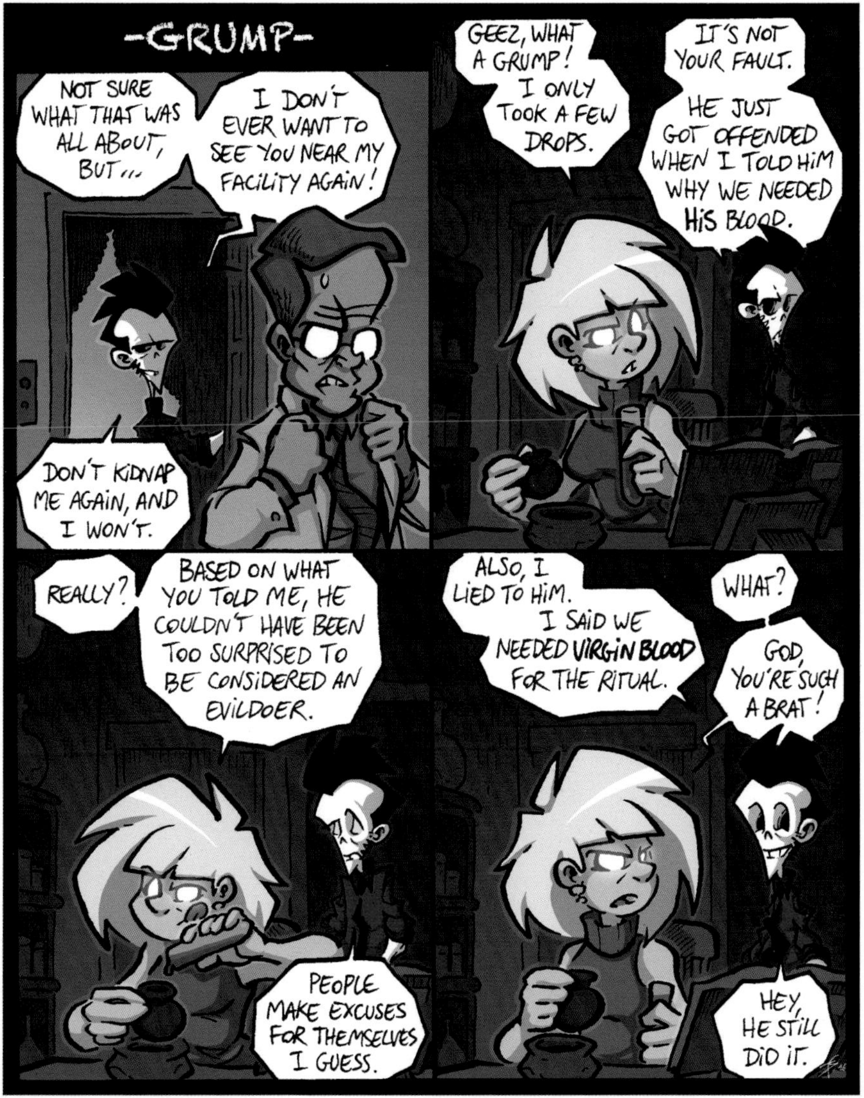
-GRUMP-
NOT SURE WHAT THAT WAS ALL ABOUT, BUT...
I DON'T EVER WANT TO SEE YOU NEAR MY FACILITY AGAIN!
DON'T KIDNAP ME AGAIN, AND I WON'T.
GEEZ, WHAT A GRUMP! I ONLY TOOK A FEW DROPS.
IT'S NOT YOUR FAULT.
HE JUST GOT OFFENDED WHEN I TOLD HIM WHY WE NEEDED HIS BLOOD.
REALLY?
BASED ON WHAT YOU TOLD ME, HE COULDN'T HAVE BEEN TOO SURPRISED TO BE CONSIDERED AN EVILDOER.
PEOPLE MAKE EXCUSES FOR THEMSELVES I GUESS.
ALSO, I LIED TO HIM.
I SAID WE NEEDED VIRGIN BLOOD FOR THE RITUAL.
WHAT?
GOD, YOU'RE SUCH A BRAT!
HEY, HE STILL DID IT.

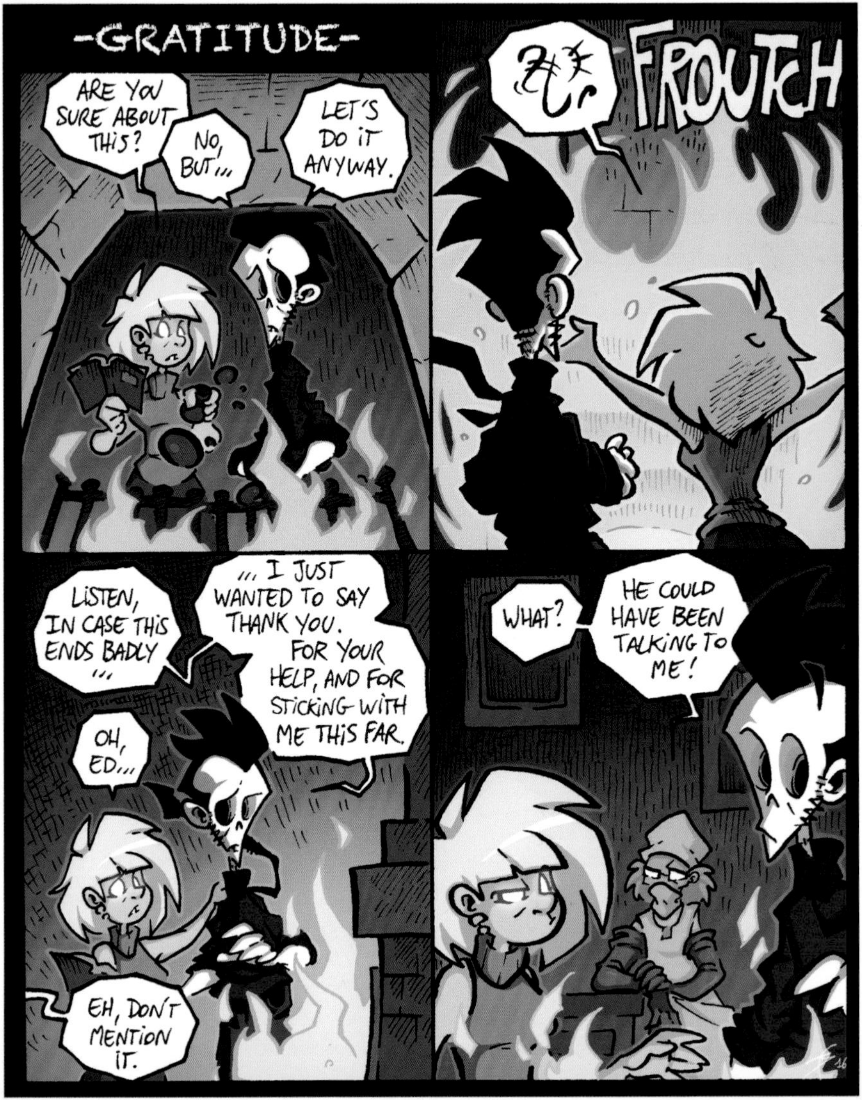
-GRATITUDE-
ARE YOU SURE ABOUT THIS?
NO, BUT...
LET'S DO IT ANYWAY.
FROUTCH
LISTEN, IN CASE THIS ENDS BADLY ...
... I JUST WANTED TO SAY THANK YOU. FOR YOUR HELP, AND FOR STICKING WITH ME THIS FAR.
OH, ED...
EH, DON'T MENTION IT.
WHAT?
HE COULD HAVE BEEN TALKING TO ME!

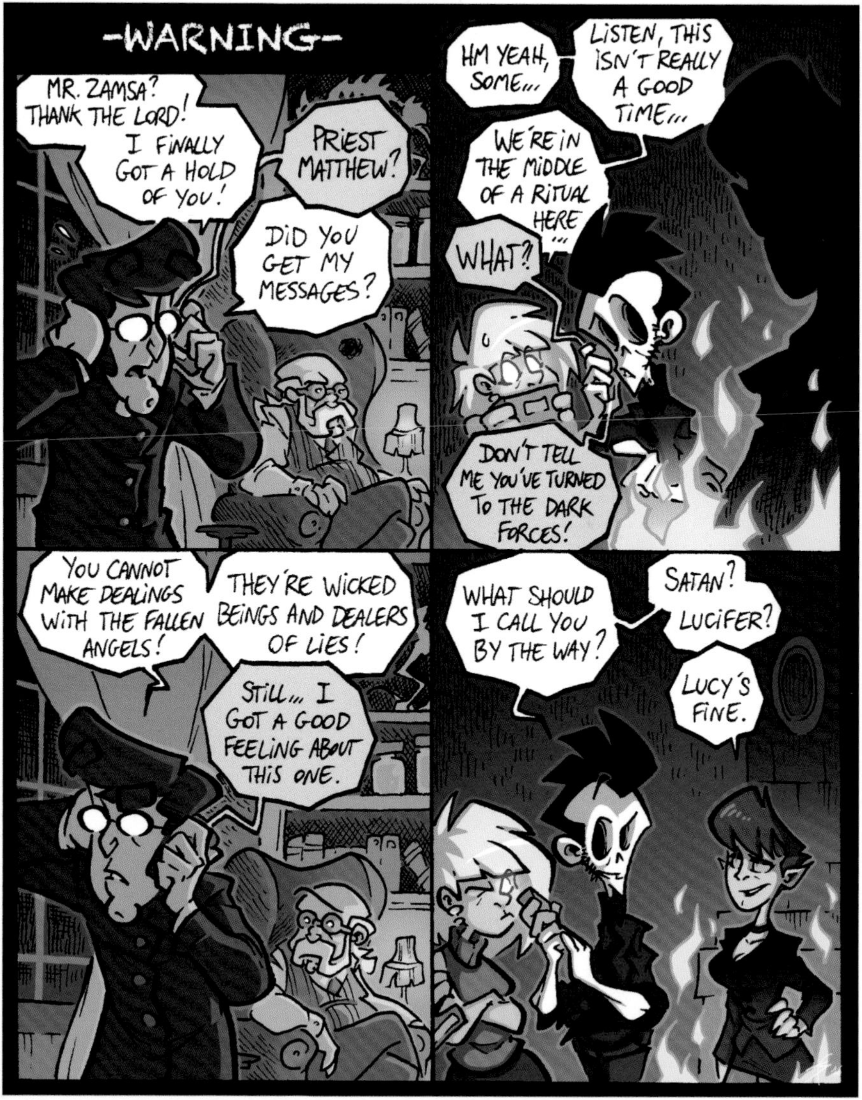
-WARNING-
MR. ZAMSA? THANK THE LORD!
I FINALLY GOT A HOLD OF YOU!
PRIEST MATTHEW?
DID YOU GET MY MESSAGES?
HM YEAH, SOME...
LISTEN, THIS ISN'T REALLY A GOOD TIME...
WE'RE IN THE MIDDLE OF A RITUAL HERE...
WHAT?!
DON'T TELL ME YOU'VE TURNED TO THE DARK FORCES!
YOU CANNOT MAKE DEALINGS WITH THE FALLEN ANGELS!
THEY'RE WICKED BEINGS AND DEALERS OF LIES!
STILL... I GOT A GOOD FEELING ABOUT THIS ONE.
WHAT SHOULD I CALL YOU BY THE WAY?
SATAN?
LUCIFER?
LUCY'S FINE.

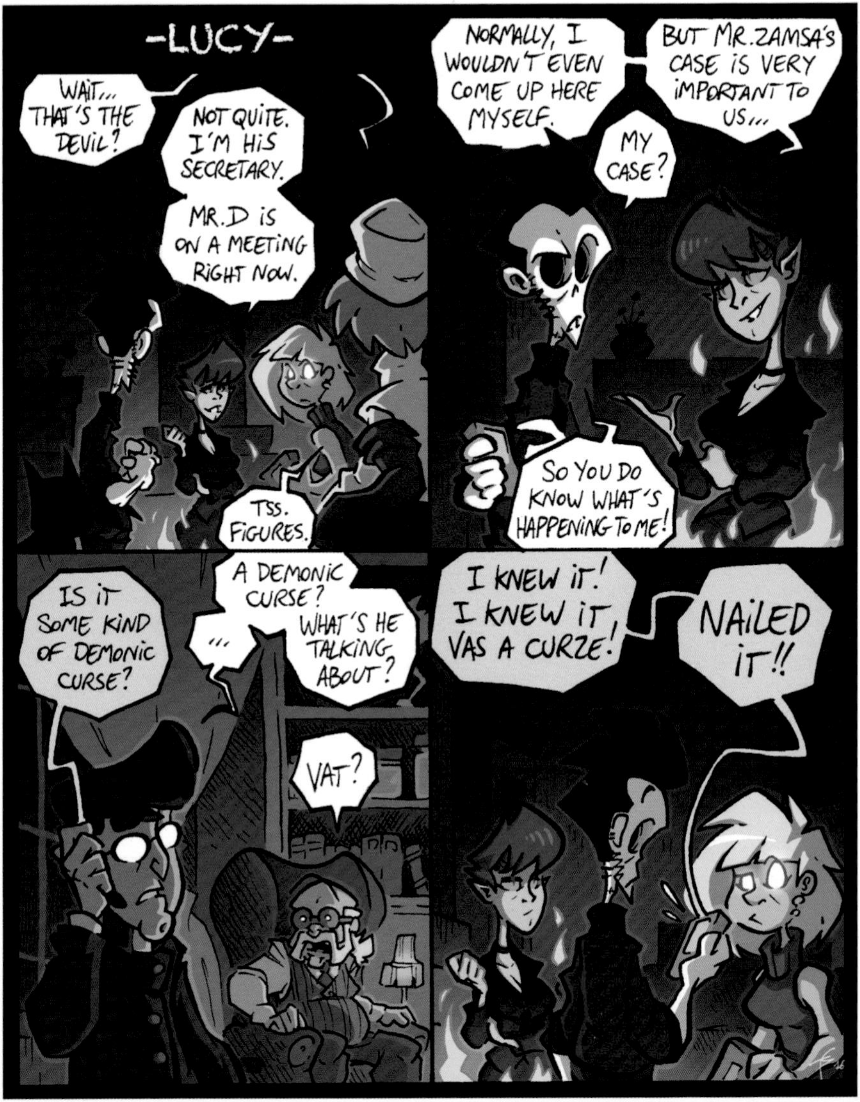
-LUCY-
WAIT... THAT'S THE DEVIL?
NOT QUITE. I'M HIS SECRETARY.
MR. D IS ON A MEETING RIGHT NOW.
TSS. FIGURES.
NORMALLY, I WOULDN'T EVEN COME UP HERE MYSELF.
BUT MR. ZAMSA'S CASE IS VERY IMPORTANT TO US...
MY CASE?
SO YOU DO KNOW WHAT'S HAPPENING TO ME!
IS IT SOME KIND OF DEMONIC CURSE?
...
A DEMONIC CURSE?
WHAT'S HE TALKING ABOUT?
VAT?
I KNEW IT! I KNEW IT VAS A CURZE!
NAILED IT!!

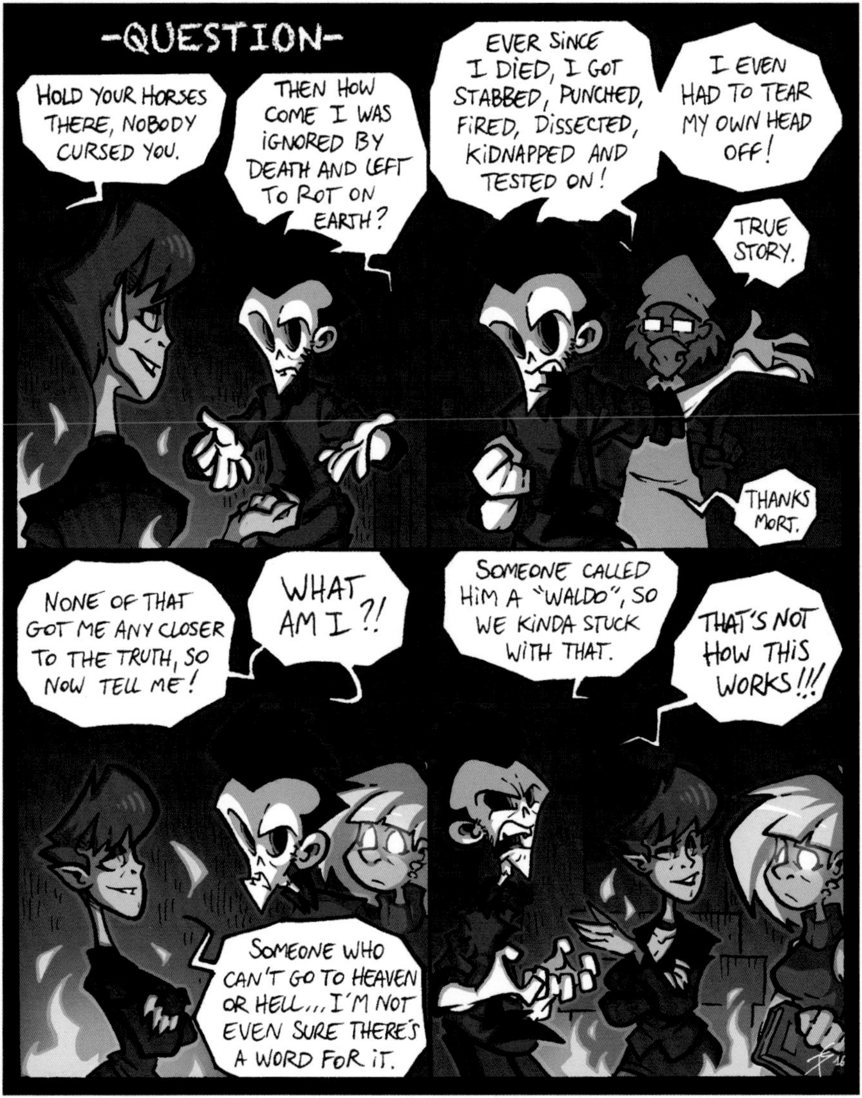
-QUESTION-
HOLD YOUR HORSES THERE, NOBODY CURSED YOU.
THEN HOW COME I WAS IGNORED BY DEATH AND LEFT TO ROT ON EARTH?
EVER SINCE I DIED, I GOT STABBED, PUNCHED, FIRED, DISSECTED, KIDNAPPED AND TESTED ON!
I EVEN HAD TO TEAR MY OWN HEAD OFF!
TRUE STORY.
THANKS MORT.
NONE OF THAT GOT ME ANY CLOSER TO THE TRUTH, SO NOW TELL ME!
WHAT AM I?!
SOMEONE WHO CAN'T GO TO HEAVEN OR HELL... I'M NOT EVEN SURE THERE'S A WORD FOR IT.
SOMEONE CALLED HIM A "WALDO", SO WE KINDA STUCK WITH THAT.
THAT'S NOT HOW THIS WORKS!!!

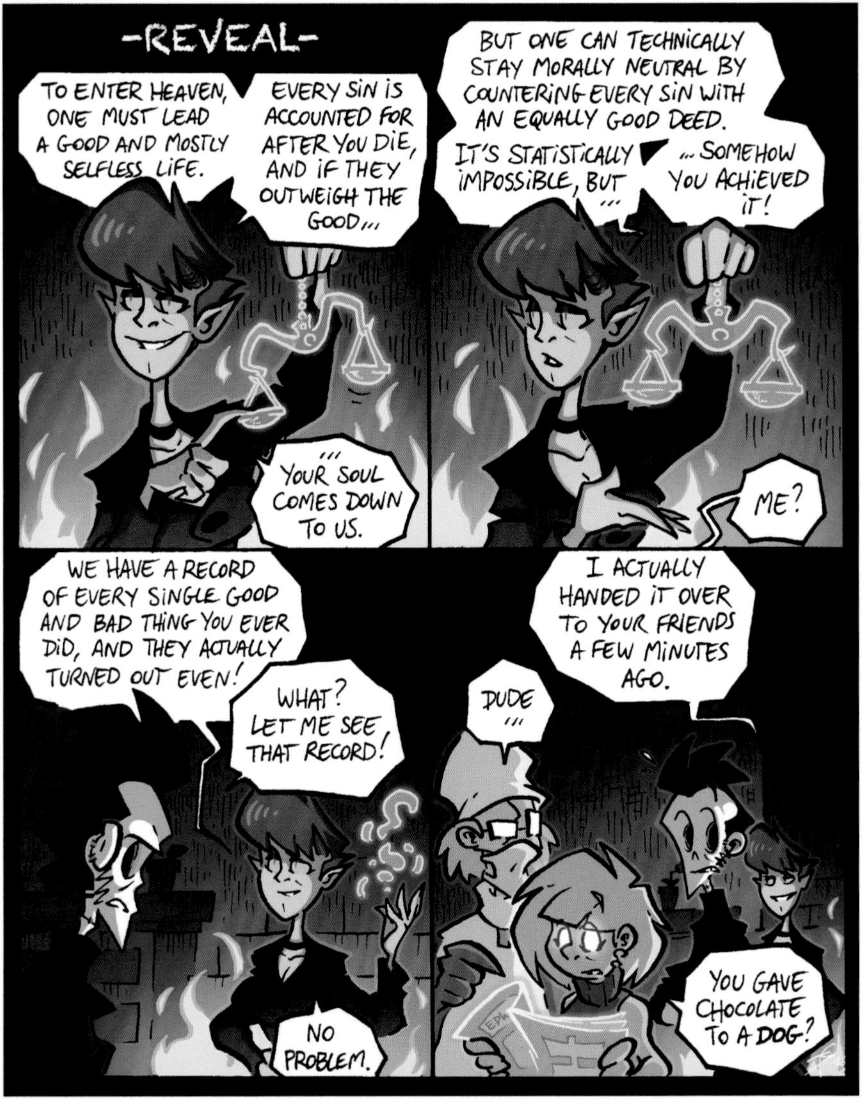
-REVEAL-
TO ENTER HEAVEN, ONE MUST LEAD A GOOD AND MOSTLY SELFLESS LIFE.
EVERY SIN IS ACCOUNTED FOR AFTER YOU DIE, AND IF THEY OUTWEIGH THE GOOD...
... YOUR SOUL COMES DOWN TO US.
BUT ONE CAN TECHNICALLY STAY MORALLY NEUTRAL BY COUNTERING EVERY SIN WITH AN EQUALLY GOOD DEED.
IT'S STATISTICALLY IMPOSSIBLE, BUT ...
... SOMEHOW YOU ACHIEVED IT!
ME?
WE HAVE A RECORD OF EVERY SINGLE GOOD AND BAD THING YOU EVER DID, AND THEY ACTUALLY TURNED OUT EVEN!
WHAT? LET ME SEE THAT RECORD!
NO PROBLEM.
I ACTUALLY HANDED IT OVER TO YOUR FRIENDS A FEW MINUTES AGO.
DUDE ...
YOU GAVE CHOCOLATE TO A DOG?

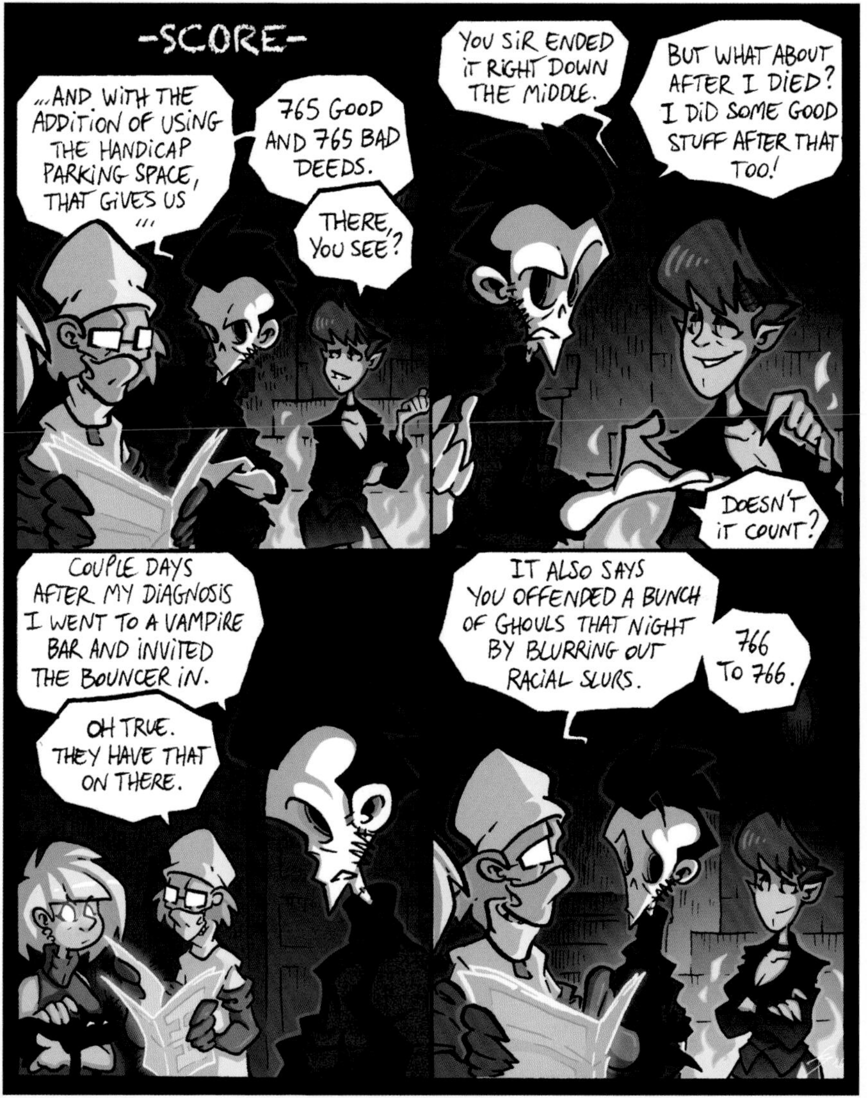
-SCORE-
...AND WITH THE ADDITION OF USING THE HANDICAP PARKING SPACE, THAT GIVES US ...
765 GOOD AND 765 BAD DEEDS.
THERE, YOU SEE?
YOU SIR ENDED IT RIGHT DOWN THE MIDDLE.
BUT WHAT ABOUT AFTER I DIED? I DID SOME GOOD STUFF AFTER THAT TOO!
DOESN'T IT COUNT?
COUPLE DAYS AFTER MY DIAGNOSIS I WENT TO A VAMPIRE BAR AND INVITED THE BOUNCER IN.
OH TRUE. THEY HAVE THAT ON THERE.
IT ALSO SAYS YOU OFFENDED A BUNCH OF GHOULS THAT NIGHT BY BLURRING OUT RACIAL SLURS.
766 TO 766.

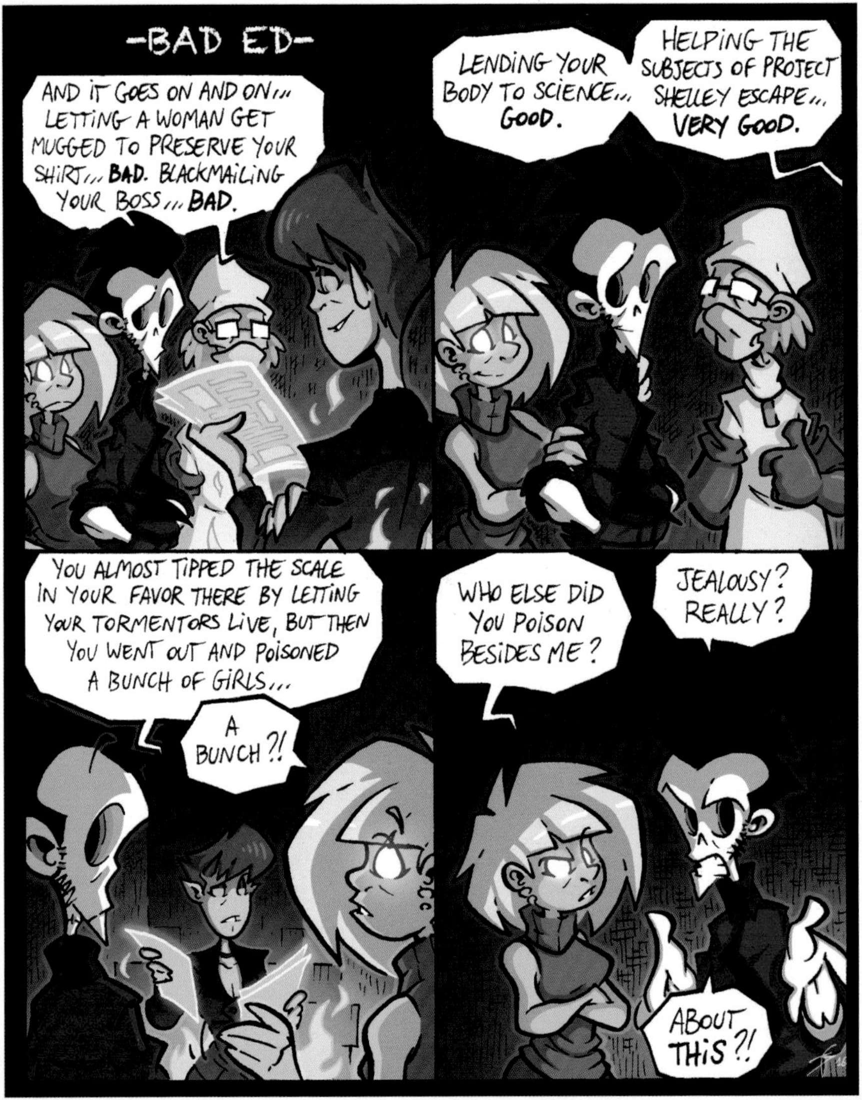
-BAD ED-
AND IT GOES ON AND ON... LETTING A WOMAN GET MUGGED TO PRESERVE YOUR SHIRT... BAD. BLACKMAILING YOUR BOSS... BAD.
LENDING YOUR BODY TO SCIENCE... GOOD.
HELPING THE SUBJECTS OF PROJECT SHELLEY ESCAPE... VERY GOOD.
YOU ALMOST TIPPED THE SCALE IN YOUR FAVOR THERE BY LETTING YOUR TORMENTORS LIVE, BUT THEN YOU WENT OUT AND POISONED A BUNCH OF GIRLS...
A BUNCH?!
WHO ELSE DID YOU POISON BESIDES ME?
JEALOUSY? REALLY?
ABOUT THIS?!

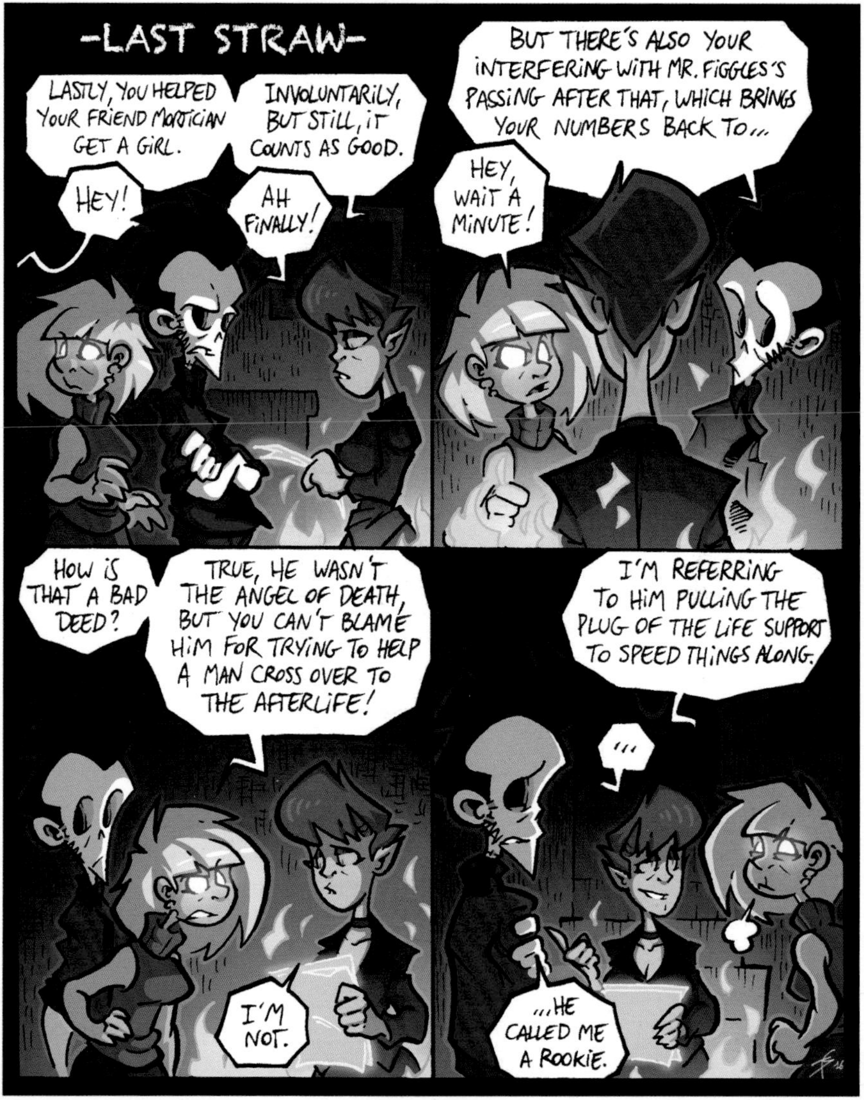
-LAST STRAW-
LASTLY, YOU HELPED YOUR FRIEND MORTICIAN GET A GIRL.
HEY!
INVOLUNTARILY, BUT STILL, IT COUNTS AS GOOD.
AH FINALLY!
BUT THERE'S ALSO YOUR INTERFERING WITH MR. FIGGLES'S PASSING AFTER THAT, WHICH BRINGS YOUR NUMBERS BACK TO...
HEY, WAIT A MINUTE!
HOW IS THAT A BAD DEED?
TRUE, HE WASN'T THE ANGEL OF DEATH, BUT YOU CAN'T BLAME HIM FOR TRYING TO HELP A MAN CROSS OVER TO THE AFTERLIFE!
I'M NOT.
I'M REFERRING TO HIM PULLING THE PLUG OF THE LIFE SUPPORT TO SPEED THINGS ALONG.
...
...HE CALLED ME A ROOKIE.

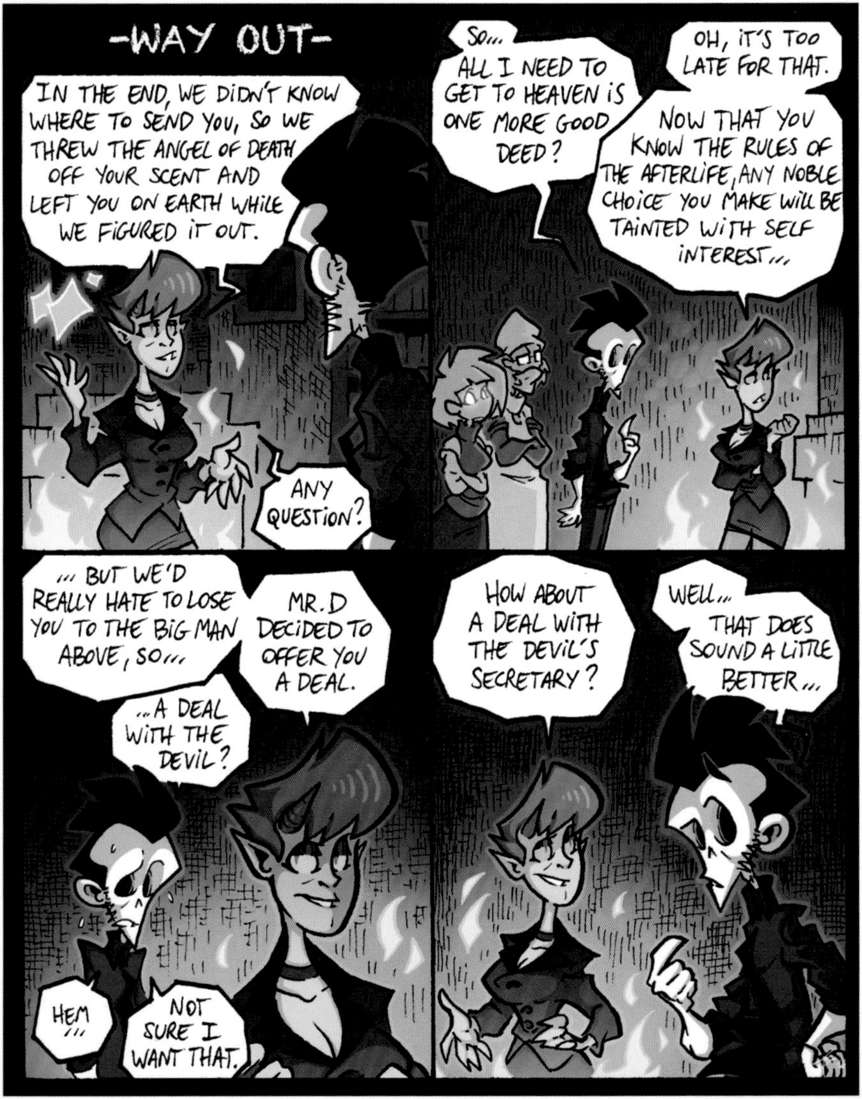
-WAY OUT-
IN THE END, WE DIDN'T KNOW WHERE TO SEND YOU, SO WE THREW THE ANGEL OF DEATH OFF YOUR SCENT AND LEFT YOU ON EARTH WHILE WE FIGURED IT OUT.
ANY QUESTION?
SO...
ALL I NEED TO GET TO HEAVEN IS ONE MORE GOOD DEED?
OH, IT'S TOO LATE FOR THAT.
NOW THAT YOU KNOW THE RULES OF THE AFTERLIFE, ANY NOBLE CHOICE YOU MAKE WILL BE TAINTED WITH SELF INTEREST...
... BUT WE'D REALLY HATE TO LOSE YOU TO THE BIG MAN ABOVE, SO...
MR. D DECIDED TO OFFER YOU A DEAL.
...A DEAL WITH THE DEVIL?
HEM ...
NOT SURE I WANT THAT.
HOW ABOUT A DEAL WITH THE DEVIL'S SECRETARY?
WELL...
THAT DOES SOUND A LITTLE BETTER...

-THE DEAL-

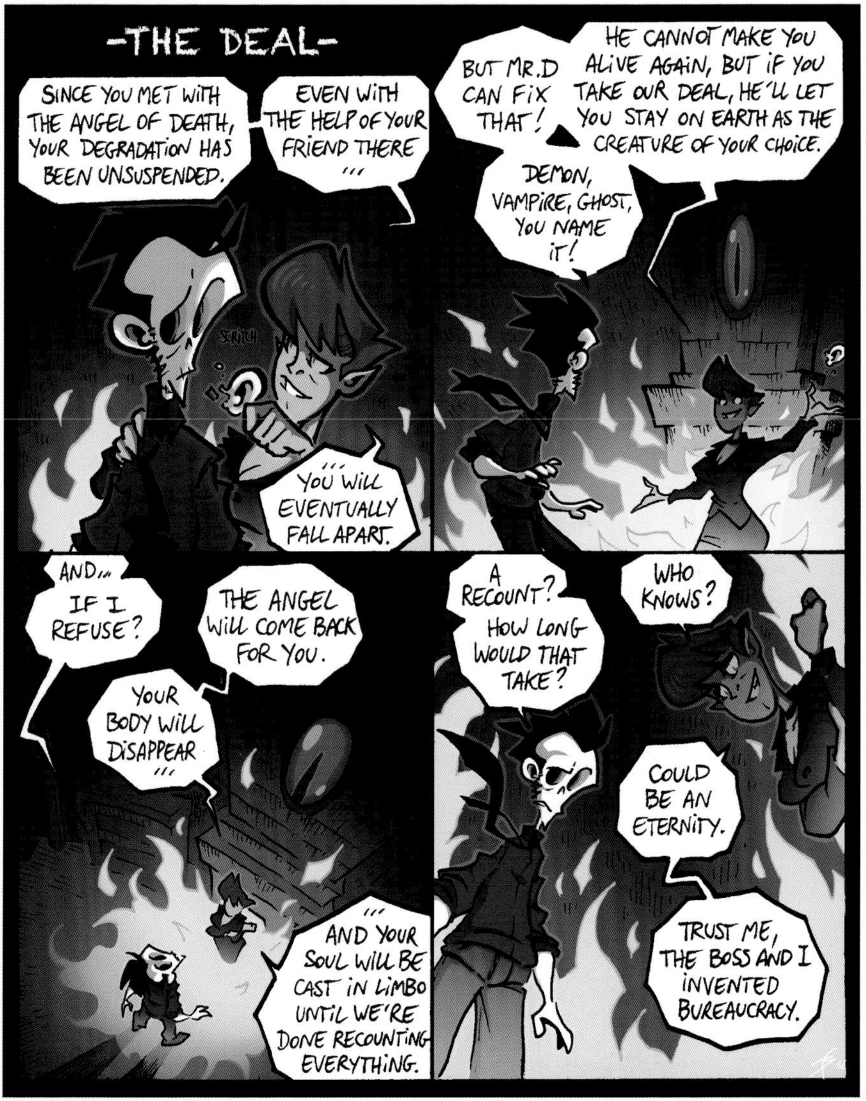
SINCE YOU MET WITH THE ANGEL OF DEATH, YOUR DEGRADATION HAS BEEN UNSUSPENDED.
EVEN WITH THE HELP OF YOUR FRIEND THERE ...
SCRITCH
... YOU WILL EVENTUALLY FALL APART.
BUT MR.D CAN FIX THAT!
HE CANNOT MAKE YOU ALIVE AGAIN, BUT IF YOU TAKE OUR DEAL, HE'LL LET YOU STAY ON EARTH AS THE CREATURE OF YOUR CHOICE.
DEMON, VAMPIRE, GHOST, YOU NAME IT!
AND... IF I REFUSE?
THE ANGEL WILL COME BACK FOR YOU.
YOUR BODY WILL DISAPPEAR ...
... AND YOUR SOUL WILL BE CAST IN LIMBO UNTIL WE'RE DONE RECOUNTING EVERYTHING.
A RECOUNT?
HOW LONG WOULD THAT TAKE?
WHO KNOWS?
COULD BE AN ETERNITY.
TRUST ME, THE BOSS AND I INVENTED BUREAUCRACY.

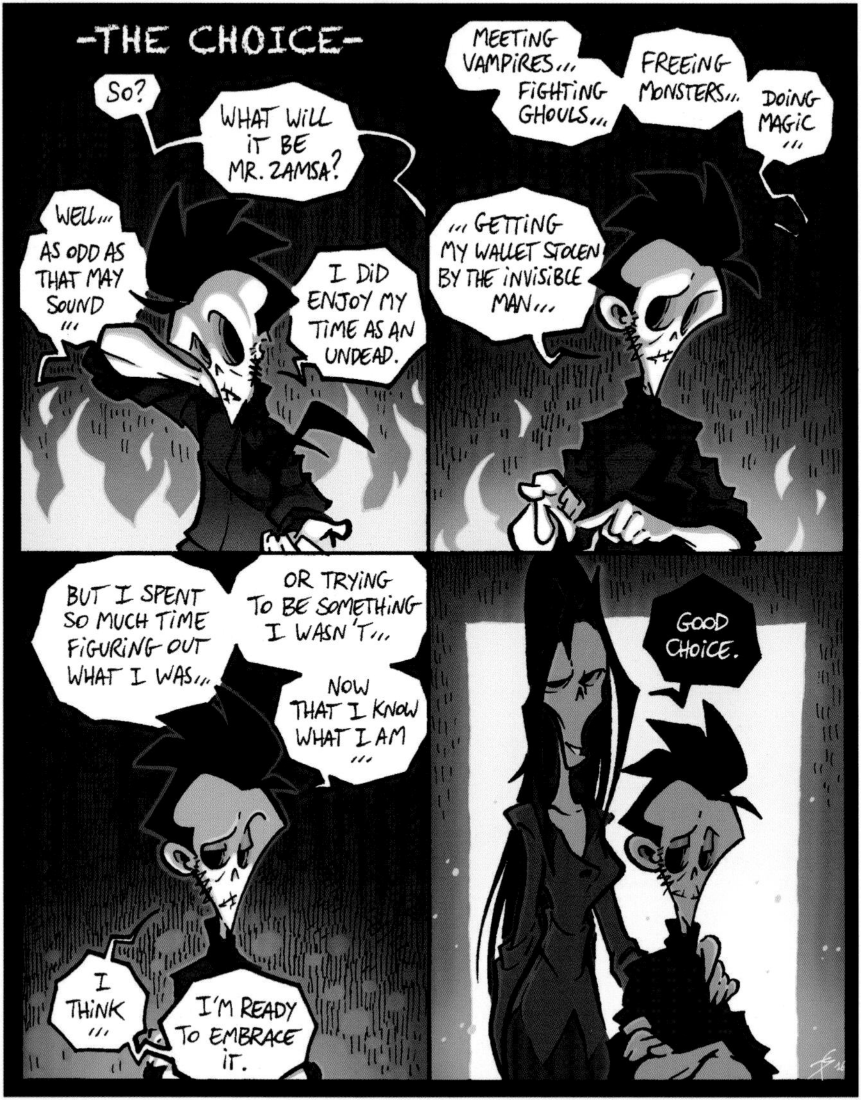
-THE CHOICE-
So?
WHAT WILL IT BE MR. ZAMSA?
WELL...
AS ODD AS THAT MAY SOUND ...
I DID ENJOY MY TIME AS AN UNDEAD.
MEETING VAMPIRES...
FIGHTING GHOULS...
FREEING MONSTERS...
DOING MAGIC ...
... GETTING MY WALLET STOLEN BY THE INVISIBLE MAN...
BUT I SPENT SO MUCH TIME FIGURING OUT WHAT I WAS...
OR TRYING TO BE SOMETHING I WASN'T...
NOW THAT I KNOW WHAT I AM ...
I THINK ...
I'M READY TO EMBRACE IT.
GOOD CHOICE.

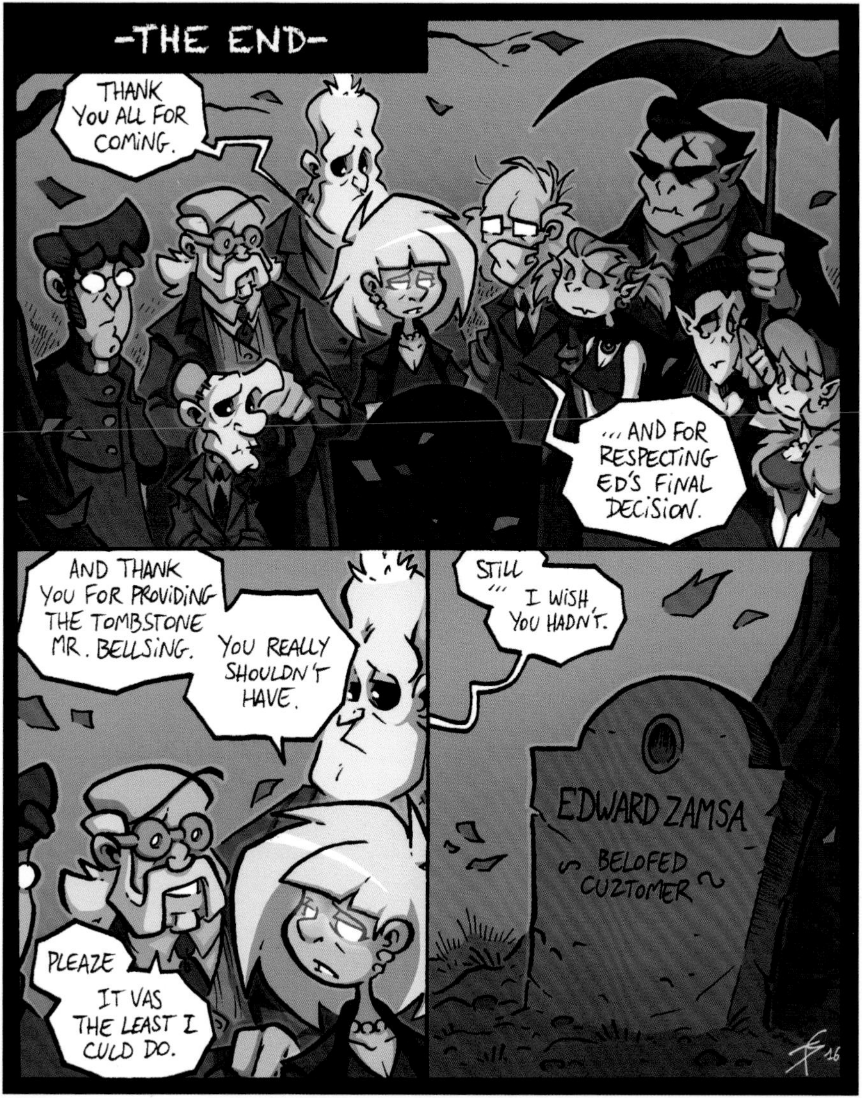
-THE END-
THANK YOU ALL FOR COMING.
...AND FOR RESPECTING ED'S FINAL DECISION.
AND THANK YOU FOR PROVIDING THE TOMBSTONE MR. BELLSING.
YOU REALLY SHOULDN'T HAVE.
PLEAZE
IT VAS THE LEAST I CULD DO.
STILL
... I WISH YOU HADN'T.
EDWARD ZAMSA
BELOFED CUZTOMER

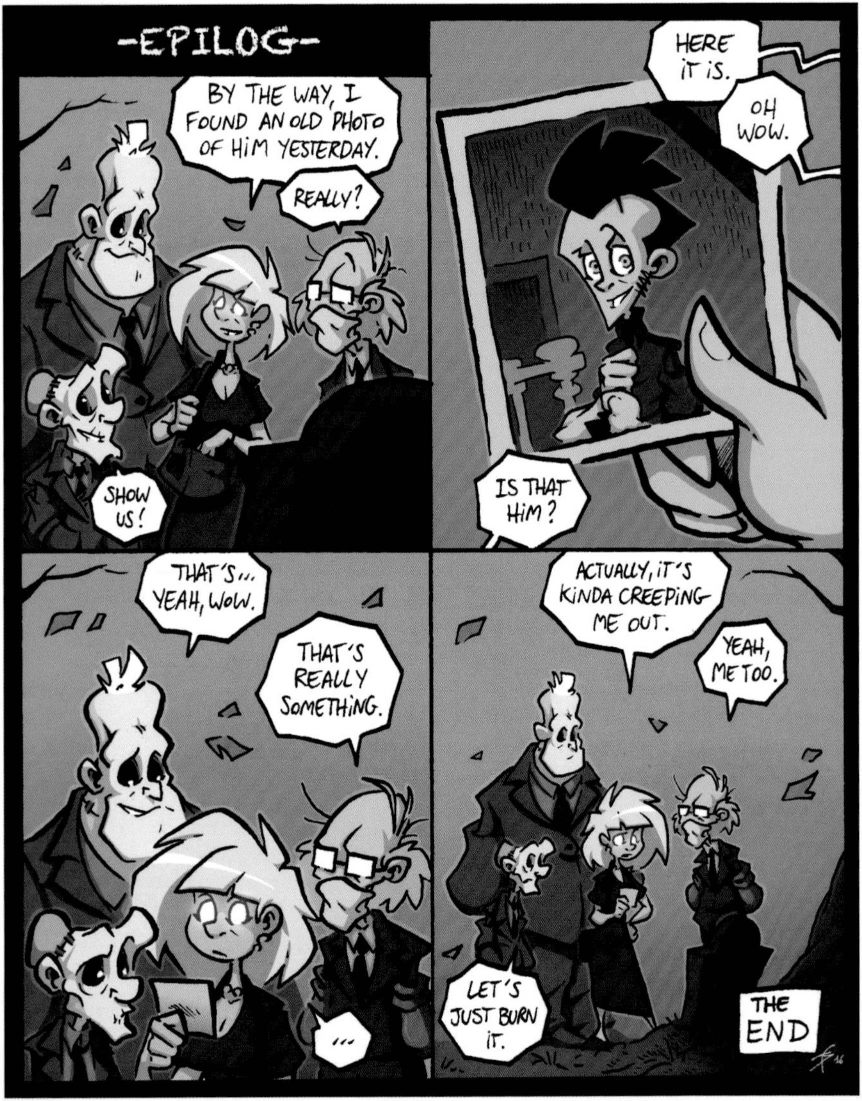
-EPILOG-
BY THE WAY, I FOUND AN OLD PHOTO OF HIM YESTERDAY.
REALLY?
SHOW US!
HERE IT IS.
OH WOW.
IS THAT HIM?
THAT'S... YEAH, WOW.
THAT'S REALLY SOMETHING.
...
ACTUALLY, IT'S KINDA CREEPING ME OUT.
YEAH, ME TOO.
LET'S JUST BURN IT.
THE END

Searching yourself
can lead to
Heaven or Hell

But it still beats
not knowing

...

and roaming
the Earth

I LEAVE YOU WITH A GAME:

IN EPISODE 55, THE INVISIBLE MAN
ALSO STOLE ED'S WATCH, AND HID IT
SOMEWHERE IN THE FOLLOWING EPISODES.

DID YOU SEE WHERE IT WENT ?

VON BELLSING,
PRIEST MATTHEW
AND LUCY
WILL RETURN IN

Concept Art
& Illustrations

THE NAME OF THE STORY WAS ORIGINALLY GOING TO BE DEAD ED, BUT I SOON FOUND OUT THAT NAME WAS ALREADY TAKEN AND CHANGED IT TO UNDEAD ED... WHICH LATER TURNED OUT TO BE TAKEN AS WELL.

IT'S HARD BEING ORIGINAL NOWADAYS.

DEAD ED

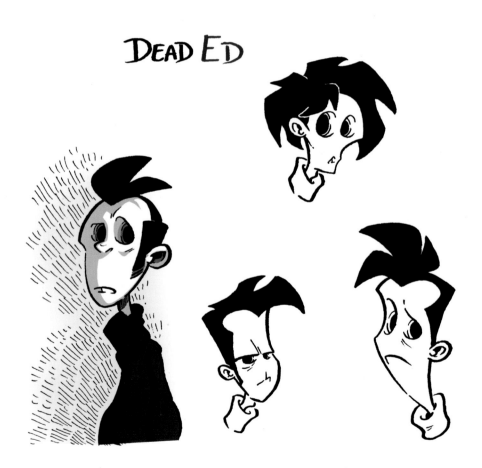

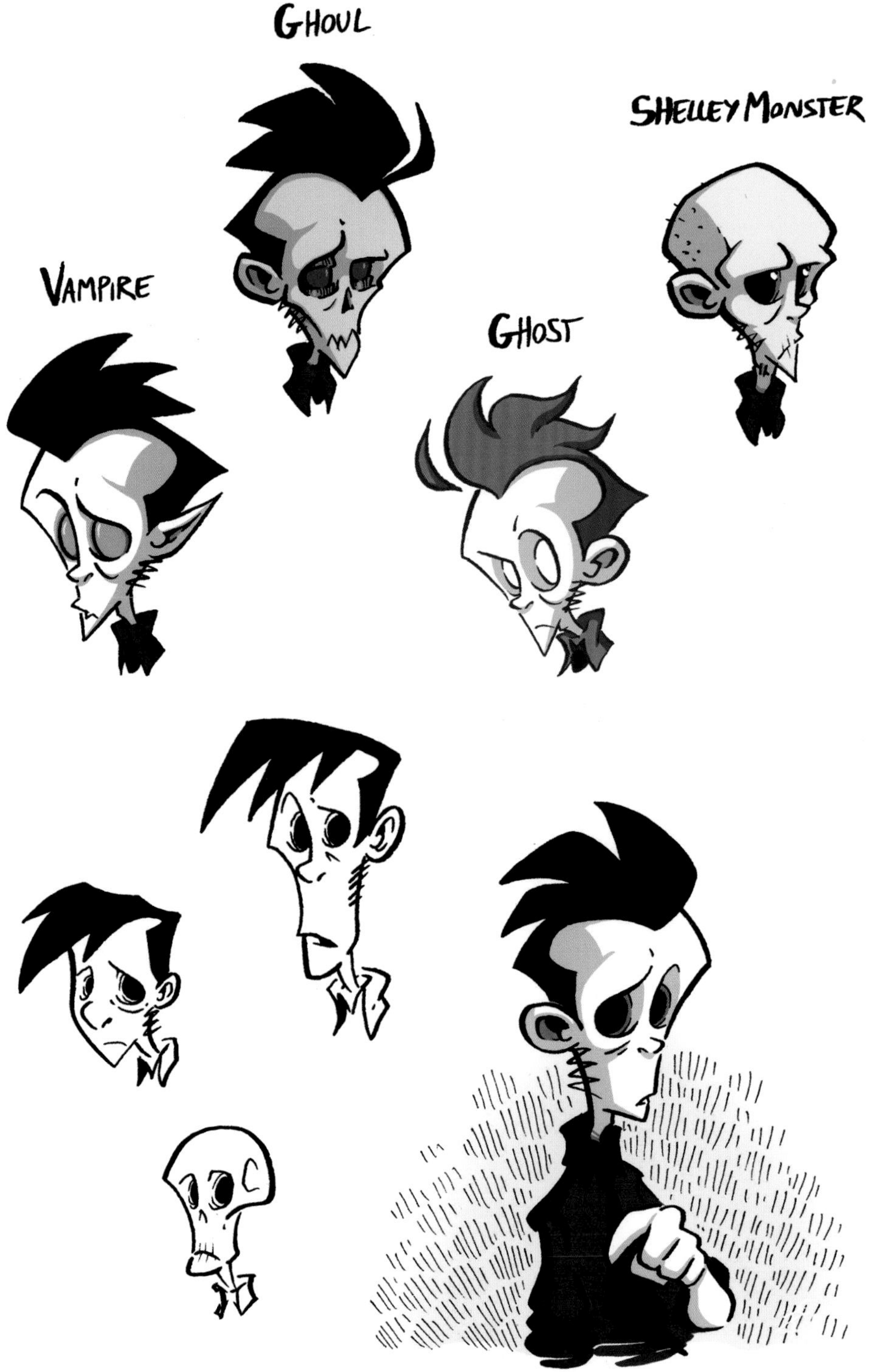
GHOUL
SHELLEY MONSTER
VAMPIRE
GHOST

ANNOUNCEMENT
SO, TELL ME...
WHAT DO YOU DO?
I... HEM.
I'M DEAD.
MOSTLY.
I SEE...
ANYTHING ELSE?
...
I GOT A FRIEND MORTICIAN.
AWW
THAT'S CUTE.
WEB TOON

BY THE TIME WEBTOON DECIDED TO TAKE UNDEADED OUT OF
THE CHALLENGE LEAGUE AND INTO THEIR SELECTION,
THE COMIC WAS ALSO AVAILABLE ON BOTH
DEVIANTART AND TAPASTIC.
SINCE IT HAD TO REMAIN
A WEBTOON EXCLUSIVE,
ALL EPISODES WERE THEN
TAKEN DOWN AND REPLACED
BY THIS ANNOUNCEMENT.

PIRATE SHARING LATER MADE IT
AVAILABLE ON SITES LIKE MANGAFOX.ME,
MYMANGAONLINE.NET, READMANGA.ME
AND ON IMGUR AND REDDIT WHERE IT GOT
HALF A MILLION VIEWS IN TWO DAYS.

UNFORTUNATELY IT WAS A WEEK
BEFORE ITS CONCLUSION...

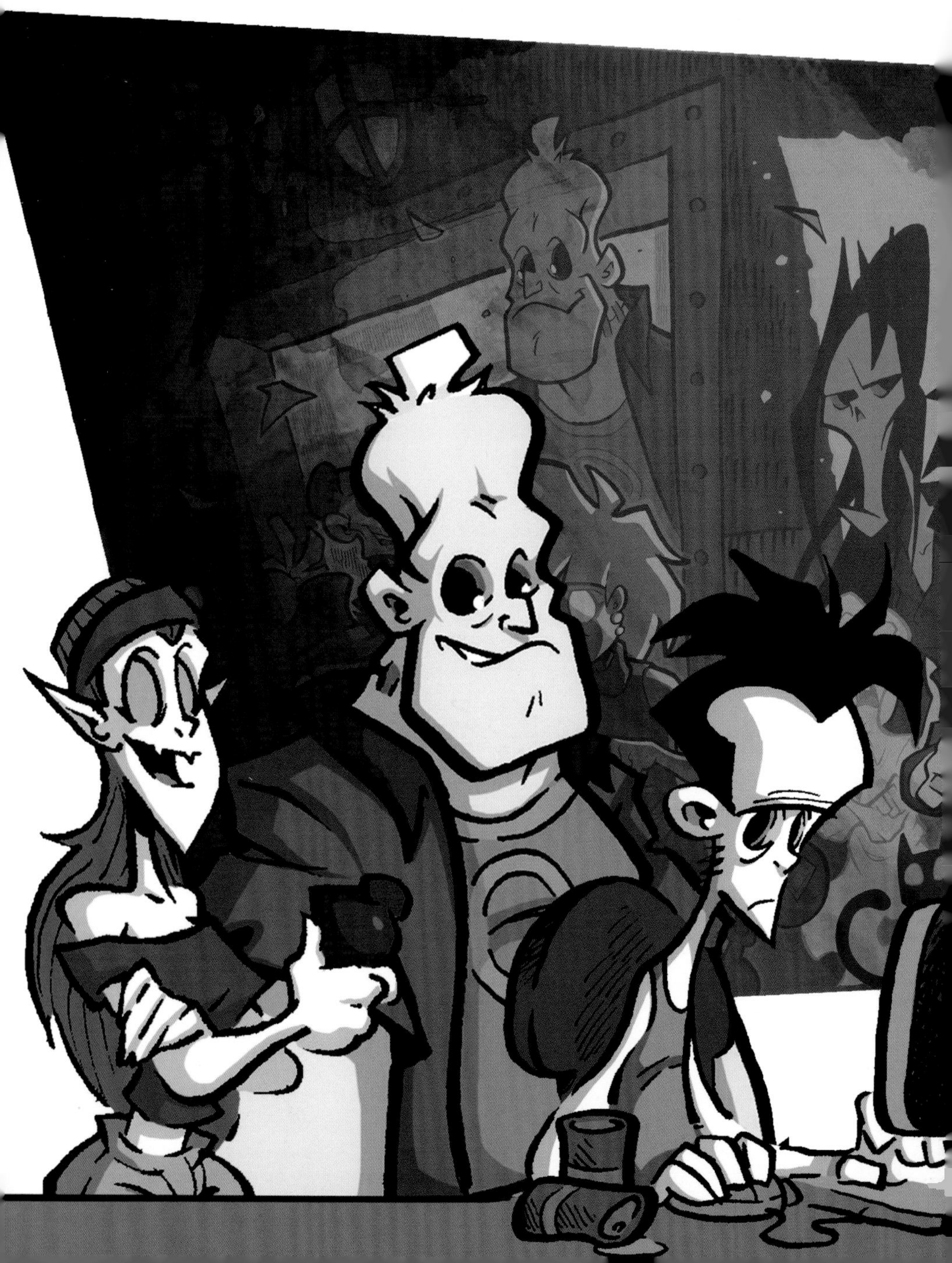

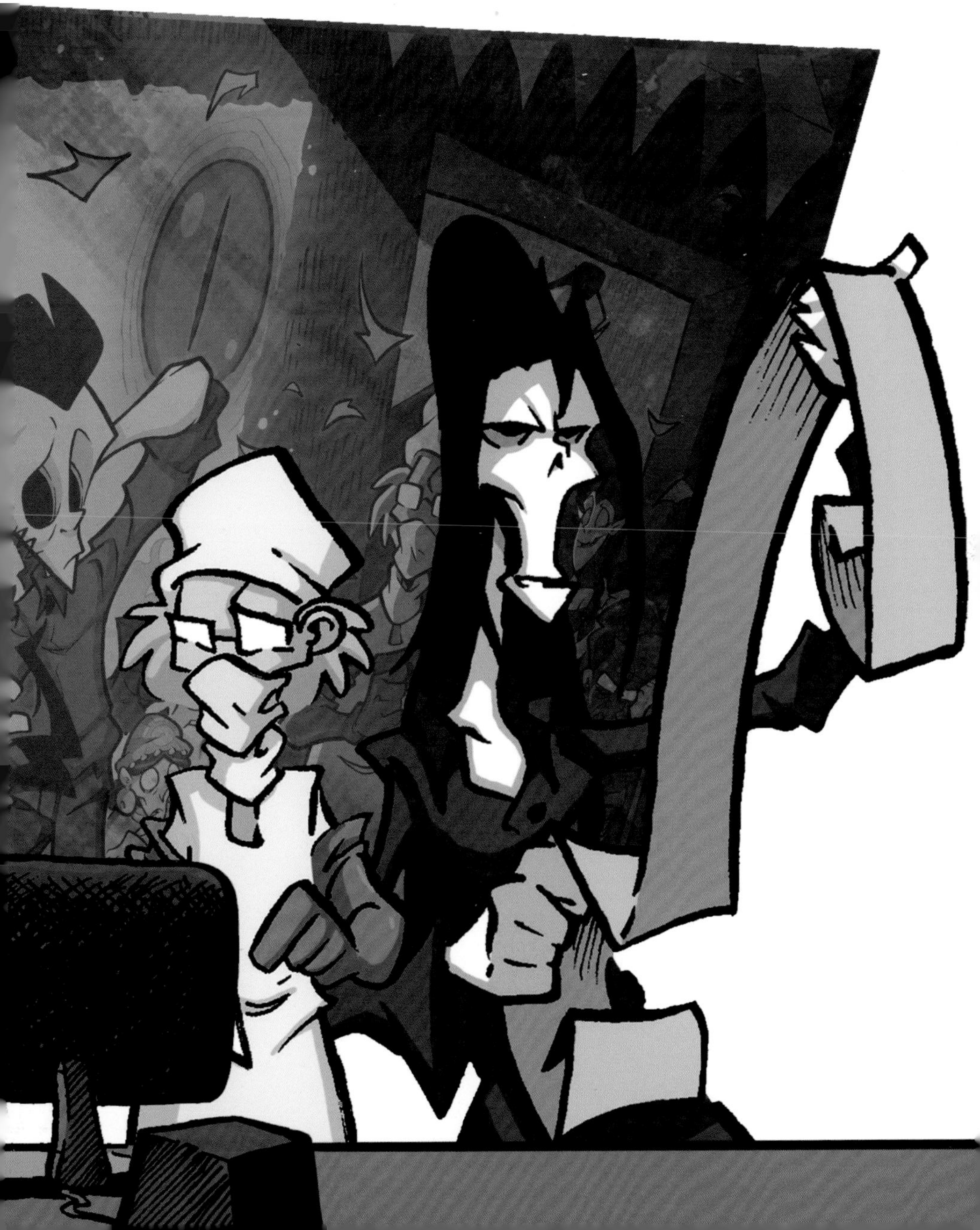

MY NAME'S ELIOTT, I'M A BONEY FRENCH CARTOONIST LIVING IN BELGIUM WITH MY WIFE AND OUR THREE HUNGRY BABIES, ONLY ONE OF WHICH IS HUMAN.

ARTISTICALLY BROUGHT INTO EXISTENCE BY BOREDOM, MY WORK IS NOW THE ONLY THING THAT KEEPS IT AT BAY, BUT THANKS TO THE WONDERS OF DIGITAL MEDIA AND MY COMPLETE DISINTEREST IN VITAMIN D, I'VE BEEN MAKING CARTOONS AND WEBCOMICS FOR OVER FIFTEEN YEARS.

SINCE *UNDEADED'S* OFFICIAL RELEASE IN 2015, I'VE BEEN PUBLISHING MY WORK ALMOST EXCLUSIVELY ON WEBTOON, BUT YOU CAN STILL FIND OTHER COMICS OF MINE ON DEVIANTART, PATREON, BLOGGER AND ON THE WALLS OF MY MOTHER'S KITCHEN.

22